CHOOSING JUSTICE

R

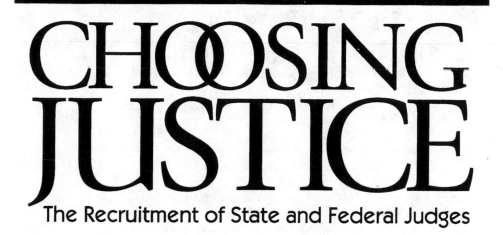

CHOOSING JUSTICE

The Recruitment of State and Federal Judges

Charles H. Sheldon
and Linda S. Maule

WSU
PRESS

Washington State University Press
Pullman, Washington

Copyright 1997 by the Board of Regents of Washington State University
All rights reserved
First printing 1997

Library of Congress Cataloging-in-Publications Data
Sheldon, Charles H., 1929-
    Choosing justice : the recruitment of state and federal judges / Charles H. Sheldon, Linda S. Maule.
    p. cm.
    Includes bibliographical references and index.
    ISBN 0-87422-152-8 (pbk. : alk. paper)
    1. Judges—Selection and appointment—United States. 2. Judges—Selection and appointment—United States—Case studies. 3. Judges—Selection and appointment—United States—States. 4. Judges—Selection and appointment—United States—States—Case studies.
    I. Maule, Linda S., 1965- . II. Title.
    KF8776.S4 1997   97-1776
    347.73'14—dc21   CIP

Dedication

To Pat

Cedric and Ian

Table of Contents

A Claudius O. and Mary W. Johnson Book

Acknowledgments

We are greatly indebted to Nicholas P. Lovrich, Jr. who, from the beginning, has been a major player in whatever understanding we have developed concerning how judges are chosen. He has been a valued member of our research team and a creative contributor to our writings. Many of the ideas presented here are his.

Also, we are indebted to the numerous judges, lawyers, public officials, bar association officials, political activists and concerned citizens who shared their intimate knowledge and informed views on judicial recruitment. In every instance, they were forthcoming in how judges are chosen and in explaining the often subtle but important nuances affecting who ultimately comes to don the robes of judicial office.

Professor Stephen Wasby's encouragement and advice got the project going, and his review of the final results was invaluable. Jean Taylor, proof reader, Glen Lindeman, editor, and Tom Sanders, director, at the WSU Press, kept us on track. Ruth Self and Rebecca Taylor did a magnificent job of preparing the final version of the manuscript. We are also indebted to the many graduate and undergraduate students at Washington State University who suffered through successive versions of our recruitment model in our courses and seminars. Unfortunately, we can blame only ourselves for any errors or misunderstandings.

Charles H. Sheldon
Washington State University

Linda S. Maule
Indiana State University

Preface

Nicholas P. Lovrich, Jr.

Judges play a crucial and special role in a Democracy. Americans pride themselves in living under a "government of laws, not of men," but at the same time they remain fully aware of the human side of the law, and the great role judges play in interpreting the law. It is not doubted that it is men and women that shape the laws of American society. Elected representatives enact the laws, administrators apply them in their work, and executives enforce those laws and are charged with the responsibility of seeing that the laws are "faithfully executed." In all of these processes of law making, law administrating, and law execution conflicts arise over the proper exercise of authority and appropriate reading of rights and duties of officials and citizens alike; the crucial nexus between government, the law and citizens is provided by judges. At least at three critical points judges bridge law and government in our system of democratic self rule.

In actual conflicts over the meaning of the law, judges decide which version is to be taken as authoritatively valid. Through a unique decisional process our trial courts, sometimes with the assistance of juries, resolve disputes between antagonists. The adversarial process featuring one attorney against another brings the facts forth—in a setting and under rules of conduct supervised by a judge—upon which the jurists and juries rely, and the judge then applies the appropriate law. In civil cases the preponderance of evidence determines the outcome, while evidence beyond a reasonable doubt convicts one who is accused of having transgressed the criminal laws. The role of the judges in both situations is to remain above the verbal fray, assuring that the fight between opposing attorneys is fair and that each side has the opportunity to present their case according to long established rules of procedure. When all the evidence has been presented and all the relevant facts have surfaced, the judge decides who is to receive a monetary award or who is to be convicted or set free. The settlement of civil and criminal disputes is the primary function of judges.

Judges not uncommonly make decisions which alternatively reinforce, establish or negate existing public policies. Trial judges most often concerned with the litigants directly before them set the framework for appeals to higher courts, which in turn consider not only the immediate litigants but on occasion decide for a considerable number of people affected by the policy. In the case of the U.S. Supreme Court, such decisions are made for an entire nation. Judges, as with legislators and executives, are indeed policy makers on many occasions. Judges are most often reluctant to recognize their role in policy making, but policymaking is indisputably a part of the functions of judging to the extent that judicial action is required to fill the interstices of authority found in our federal and state constitutions, in statutes, and in long-standing (or more recently established) legal precedents. Moreover, in American jurisprudence the special status of substantial authority implied by the phrase "on the policy making level" is signaled by phrases such as "exercise of discretion" and "exercise of judgment," phrases which are indisputably descriptive of most of the performance of those persons within the judicial branch who serve as judges.

Judges provide much of the continuity with the past which is essential to the maintenance of confidence in the public institutions of a sometimes volatile democracy. The authority surrounding the actions of legislators, of bureaucrats, and even of elected executives is transitory—as it should be in a democracy. These electorally accountable officials must react to the immediate needs, passions, and prejudices of their respective publics. In contrast, the authority of judges represents a constancy in time and space that is absent from the enactments of other legitimate voices of political authority. Judges are called upon to blend the past with the present, and in the process set a firm societal and legal foundation for the future. Courts are expected to rise above the short-term expediencies characteristic of the incumbents of other democratic political institutions in America. Judges thereby provide ideological unity to the law. In our system of government the combination of written constitutions, administrative codes, and statutes applied through *stare decisis* combine to supply the constancy that a "government of laws" requires.

As judges settle disputes, make public policy, and weave the past into the fabric of the present, they are confronted with a dilemma that does not face other policy makers. To settle the conflicts that arise between citizens, and between the government and citizens, judges must remain aloof from the parties to the dispute. Objectivity is essential for them to weigh each side's arguments and render a fair decision. Further, judges on occasion must defy the strident shouts of the majority in order to protect the individual or the isolated, feared or disliked minority. Judges must be independent. The "rule of law" dictates an independent stance. However, equally as important, judges must be accountable for those disputes that they settle involving a public policy issue. In a democracy, those who make policy must be accountable to the citizenry for those authoritative decisions. Majoritarian democracy dictates such responsibility. In the first case, an American judge is required to appear insensitive and arrogant; in the second, she or he is well advised to appear compliant and submissive to the will of the people. It is no mean task for judges to balance these contradictory dictates constituting the judicial dilemma.

In practice, this difficult balance is achieved when a judge somehow senses the nature of the culture of his or her constituency and blends that understanding with the dispassionate application of the law. Alternatively, this balance comes over time, with the judge ruling strictly in accordance with the law most of the time but rendering a number of decisions tempered with her or his understanding of the political culture of the civil community. Sufficient confidence in the courts is built up over time where this balance is achieved, permitting a well-considered and timely unpopular decision to be made concerning an important principle of civil liberty or governmental authority or economic commerce.

To a considerable extent, then, studying how judges are recruited and learning what implications different methods and processes hold for the achievement of this critical balance could add very importantly to our comprehension of democratic politics in America. The conflicting dictates of the judicial dilemma, and how they are resolved, is a question at the core of our political system. It would seem that the *ideal* selection process shapes the views of the judge in two ways. The particular system of selection employed insures that those individuals seeking the robes of office who are lacking requisites are winnowed out while others with the attitudes and views that lend themselves to resolving the judicial dilemma in a balanced way survive the selection process and are placed on the bench. The recruitment system must select characteristic judges and reject the uncharacteristic judicial candidates. However, equally as important, the person who survives the recruitment process necessarily learns something very important from that experience. He or she learns what is expected of them as a judge. If those who select judges demand accountability as a prerequisite for a judgeship, the candidate who is finally selected learns that his or her position is regarded as a representative position; more likely than not she or he will behave accordingly. If, in contrast, those who are involved in the selection process represent a broad range of actors, in toto they serve as a microcosm of the political culture of the jurisdiction for whom the judge will have responsibility for balancing the need for stability and change, the need for independence and accountability, and the need to make judicious use of his or her policymaking prerogative.

Judicial recruitment is indeed a complicated process, too often involving a complex mixture of legal philosophy, politics and ideology. A segment of the political system may attempt to pursue its interest by placing judges on the bench that are sympathetic to—or at the very least neutral toward—the interest in question. Success for the judge recruited in this setting pushes her or him toward the accountable end of the judicial dilemma continuum. Other interests work toward the establishment of an isolated and independent judiciary, and seek to establish methods of selection that are shielded as much as possible from public involvement. Experience has shown, however, that it is not altogether clear which formal method of selection produces either disproportionate accountability or independence. The problem is perhaps likely not to be understood from a study of the formal process through which a judge is recruited, but rather that we have not yet correctly viewed the judicial recruitment experience in the first place.

What is needed to understand the most profound effects of judicial recruitment—how it influences attitudes on the judicial dilemma—is a research model of judicial recruitment that allows the accumulation of comparative evidence over diverse jurisdictions and over time, and the application of that model to an empirical base of evidence systematically collected to test that model. The authors have indeed constructed such a model, and they have subjected it to a range of empirical testing that appears most promising. The model remains exploratory at this early stage of research, but promising avenues for meaningful data gathering and further analysis are clearly indicated.

Beginning in 1984, we began surveying voters in Oregon and Washington with the objective of understanding how the electorate responded to judicial candidates in nonpartisan primary and general elections. Through each subsequent survey we perfected our survey instrument, expanded our universe to include candidates for judicial election and appointment, and in one election we included judicial election campaign managers. We were struck with the wide variety of views and perspectives represented in these campaigns, among these candidates, and among voter reactions. All of these observations were recorded in the nonpartisan election systems of Oregon and Washington, however, hence limiting the extent to which findings noted here can be more broadly generalized. During the course of analyses performed on these empirical data, we were confronted with two principal questions: What did these highly different selection experiences in supposedly identical selection systems have in common? and Did these commonalties identified within nonpartisan election systems show up in other judicial recruitment experiences?

This book is an attempt to provide answers to these two questions. The authors succeed in identifying what all recruitment systems—federal and state— hold in common. By comparing systematic variations in the intensity of these common traits they have, quite possibly, discovered a key to our understanding of what factors are associated with the achievement of an appropriate balanced viewpoint among judges on the judicial dilemma. At the very least, this volume will encourage a new interest in research on how judges are selected, and provide a powerful model for exploring this important phenomenon in American politics.

Introduction

Laws are crucial to any concept of justice, but it is those who apply the laws that actually give shape to whatever degree of justice is attained. Maurice Rosenberg has captured this idea well:

> Justice is an alloy of men and mechanisms in which, as Roscoe Pound remarked, "men count more than machinery." Assume the clearest rules, the most enlightened procedures, the most sophisticated court techniques; the key factor is still the judge....The reason the judge makes or breaks the system of justice is that rules are not self-declaring or self applying. Even in a government of laws, men make decisions.[1]

And those decisions tell us much about justice.

Judges settle disputes involving individuals, governments and private entities. Further, in settling disputes, judges on occasion establish, reinforce or negate public policies. As they resolve disputes, judges are substituting "the notion of right for that of violence."[2] As they shape policies in the process of resolving disputes they confront issues that trouble society, occasionally substituting their view of what society needs for that of elected representatives. Those who preside over American courts—federal or state, appellate or trial—carry a heavy burden.

To resolve issues that litigants bring to the courts fairly, judges must remain objective as they weigh the arguments presented to them. However, it is naive to think that judges merely apply relevant law to clear facts. They exercise choice, searching for the best fit between the sometimes inapplicable or confusing law and disputed case facts. However, as they come to judgment, responsible judges must remain independent from the interests of the contending parties in order to be as objective as possible. The rule of law dictates this independence on the part of the judiciary.

Sometimes these contending interests require judges to confront issues generated by the community's history, economy, politics, or social structure. In

---

[1] Maurice Rosenberg, "The Qualities of Justice—Are They Strainable?" in Glenn R. Winters (ed.), *Judicial Selection and Tenure* (Chicago: American Judicature Society, 1973), p. 1.

[2] Edward M. Martin, *The Role of the Bar in Electing the Bench in Chicago* (Chicago: University of Chicago Press, 1936), p. 3.

resolving these issues judges shape policies rather directly.   In such circumstances democracy dictates that judges, like other public officials, be somehow accountable to the community for those decisions.   Judges may draw upon their experiences and knowledge to determine what coincides with the needs of the community.   Alternatively, they may assess the prevailing sentiments of the people in attempting a resolution.   Yet again, they may simply ignore society and rely upon the narrow dictates of the law, no matter the consequences to the community.   Finally, judges could put these considerations aside and turn to their own views of right and wrong to decide between parties.   Whatever the ultimate source of judgment, however, accountability is required.   A judge's perception of what is best for the community, her own common sense, his view of what the law requires, or her feeling for what is right must be susceptible to challenge by those in the community beyond the bench.   Majoritarian democracy demands no less.

How a judge balances these two conflicting demands—that of objectivity in the resolution of disputes and that of accountability when making or shaping policies—determines the degree of justice enjoyed by that community.   The issue for us is how do we pick those that can best fashion a balance between judicial independence and public accountability? This idea of "balance" is the beginning point of our analysis.

Two major forces shape how successful judges are in remaining objective and in defining the needs of society.   Initially, judges bring with them to the bench years of training and experience and a set of personal attributes.   These characteristics give judges their particular outlook on society, law and politics.   However, this outlook is tempered by the demands and constraints of a judgeship.   A judge is a distinct person, but a judgeship provides limits on and opportunities for the actions of that person.   This volume is concerned with the first half of the judging formula; how judges are recruited and how the recruiting processes experienced contribute to the views judges have concerning accountability and independence.

Unfortunately, research on judicial recruitment has not indicated clearly the one best way to select judges.   The difficulty in doing so relates to determining how to measure such factors as "integrity," "temperament," "intellect" or "impartiality."   It is also difficult to determine what background factors lend themselves best to judging.   For example, is having practiced with a large law firm better than having worked in the county prosecutor's office?

Some form of election or appointment is part of all the varieties of formal methods for selecting judges.   Advocates of the popular election of judges adopt Thomas Jefferson's compelling statement:

> I know of no safe depository of the ultimate powers of
> society but the people themselves; and if we think them not
> enlightened enough to exercise their control with wholesome
> discretion, the remedy is not to take it from them, but to
> inform their discretion with education.[3]

Those advocating appointments with long tenure favor Alexander
Hamilton's view that they would contribute "to the independent spirit
in judges which must be essential to the faithful performance of so
arduous duty."[4] Jefferson advocated accountability; Hamilton urged
independence. Both were right, but the need is for balance over time
between these two desiderata.

Judicial recruitment involves more than simply the act of voting
in an election or the formal appointment of an aspirant to the bench.
Elections require campaigns, the framing of issues, fundraising,
organization, advocates, opponents and considerable personal
commitment. Appointments require access to the appointing
authorities, well-placed supporters, public endorsements, petitions,
interviews and political experience. Oftentimes timing and luck play
a major role in both elections and appointments. How these and
other selection process requirements mesh, constituting a
recruitment experience, determines the winner and the loser. Also,
the experience determines which personal attributes are brought to
the bench to be matched with the demands of the office.

For a detailed picture of recruitment, we need to understand
what happens from the very beginning. We are attempting to provide
a framework in this volume that will assist in viewing judicial
recruitment from the beginning to the end, and help in gaining some
additional understanding of how that recruitment sequence can
contribute to a proper balance between independence and
accountability.

Volcansek and Lafon have written that

> The judiciary of a nation, as any other governmental
> institution, is affected by the culture in which it is located.
> Innovations and experiments in judicial structures and
> judicial powers have been resilient in some cultures...and
> short lived in others. Implicit in the question of the role and

---

[3] Thomas Jefferson, *Notes on the State of Virginia* (1779), quoted in Fawn M. Brodie,
Thomas Jefferson: An Intimate History (New York: Bantam Books, 1974), p. 602.
[4] Alexander Hamilton, "Federalist No. 78," in *The Federalist Papers* (New York:
Mentor Books, 1961), p. 469.

> power of the judiciary in a country's scheme of political
> power distribution is the issue of who names the judges.[5]

They are suggesting that those concerned with selection reform may be mistaken in searching for a system of selected judges that would fit all states and jurisdictions. Certainly, if a community's culture is reflected in some way in its court system, likely this reflection is at least partially formed during the judicial recruitment process, affecting it significantly from beginning to end. The successes of appointment of judges in one jurisdiction need not be similarly successful in another appointment system. We do not assume that our single-state case study of nonpartisan elections in Washington exhausts the forms it will take in other nonpartisan systems. However, the Washington experience may well possess shared characteristics of the often complicated and detailed selection process that can be found in Texas, Colorado, or the Fifth Circuit of the federal bench if one looks beyond the formal constitutional rules for selecting judges. A close look at the informal process may indeed reveal that state and federal recruitment systems are more alike than they are dissimilar. Our goal is to look at the informal and often ignored (but important) aspects of recruitment and to discover some commonalities that permit useful analysis.

---

[5] Mary L. Volcansek and Jacqueline Lucienne Lafon, *Judicial Selection: The Cross-Evolution of French and American Practices* (Westport, CT: Greenwood Press, 1988), p. 1.

Chapter One

A Short History of Judicial Selection

The history of the processes by which state and federal judges have been selected represents the intersection of law and politics, and whether at that point
justice is served. It is judges who determine at which point the two forces will
cross.[1] As expressed by Justice Benjamin Cardozo, "There is no guarantee of
justice...except the personality of the judge."[2] How to select those with the requisite personality is at the heart of any system of justice. In the beginning, the
leaders of the American revolution understood this.

> American statesmen were not naive; they knew it mattered what
> judges believed and who they were. How judges were to be chosen
> and how they were to act was a political issue in the Revolutionary
> generation, at a pitch of intensity rarely reached before or since.[3]

The History of State Judicial Recruitment

Those who designed the new governmental structures were determined to ensure that judges were both part of representative government and servants of the
law. This had not been their experience as colonists. A revulsion against and an
attraction to the English judicial experience shaped both federal and state selection systems. This schizophrenic tug-of-war came from what the Americans
knew of the history of the struggle between English monarchs and judges, their
experiences of the legal system during the colonial period, and their understanding of the potential a common law legal system held for a new democracy.[4]
This knowledge made it clearly understood that independence was to be of fundamental importance to state judiciaries and later to the federal bench.

---

[1] Mary L. Volcansek and Jacqueline Lucienne Lafon, *Judicial Selection: The Cross-Evolution of French and American Practices* (Westport, CT: Greenwood Press, 1988), p. 1.

[2] Benjamin N. Cardozo, *The Nature of the Judicial Process* (New Haven, CT: Yale University Press, 1922), pp. 16-17.

[3] Lawrence M. Friedman, *History of American Law* (New York: Simon and Schuster, 1985), p. 124.

[4] Evan Haynes, *The Selection and Tenure of Judges* (The National Conference of Judicial Councils, 1944), pp. 51-79.

> Undoubtedly, awareness of political manipulation of judges and jus-
> tice by the Crown and the insecurity of tenure of jurists had an effect
> on...the framers of both state and national constitutions.[5]

Sharpening this awareness was the experience the colonies had with colonial governors who ignored judicial rulings and often created courts in order to
appoint their friends and supporters, regardless of their qualifications.[6] Those
fashioning the new state basic laws understood that only through separation
from the executive was an independent judiciary possible. Assuring judicial
independence would permit Americans to enjoy the benefits of English common
law and individual rights. Thus the schizophrenia over the proper role of judges
resulted from a belief in the English system of law and courts but a rejection of
how the system had actually operated in the colonies.

The Articles of Confederation brought the thirteen original colonies
loosely together but provided for no judiciary beyond that which the states had
designed for themselves.[7] Each state had an appointed judiciary, selected either
by the legislature, or by the governor who had been selected by the legislature
or who remained under the close scrutiny of the legislature. The involvement of
the legislature in the appointment of judges assured the desired independence
from the executive, for, as yet, the idea of a tri-partite separation of powers that
placed courts apart from but equal to both executive and legislative branches
had not fully evolved. The principle of republicanism or representative democracy put the governing emphasis upon the legislative branch, and, consequently,
much of fine tuning of state judiciaries was left to the legislature. However, the
basic principles were outlined in the new state constitutions.[8]

---

[5] Volcansek and Lafon, *Judicial Selection*, p. 19.

[6] The Declaration of Independence confirmed the colonial practices with its condemnation of the
British monarch:

> "He has obstructed the Administration of Justice, by refusing his Assent to Laws for estab-
> lishing Judiciary Powers."
> "He has made Judges dependent on his Will alone, for the tenure of their offices, and the
> amount and payment of their salaries."

[7] Congress under the Articles of Confederation established a special court to try crimes on the high
seas and prize cases. The special Court of Appeals had a shaky appellate jurisdiction over state
courts in such matters and over its existence heard 56 cases. But predictably, the states persisted in
their resistance to any national control. See Julius Goebel, Jr., *History of the Supreme Court of the
United States: Antecedents and Beginnings to 1801* (New York: Macmillian, 1971), p. 172.

[8] For example, the Massachusetts Bill of Rights of 1780 declared that "It is the right of every citizen to be tried by judges as free, impartial, and independent as the lot of humanity will admit....
[T]he judges of the supreme judicial court should hold their offices as long as they behave themselves well; and they should have honorable salaries ascertained and established by standing laws."
Henry Steele Commager (ed.), *Documents of American History* (New York: Crofts, 1944), pp.
109-110.

If independence could be assured and popular support developed through the participation of the legislature in the process, then the British practice of appointing judges was acceptable. Judges in eight states (Connecticut, Delaware, Georgia, New Jersey, North Carolina, Rhode Island, South Carolina and Virginia) were appointed by the legislature and in the remainder (Maryland, Massachusetts, New Hampshire, New York and Pennsylvania) judges were appointed by the governor but only with the approval of a special council elected by legislators or appointed to serve as a check on the governor.[9]

Judicial independence meant more than assuring legislative involvement in appointments. The English and colonial experiences had taught the Americans that a secure tenure for judges was essential. Tenure was commonly awarded "for good behavior" although, again, the legislature could intervene. Impeachment and removal by legislative resolution or by some special body were part of state provisions. Upper limits were placed on age and controls over salaries and fees remained in the hands of the legislature, although the remuneration was to remain fixed or "adequate," providing some security.[10]

The influence of both the English experience and imitation of other states dictated the selection choices for several decades. The new states that entered the Union between 1776 and 1830 all adopted the selection schemes that their thirteen predecessors enjoyed. Five new states (Alabama, Illinois, Mississippi, Ohio and Tennessee) relied upon the legislature for appointments. Six others (Indiana, Kentucky, Louisiana, Maine, Missouri and Vermont) adopted appointment by the governor with either legislative advise and consent or approval from a legislative council.

The demise of the Federalists and the rise of Jeffersonian Democracy helped ease states into the Jacksonian period by emphasizing representative bodies and citizen participation.[11] Jacksonian democracy meant that the average citizen could not only use the extended franchise to pick his leaders, but he could share responsibility for governing. Egalitarianism, political efficacy, self-government and populism constituted Jacksonian principles. The election of judges by citizen voters and shorter tenures were the forms the movement took on in the judiciary. However, as Lawrence Friedman observed, the Jacksonian movement "did not mean, that every man could or should be a judge. Jackson himself, for example, did not appoint the common man to the bench."[12] Perhaps most of the lower court judges, especially justices of the peace or probate judges, were laypersons and even prior to the Jacksonian period were elected by

---

[9] For a compilation of original state provisions for judicial selection see Haynes, *The Selection and Tenure of Judges*, pp. 101-135.

[10] Ibid., 22-23.

[11] James Willard Hurst, *The Growth of American Law: The Law Makers* (Boston: Little Brown, 1950), p. 140.

[12] Friedman, *History of American Law*, p. 127.

the people. For example, in Vermont in 1777 every "freeman" had the "liberty of choosing the judges of inferior court of common pleas."[13]

Coupled with the Jacksonian movement was a variety of other factors which encouraged more popular control of judges. The few occasions when state judges exercised judicial review, challenging and in some cases negating legislative enactments, they invited closer popular scrutiny. Also, the common law had developed so that some feared courts were usurping the law-making powers of the legislature.

> To the extent that the courts were thought of as entrusted with powers which we should now regard as purely legislative, it was not unnatural to argue that they should somehow be subject to popular control.[14]

Jacksonian democracy and the movement into the agrarian and individualist West meant "the rule of the majority rather than that of property" and the rejection of the "[r]ule by the few, the well educated or well born."[15]

Impeachment had proven to be too difficult to punish arrogant judges, making elections and shorter terms acceptable alternatives.[16] The legal profession, reaching the same conclusion but for different reasons, saw popular election as an opportunity to provide the judiciary with its own separate constituency, thus ensuring it some measure of independence from the legislature.[17]

The swing away from legislative control over judicial selection was neither complete nor abrupt. Mississippi, which had originally adopted selection by legislative appointment with tenure during "good behavior," changed in 1832 to the popular election of judges with six-year terms. In 1846 New York followed suit, changing over to the popular election of all judges. Just over half of the 29 states that were part of the Union in 1846 adopted popular election of judges and every state admitted since 1846 followed suit for some if not all judges.[18] Those states, apparently satisfied with legislative selection, added restraint by shortening the terms for judges.

---

[13] Ibid., 126. Georgia in 1812 chose lower trial court judges by popular election; in 1816 Indiana followed the practice, joined by Michigan in 1836.

[14] Haynes, *The Selection and Tenure of Judges*, p. 96.

[15] Quoted in Volcansek and LaFon, *Judicial Selection*, p. 89.

[16] Impeachment was not totally ineffective but was viewed as a drastic solution that elections could more easily correct. See Friedman, *History of American Law*, pp. 129-130.

[17] Kermit L. Hall, "Progressive Reform and the Decline of Democratic Accountability: The Popular Election of State Supreme Court Judges, 1850-1920," *American Bar Foundation Research Journal* (1984): 347.

[18] Haynes writes that "In the year 1850 alone, seven states changed to popular election of judges; and thereafter, year by year until the Civil War, others followed." Haynes, *The Selection and Tenure of Judges*, p. 100. Imitation was among the reasons for the surge toward popular election of judges in some of the newer states. Older states had adopted elections, newer states followed suit.

Of course, the popular election of judges soon meant partisan elections. Party list ballots and partisan slates permitted voters to mark the ballot once to cast a vote for all party candidates, including judges, and, in effect, making parties responsible for recruiting judges. Political party conventions nominated judges and party loyalists elected them. Unfortunately, cronyism, payment of political debts, and political trading permeated much of the judicial selection process.

At the beginning of the twentieth century, statutory law began to replace common law doctrine, removing judges from many policy areas. The Progressive Movement gained a hold on politics with reforms like initiative, referendum and recall, primary elections, administrative regulation, and nonpartisanship. Coincidentally, the legal profession organized at the national but more importantly at the state level, to further the interests of lawyers. This interest extended to the recruitment of judges. Initially the bar could only hope that the political party would insist that candidates have some minimum qualifications.

> The bar associations generally did not try directly to influence the party leaders' choice of candidates; frequently, therefore, the bar found itself in the not-too-happy position of publicly recommending that the people accept the lesser evil.[19]

However, the election of political hacks to the bench, scandal, control by political machines and evidence of corruption especially in the big cities tarnished the judiciary. Judges and partisan politics were too closely aligned. Roscoe Pound's much referenced but little read 1906 address to the American Bar Association was symptomatic of the dissatisfaction with the prevailing system of electing judges. Although wide ranging, his speech pointed out that a cause of dissatisfaction with the American judicial system was due to "[p]utting courts into politics, and compelling judges to become politicians, [and] in many jurisdictions [this] has almost destroyed the traditional respect for the Bench."[20] According to Pound, most destructive was the popular election of judges. The push for reform gained momentum with the formation of the American Judicature Society in 1913. Rationalizing judicial administration and removing partisan politics from the selection of judges constituted its primary objectives.

Reform efforts followed two paths. One direction urged the adoption of nonpartisan elections of judges, which was supported by Progressives and bar associations. In the view of the Progressives, partisanship had little to do with judging and often resulted in placing unqualified jurists on state benches. For the lawyers the hope was that as political parties were removed from the election of judges, bar associations would be drawn into the vacuum. Judges in

---

[19] Hurst, *The Growth of American Law*, p. 130.

[20] "The Causes of Popular Dissatisfaction with the Administration of Justice," reprinted in *Journal of the American Judicature Society* 28 (1937): 178.

Cook County, Illinois or Chicago ran for office on a nonpartisan platform as early as 1873. However, not until the second decade of the century did nonpartisan judicial elections attract a significant number of jurisdictions. By 1927, 12 states employed the method.[21]

The other path led to the commission plan pushed by the American Judicature Society, judges and some reform minded lawyers. Nonpartisanship prevailed initially but the commission or Missouri plan gained momentum in the latter half of the twentieth century. Although it removed the direct influence of political parties from the process and although the voters were still involved in selecting their judges, dissatisfaction with the results of nonpartisan contests was voiced. The roll-off (voters who do not cast ballots for judges) increased with the removal of the political party label. Voters were expected to cast an informed vote but very little information was available. It was feared that special interests such as insurance companies, big business, labor unions or segments of the legal profession would determine close races. It was also felt that the quality of those elected had deteriorated. William Howard Taft, then ex-President and soon to be Chief Justice, addressed the American Bar Association in 1913, arguing that nonpartisanship had failed. Unqualified judges were being elected who were unable even to gain partisan support but could, through vigorous and deceptive campaigning, gain a judgeship.

Unnoticed in the reform was the fact that partisanship entered nearly as strongly and more surreptitiously through gubernatorial appointments used to fill vacancies caused by deaths, resignations or removals. Partisan considerations not only weighed heavily in governors' choices, but those appointed had the advantage of incumbency when they eventually had to face the voters to retain their positions.

Many lawyers and judges felt ill-at-ease with any form of popular election of judges - partisan or nonpartisan. In 1913 Albert M. Kales proposed a system of selecting judges around which the American Judicature Society rallied and in 1937 a "merit plan" similar to what Kales had proposed was endorsed by the American Bar Association.[22] In 1940, Missouri became the first state to adopt a

<hr>

[21] Larry C. Berkson, "Judicial Selection in the United States: A Special Report," in Elliot Slotnick (ed.), *Judicial Politics: Readings from Judicature* (Chicago: American Judicature Society, 1992), p. 58.

[22] Albert M. Kales was director of research for and one of the founders of the American Judicature Society. His proposal would have vacancies filled by appointment by a high elected official (he preferred an elected chief justice) from a list of names submitted by a commission "which would have an affirmative responsibility to seek out the best available judicial talent." The commission would be composed in part of "high judicial officers" and in part of laypersons. If a further check was needed, the legislature could confirm the appointee. After a period of time, the reappointment could be made by going through the same screening and appointment process again or the appointee would run on his or her record in an uncontested election. Glenn R. Winters, "Selection of Judges - An Historical Introduction," *Texas Law Review* 44 (1966): 1081, and "Judicial Selection and Tenure," in Winters (ed.), *Judicial Selection and Tenure* (Chicago: American Judicature Society, 1973), p. 19.

version of the plan which has subsequently been referred to as the Missouri Plan. California had earlier considered a similar system and finally instituted a plan that had elements of the Missouri plan.[23] The plan involves a nominating commission composed of lawyers, laypersons and judges. The commission evaluates candidates and nominates three or so names from which the governor appoints. After a short period of probation, the voters are asked whether to retain the judges who run on their record in an unopposed retention election. The plan was designed to combine the better parts of all the other selection systems. Politics, partisan or otherwise, was to be removed from the recruitment process.[24]

Versions of the Missouri plan and non-partisan elections now dominate the formal state selection methods. Twenty states elect some or all of their judges by means of nonpartisan elections. Twenty-three states use the Missouri plan to select some or all of their jurists. The trend now favors the Missouri plan.

The evolution of state judicial selection methods from appointments through legislative, partisan and non-partisan elections to the merit plan, was not clean and consistent. As one method became popular some of the old methods persisted, due to entrenched political interests, some satisfaction with what existed, or possibly inertia. To understand the particular mix in any one state, a review of its history is called for.[25]

As the formal methods of recruiting state judges shifted, those who participated in the selection, those who were represented, and those who had access to judicial office correspondingly shifted. The equilibrium between who participated in selection, the degree of representativeness of those selected and the openness of access reflected the politics of the moment.[26]

The selection debate over the past 200 years has largely been confined to whose politics is to be included or excluded from choosing judges. Initially, the goal was to strengthen the legislature's role in picking and dismissing judges and weaken the role of the executive. Later political parties replaced the legislature as the lead player in the selection drama. Fear of party politics led to nonpartisan elections which were designed to encouraged the citizen-voter to be involved but rather brought interest groups, especially bar associations, into recruitment. Next, but not finally, some of the voters' influence was sacrificed and the legal profession's role increased through the Missouri plan. The upshot

---

[23] Rather than having a nominating commission, the California version has a confirming body which has some influence as a threat after nominations have been made.

[24] The definitive analysis of the Missouri plan is Richard A. Watson and Rondal G. Downing, *The Politics of the Bench and the Bar* (New York: Wiley and Sons, 1969).

[25] Bradley C. Canon, "The Impact of Formal Selection Processes on the Characteristics of Judges—Reconsidered," *Law & Society Review* 6 (1972): 579.

[26] Charles H. Sheldon and Nicholas P. Lovrich, "State Judicial Recruitment," in John B. Gates and Charles A. Johnson (eds.), *The American Courts: A Critical Assessment* (Washington, D.C.: CQ Press), p. 166.

is that in states today there is a mix of methods and often even within a single state. Nonetheless, it is most likely that the same traditional groups are involved to varying degrees in recruiting judges along with a collection of newer groups. All are attempting to exert some influence over who finally dons the robes of judicial office.

The debate among those seeking influence is often couched in promoting the "best" candidates to the state benches, but, underlying the debate is a desire to promote those who appear to "best" represent particular interests. The need is for the debate to be more attentive toward determining which system better balances the need for some accountability against the equally important need for judges to be independent. It must be recognized that this may mean different processes in different jurisdictions.

The History of Federal Selection

Although federal recruitment has been a product of the same forces that shaped state selection, it has formally remained the same since 1789. However, the shifts have been significant within the broad outlines of formal constitutional provisions.

Constitutional Beginnings of Federal Judicial Selection

During the Constitutional Convention, little debate ensued over the tenure to be enjoyed by judges and whether they should be appointed or elected to their posts. The English example and their own colonial experiences compelled the framers to provide federal judges with a high degree of independence. They unanimously agreed that both inferior and Supreme Court judges should be appointed and should hold their offices during good behavior. They wished to insulate the federal judiciary from political manipulation to secure "a steady, upright, and impartial administration of the laws."[27] They feared that judges, who held their offices by temporary commissions, would refuse to adhere to the Constitution in an "inflexible and uniform" manner. Moreover, "periodical appointments, however, regulated or by whomever made, would be fatal to [the judges'] necessary independence."[28] Therefore, from the outset, the framers regarded federal judges as unique from other government officials. As Henry Abraham notes, when it came to the judiciary, the delegates did not even consider let alone advocate "representativeness"; it was an important democratic principle reserved to the legislature.[29]

---

[27] Cited in William P. Rogers, "Judicial Appointments in the Eisenhower Administration," *Journal of the American Judicature Society* 41 (1957): 41.

[28] Ibid.

[29] Henry J. Abraham, "A Bench Happily Filled: Some Historical Reflections on the Supreme Court Appointment Process," *Judicature* 66 (February 1983): 284.

Whereas a sense of comity existed concerning the tenure and appointment of federal judges, intensive debate characterized the framers' efforts to determine who would appoint the principal officers of the new government, including judges.[30] Was Congress or the Executive to have prime responsibility? On one side were those who feared tyrannical tendencies in the executive and on the other those who advocated a strong, energetic [President]."[31] One faction, including George Mason of Virginia and John Rutledge of South Carolina, wanted to curb the monarchical excesses of the chief executive by vesting the appointment power in the Senate.[32] They felt to grant "so great a power in any single person" would make the people think that the Convention was "leaning too much toward Monarchy."[33] They also viewed the Senate, with its plural membership, as being more effective at gathering information on potential nominees than a solitary official.[34]

Another group, headed by Alexander Hamilton and James Madison, in contrast, argued that placing the appointment power in the national legislature would make the government's principal officers dependent upon Congress.[35] They felt that the President would be "more qualified and more responsible in making appointments than a numerous body."[36] In addition, they viewed the cabal, machinations and intrigue that had pervaded the state legislatures as more of a threat to the new government than a single executive officer exercising despotic power.[37]

The resolution authorizing the Senate to appoint judges was debated vigorously.[38] The proposal was criticized on the grounds that it would be difficult

---

[30] See James Madison, *Notes of the Debates in the Federal Convention of 1787*; Henry Cabot Lodge (ed.), *The Federalist*; Charles Warren, *The Making of the Constitution*; Joseph P. Harris, *The Advice and Consent of the Senate*; Henry J. Abraham, *Justice and Presidents: A Political History of Appointments to the Supreme Court*; and Howard Ball, *Courts and Politics: The Federal Judicial System*.

[31] Abraham, "A Bench Happily Filled: Some Historical Reflections on the Supreme Court Appointment Process," 284.

[32] See Thomas Jefferson's list of grievances in the *Declaration of Independence*. David M. O'Brien, *Judicial Roulette: Report of the Twentieth Century Fund Task Force on Judicial Selection* (New York: Priority Press, 1988).

[33] Quoted in Harris, *The Advice and Consent of the Senate*, p. 20.

[34] Ibid., 17.

[35] Ibid., 17-18.

[36] Ibid., 18.

[37] In opposing the appointment of judges by the legislature, Madison contended that "besides the danger of intrigue and partiality, many of the members [are] not judges of the requisite qualifications." Ibid., 20.

for a body so great in number to make a good choice. Another suggestion favored granting the executive the sole authority to appoint judges. However, each time the proposal came up for a vote, the Convention defeated it.[39] Later Nathaniel Gorham authored a motion supporting the appointment of judges by the executive with advice and consent of the Senate.[40] Twice the framers rejected this motion.[41] Madison introduced a similar proposal—the appointment by the President, subject to disapproval by two-thirds of the Senate. The framers never voted on this measure. Madison then modified his initial proposal, requiring only a simple majority in the Senate to reject a nomination. However, this provision lost by a vote of six to three.[42]

On July 21, 1787, the Convention approved appointment by the Senate as the mode for selecting judges.[43] Debate, however, erupted when the Committee of Eleven proposed that the President should nominate, and by and with the advice and consent of the Senate, appoint Judges of the Supreme Court, as well as all other Officers of the United States.[44] Supporters of an "energetic executive" objected to the decision, arguing that it placed too much power in the Senate. Despite his previous support for vesting the appointment power solely in the executive, Gouverneur Morris supported the committee's proposal, reasoning "that as the President was to nominate there would be responsibility, and as the Senate was to concur, there would be security."[45]

After further debate, the committee amended the proposal, granting the President the authority to make recess appointments while the Senate was not in

---

[38]   Ibid., 19. The method by which judges were to be selected was subjected to intensive floor debate for a total of twelve days in June, July, August and September. Abraham, "A Bench Happily Filled: Some Historical Reflections on the Supreme Court Appointment Process," 284.

[39]   Ibid., 19.

[40]   O'Brien, *Judicial Roulette*, p. 30.

[41]   Harris, *The Advice and Consent of the Senate*, p. 20; according to O'Brien, Gorham's motion lost on a tie vote, p. 30.

[42]   O'Brien, *Judicial Roulette*, p. 30.

[43]   Charles Black, "A Note on Senatorial Consideration of Supreme Court Nominees," *Yale Law Journal* 79 (1970): 660.

[44]   Ibid., 660. Interestingly, Chase contends "that it is unclear why the Founding Fathers granted the Senate the power to advise and give consent to appointments." The records of the Convention clearly suggest that it was a compromise that fit nicely with the general theory of "checks and balances." Also Chase, more accurately, asserts that "it is equally unclear how they expected the Senate to perform these functions." Harold W. Chase, *Federal Judges: The Appointing Process* (Minneapolis: University of Minnesota Press, 1972), p. 188.

[45]   Quoted in Harris, *The Advice and Consent of the Senate*, p. 24. The final version found in Article II, Section 2 of the Constitution reads in part: the President "shall nominate, and by and with the Advice and Consent of the Senate, shall appoint Ambassadors, other public Ministers and Consuls, Judges of the Supreme Court, and all other Officers of the United States, whose Appointments are not herein otherwise provided for, and which shall be established by law."

session.[46] On September 7, the framers agreed to the amended provision.[47] A final change, however, occurred on the next to last day of the Convention. The delegates agreed to a clause proposed by Gouverneur Morris authorizing Congress to vest the appointment of inferior officers "in the President alone, in the Courts of Law, or in the heads of Departments."[48]

During the ensuing debates over the ratification of the Constitution by the states, the method designated for appointing judges received little attention.[49] Alexander Hamilton, however, did discuss the appointment power in The Federalist, Nos. 66, 72, 76, and 77. He described, in Federalist No. 76, the Senate's role in the selection of federal judges as a "check upon a spirit of favoritism in the President...one that would tend greatly to prevent the appointment of unfit characters from State prejudice, from family connection, from personal attachment, or from a view of popularity."[50] However, according to Henry Abraham, the framers feared favoritism from a 'partial' Senate more than the President. John Adams, who did not attend the Constitutional Convention, maintained that "partisan considerations rather than the fitness of the nominees would often be the controlling consideration of the Senate in passing on nominations."[51] However, in No. 77, Hamilton made the argument that the Senate would not exert undue influence on presidential nominations.

The First Congress convened on March 4, 1789, to give life to the broad governmental framework laid out by the Constitution. One of the first duties of the Senate was to establish a national judiciary.[52] The Constitution had only

[46] O'Brien, *Judicial Roulette*, p. 31. Article II, Section 3 gives the President power to make recess appointments. Controversies have arisen over the extent to which Presidents have the power to ingeniously expand on the meaning of recess appointments to the Supreme Court and other federal courts. According to Chase, some argue that the President can fill only a vacancy that happened to occur during a recess; whereas, others argue he can also fill vacancies that happen to exist during a recess. See in Harold W. Chase, "Federal Judges: The Appointing Process," *Minnesota Law Review* 51 (1966): 193.

[47] Charles Black argues that the last vote must have meant that those who wanted appointment by the Senate alone--and in some cases by the whole Congress--were satisfied that a compromise had been reached and did not think the legislative part in the process had been reduced to a minimum. Black, "A Note on Senatorial Consideration of Supreme Court Nominees," *Yale Law Journal* 79 (March 1970): 661.

[48] O'Brien, *Judicial Roulette*, p. 31.

[49] Abraham, "A Bench Happily Filled: Some Historical Reflections on the Supreme Court Appointment Process," 285.

[50] Lodge, *The Federalist*, pp. 474-475.

[51] Abraham, "A Bench Happily Filled: Some Historical Reflections on the Supreme Court Appointment Process," 285.

[52] On April 7, 1789, the Senate appointed a Special Judiciary Committee. The Committee of 1789 consisted of ten men (one from each state), comprising one half of the Senate membership. See Charles Warren, "New Light on the History of the Federal Judiciary Act of 1789," *Harvard Law Review* 37 (1923): 57-58.

provided that "the judicial Power of the United States shall be vested in one Supreme Court, and in such inferior Courts as the Congress may from time to time ordain and establish." It did not dictate, however, the size of the Supreme Court, and it only briefly outlined its jurisdiction. Moreover, it was absolutely silent about how Congress ought to organize lower courts, if it determined them necessary. Therefore, the Senate's Special Judiciary Committee of 1789, and Oliver Ellsworth, William Patterson, and Caleb Strong in particular, were handed the important task of

> settling the composition of the Supreme Court, of organizing inferior
> federal courts, of forming modes of procedure, and most important of
> all, of establishing the extent of the Supreme Courts appellate juris-
> diction, both with reference to state and inferior federal courts.[53]

On September 24, 1789, after spending a half a year on its composition, Congress passed the Judiciary Act of 1789. According to Justice Brown the Judicial Bill was "probably the most important and the most satisfactory Act ever passed by Congress," and that the "wisdom and forethought with which it was drawn have been the admiration of succeeding generations."[54] The Act provided that the Supreme Court should consist of a Chief Justice and five Associate Justices, any four of whom should be a quorum. It also created a lower court system and defined the appellate jurisdiction of the Supreme Court.

On the day that Washington[55] approved the Judiciary Act, he also sent to the Senate his nominations for Chief Justice and five Associate Justices. Washington's correspondence illustrates how seriously he took the important task of selecting the nation's judges. In a letter to his future Attorney General, Edmund Randolph, he wrote:

> Impressed with a conviction that the true administration of justice is
> the firmest pillar of good government, I have considered the first ar-
> rangement of the judicial department, as essential to the happiness of
> the country and the stability of its political system. Hence, the selec-
> tion of the fittest characters to expound the laws and dispense justice
> has been an invariable subject of anxious concern.[56]

In writing to John Jay, his nominee for Chief Justice, he stated:

> In nominating you for the important station which you now fill, I not
> only acted in conformity to my best judgment, but I trust I did a

---

[53]   William Mitchell, "The Supreme Court in Washington's Time," *American Bar Association Journal* 18 (1932): 341.

[54]   Quoted in Warren, "New Light on the History of the Federal Judiciary Act of 1879," 52.

[55]   Washington is the only President to fill at one time every seat of the Court. Only four Presidents since Washington--Jackson, Lincoln, Taft and Roosevelt—have appointed even a majority of the members of the Court, and their appointments were not simultaneous.

[56]   Quoted in Mitchell, "The Supreme Court in Washington's Time," 341.

grateful thing to the good citizens of these United States; and I have
full confidence that the love which you bear to our country, and a desire to promote the general happiness, will not suffer you to hesitate a
moment to bring into action the talents, knowledge and integrity
which are so necessary to be exercised at the head of that department
which must be considered the keystone of our political fabric.[57]

To another he wrote:

Considering the judicial system as the chief pillar upon which our
national government must rest, I have thought it my duty to nominate, for the high offices in that department, such men as I conceived
would give dignity and lustre to our national character.[58]

Washington's first six appointees to the Supreme Court had a sterling national reputation and were in the prime of their life, the oldest being fifty-seven
and the youngest thirty-eight. All but two had previous judicial experience.
Washington first selected John Jay of New York, then Secretary of Foreign Affairs, for the Chief Justiceship; he then chose John Rutledge, William Cushing,
James Wilson, John Blair and James Iredell to fill the Associate positions. The
Senate swiftly confirmed each nomination.[59]

What criteria or standards did Washington heed when screening prospective nominees to the federal bench? Turning to the Constitution would not have
assisted him, because it is virtually silent on the topic of judicial qualifications.
Of all three branches of government, the Constitution devotes the least attention
to the judicial branch. It does not even dictate minimum age, citizenship, and
residency qualifications for Supreme Court Justices; nor does it require the candidate to be a lawyer. Moreover, although it briefly mentions the Chief
Justiceship in Article I, it does not delineate how the Chief Justice should be
selected or how long he should serve. For instance, "Chiefs could have been
designated for fixed terms coinciding with the terms of presidents, or chiefs
might have been chosen by the Court, itself, rather than imposed from outside."[60]

The debates at the Constitutional Convention, over which Washington
presided, would have been equally unenlightening. According to Henry
Abraham, "while the question of the methodology to be employed for judicial
appointments was subjected to intensive floor debate...criteria for such
appointments were neither debated, nor did they appear to loom as a matter of

---

[57] Ibid.

[58] Ibid.

[59] Ibid.

[60] John R. Vile, "The Selection and Tenure of Chief Justices," *Judicature* 78 (1994): 98.

either significance or puzzlement."[61] The few delegates who addressed the issue of criteria seemed to assume that merit, as opposed to favoritism, would govern appointments. Alexander Hamilton maintained that "the Senate whatever its stance on a particular nominee might be, would be guided by a candidate's merit."[62] Moreover, the framers did not foresee the rise of political parties, and therefore, did not find it necessary to address whether partisan considerations should play a role in the appointment process.[63] Thus, if the debates during the Convention or provisions in the Constitution offered Washington any guidance, it was to reconfirm the contention that merit, not representativeness,[64] was to be the sole criterion for selecting judges.

In screening judicial candidates, however, Washington went beyond the standard of mere competency. According to Henry Abraham, he "probably more than any other president, not only had a septet of criteria for Court candidacy, but adhered to them predictably and religiously."[65] His criteria included the following: (1) support and advocacy of the Constitution; (2) distinguished service in the Revolution; (3) active participation in the political life of state or nation; (4) prior judicial experience on lower tribunals; (5) either a "favorable reputation with his fellows" or personal ties with Washington himself; (6) geographic suitability; and (7) love of our country.[66] Of the seven, the first was the most important—Washington sought only ardent Federalists to fill each vacant judgeship. Thus, as Howard Ball notes, the nation's first President "began the process of politicization of the judicial branch."[67]

Although the Constitution lacked explicit guidelines, permitting the appointment process to evolve naturally and to develop its own set of customs and conventions, Washington's appointments provided a strong beginning. Designating district court judges as "Other Officers" and establishing "senatorial courtesy" were significant conventions that emerged during Washington's presidency. However, in the early years of the Republic the President made few judicial appointments; thus, there was little incentive to formalize or institutionalize the recruitment process.[68] The real difficulty arose from a lack individuals

---

[61] Abraham, "A Bench Happily Filled: Some Historical Reflections on the Supreme Court Appointment Process," 284.

[62] Ibid., 285.

[63] Ibid.

[64] According to Abraham, "representativeness" was to be reserved to the legislature. Ibid., 284.

[65] Abraham, *Justices and Presidents*, p. 71.

[66] Ibid., 72.

[67] Howard Ball, *Courts and Politics: The Federal Judicial System* 2 ed. (Englewood Cliffs, NJ: Prentice-Hall, 1987), p. 175.

[68] Rogers cites Senator Breckenridge's statement that "the time will never arrive when America will stand in need of thirty-eight federal judges," to support his contention that numerically judicial

willing to serve due to the arduous requirements of circuit riding and a paltry salary.[69] However, as Congress increased the number of judgeships, and the number of political actors involved in judicial selection increased, the need for regularized procedures became more pronounced. These procedures are detailed in chapters 8, 9, 10, and 11, but the conflict over the appropriate role of the Senate and the President in the process still remains. Much of the debate today is simply a repeat of what concerned the Founders in Philadelphia more than 200 years ago. In a real sense, the evolution of the recruitment of federal judges has been how the President and the Senate play out their respective roles.

---

selection could not have posed a problem during Washington's presidency. Rogers, "Judicial Appointments in the Eisenhower Administration,": 38.

[69] Ibid.

Chapter Two

A Model for Understanding Judicial Recruitment

The Judges' Dilemma

According to the precepts of democracy, public officials should be responsible to the public for the policies they establish and the rules they administer. In theory, this is the meaning of majoritarian rule and representative democracy. At the same time, however, the weak, the isolated, the shunned and unconventional individual or politically ineffective and potentially vulnerable political minority must be protected from the overwhelming political power of the majority.[1] Protecting minority rights is as much a part of the tenets of democracy as is majority rule. Those who make public policy must be held accountable, but their public policies must not breach the wall separating inalienable rights from everyday politics. Conflicts arise from time to time when the majority demands that the minority relinquish some of its rights, or denies it some rights granted to the majority. A viable democratic political system is designed to ensure that not only are the majority's demands considered, but that checks are placed on the scope of the policy responses generated by those demands.

Elections, interest group politics, public opinion, media attention, and party discipline all are methods of holding public officials accountable to the needs and wants of the majority, or segments thereof. The minority is best protected when the majority exercises restraint; when government officials, especially judges, carefully consider responses to the majority. The courts' role in

---

[1] Illustrative of this concern by the Supreme Court is found in footnote 4 in *U.S. v. Carolene Products Co.*, 304 U.S. 144 (1938):

> There may be narrower scope for operation of the presumption of constitutionality when legislation appears on its face to be within a specific prohibition of the Constitution, such as those of the first ten amendments, which are deemed equally specific when held to be embraced within the Fourteenth.
>
> It is unnecessary to consider now whether legislation which restricts those political processes which can ordinarily be expected to bring about repeal of undesirable legislation, is to be subjected to more exacting judicial scrutiny under general prohibition of the Fourteenth Amendment than are most other types of legislation.
>
> Nor need we inquire whether similar considerations enter into the review of statutes directed at particular religions...or racial minorities...whether prejudiced against discrete, and insular minorities may be a special condition which tends seriously to curtail the operation of those political processes ordinarily to be relied upon to protect minorities, and which may call for a corresponding more searching inquiry. p. 152.

the process, however, places them in a dilemma unique to the judiciary. Judges settle disputes, and in the process they occasionally affirm, reaffirm or deny public policies as established by the legislature or as administered by the executive. Judges, thus, on occasion are policy makers. According to Gates and Johnson:

> American courts do make public policy...much of this policy is politically significant and enduring. Regardless of the type of court (trial or appellate) or its level in the federal system (state or federal), judicial bodies make authoritative decisions that allocate societal resources, values and costs.[2]

Judges have also confirmed that making or shaping policy is what they do. In **Gregory v. Ashcroft** the U.S. Supreme Court was confronted with the question of whether judges were properly considered to be policy-makers.[3] The Court, in an opinion authored by Justice O'Connor, observed (as had Benjamin Cardozo) that:

> Each [common-law judge] indeed is legislating within the limits of his competence. No doubt the limits for the judge are narrower. He legislates only between gaps. He fills the open spaces in the law.... [W]ithin the confines of these open spaces and those of precedent and tradition, choice moves with a freedom which stamps its action as creative. The law which is the resulting product is not found but made.[4]

Accepting this, the judicial dilemma places judges in a position where other public officials are found at their peril. The position requires that some sort of balance be reached between the two conflicting but essential demands placed on the American judiciary. On the one hand, judges must be **accountable** to the public or to its representatives for the policy decisions they make; majoritarian democracy demands no less. On the other hand, judges must be **independent** from political pressures and public outcry in order to settle disputes between parties fairly, to protect the individual and minority from the un-

---

[2] John B. Gates and Charles A. Johnson (eds.), *The American Courts: A Critical Assessment* (Washington, D.C.: CQ Press, 1991), p. 1.

[3] 111 S.Ct 2395 (1991). If, indeed, judges were properly considered to be policy makers, then they were exempt from the provisions of the Federal Age Discrimination in Employment Act and thus could be required to retire at a state constitution-mandated age of 70 in Missouri. The argument was made that besides judicial review and common law powers which affect policy, appellate judges supervise much of what lower courts do, court rules are promulgated by high courts, and the legal profession is regulated and disciplined by courts. However, what remained an established fact is that judges exercise discretion when deciding.

[4] Ibid., p. 2412 from Benjamin Cardozo, *The Nature of the Judicial Process* (New Haven: Yale University Press, 1921), pp. 113-115. The **Gregory** court recognized judges as policy makers and they were thus required to follow Missouri's mandatory retirement age.

warranted demands of the majority, and to assure stability to the law; such is the meaning of "rule of law."

The judges' dilemma becomes increasingly more complicated as one ponders its elements. To whom should the judges be accountable? From what interests or from whom should they remain independent? These are among the difficult questions which arise. Judicial accountability can take two forms which, of course, have their counterparts at the independence extreme. Judges who respond to **public accountability** weigh the demands of the community, state or nation through the ballot box, public opinion, their own experiences or impressions of what the media report.[5] Judges who ignore these demands rely on traditions of independence, isolating themselves from the community and the public.[6] Equally salient, **political accountability** comes to bear when legislatures, governors or executive agencies demand consideration—if not satisfaction—from those on state benches. By ignoring or resisting these pressures or temptations, judges display political independence.

Conceivably, judges might experience a significant degree of independence from the public but nonetheless be politically obligated to a governor for their appointment. In such a situation political accountability would remain. In other situations, however, the pressures of both versions of accountability may be largely absent, giving judges a high degree of independence. Given these equally desirable but conflicting demands placed on judges, ideally a *balance* should be sought.

Judicial Selection as a Major Factor

Judicial selection bears directly on the particular weight given accountability or independence. The various methods by which judges are recruited are either designed to or inadvertently lead to an enhancement, impediment or a balance between one or the other of the competing demands. Judges are often elected or defeated, appointed or rejected, because they support certain policies, share with their constituency particular views regarding political or legal issues, or possess characteristics with which voters can identify (such as local origins, gender, or ethnicity). Paradoxically, nearly all observers recognize the need for judges to be independent from the other branches of government as well as from the strident cries of the public or the pressures of special interests. If, during selection,

[5] Stephen Wasby's version of judicial accountability is appropriate. "Generally...accountability...mean[s] keeping an institution's decisions in line with community political or social values and otherwise imposing constraints on the courts' exercise of discretion." "Accountability of Courts" in Scott Greer, Ronald Hedlund, and James Gibson (eds), *Accountability in Urban Society* (Beverly Hills: Sage, 1978), p. 145.

[6] The traditions of independence would compel judges to follow closely precedent, construe statutes rather than exercise constitutional review, change law only incrementally, observe higher court rulings strictly and reach unanimity on appellate benches with few dissents and separate concurrences. Often the doctrine of the political questions may be invoked whereby courts refuse to decide the case.

a judge has few obligations to others for his or her election or appointment, independence is enhanced.

Because of the centrality of the recruitment process to the issue of judicial independence, scholars and politicians alike have focused on understanding how the various methods of judicial selection shape those who survive the process. Do certain systems make judges more accountable—and if they do, to whom or to what interests are they more likely to be responsive? Does selection set them largely free from public responsibilities? What do we really know about how methods of selection affect the proclivities of judges?

Judicial Selection Scholarship

A thriving cottage industry has evolved among scholars researching how recruitment practices affect judges. Unfortunately, on a subject so important there is a lack of reliable evidence which might guide those who wish either to reform or to prevent change in the selection process. In 1957 James Willard Hurst aptly observed:

> The methods and ideas concerning the selection and tenure of judges
> in the United States present a story that can be told briefly. But for
> lack of satisfactory evidence by which to weigh the results, the story
> is disappointingly abstract and barren.[7]

After over four decades of collective effort since Hurst's remarks, the story remains alarmingly confusing and all too brief. Scholars have been forced to conclude as Larry Baum did in 1995:

> Despite the heated debate about how to select judges, it is not clear
> that formal systems make an enormous difference.... Nor do formal
> systems for selecting judges necessarily produce systematic differ-
> ences in the policies that courts adopt.[8]

Not only have students of courts been unable to reach any firm conclusions regarding the effects of formal methods of selection, but no overall framework by which we can view judicial recruitment has been developed. Elliot Slotnick recently concluded that the study of judicial recruitment "is not an area where great theoretical advances of broad interest and applicability are likely to be made" and scholarly works "have tended to take place in limited research contexts where analysts have viewed the trees but not the forest."[9]

---

[7] James Willard Hurst, *The Growth of American Law* (Boston: Little Brown, 1957), p. 122.

[8] Lawrence Baum, "Electing Judges," in Lee Epstein, *Contemplating Courts* (Washington, D.C.: CQ Press, 1995), p. 42. See, however, Daniel R. Pinello, *The Impact of Judicial Selection Method on State Supreme Court Policy* (Westport: Greenwood Press, 1995).

[9] Elliot Slotnick, "Review Essay on Judicial Recruitment and Selection," *Justice System Journal* 13 (1988): 121.

Several explanations might be suggested to account for the lack of prog-ress in our understanding of judicial recruitment. Much attention is diverted away from objective research because of the "politics" surrounding judicial se-lection. Instead of searching for a way to confront the judicial dilemma, many selection advocates are striving to place on federal and state benches those who will further (or at least not hinder) their special interests. Lawyers' professional organizations would like more control over judicial selection. Politicians typi-cally seek to bring more partisanship into the equation. Good government re-form groups unfailingly strive to take politics out of consideration. The problem is that objective analysis often gives way to political advocacy.

Aside from the political aspects of the selection processes, those attempt-ing to view these processes objectively are also confronted with considerable analytical problems. Scholars recognize, but fail to account for the fact that judicial recruitment is a complicated process. At first appearance the various methods of bringing lawyers to the state and federal benches fall into five seemingly simple categories: 1) merit systems involving a nominating commis-sion; 2) gubernatorial or presidential appointments; 3) partisan elections; 4) non-partisan elections; and, 5) legislative election.

A closer look at each of these five methods reveals a more complex pic-ture, however. Often judges on trial courts of general jurisdiction are selected by methods different from those used to select appeals judges in the state.[10] The federal judiciary is one clear example, as district court judges are products of senatorial courtesy or some partisan version of it while appointments to the Su-preme Court are characterized by presidential preferences and Senate acquies-cence. In addition, Court of Appeals judges are products of a senatorial preference often as strong as that felt in appointments of federal district judges. States and their senators commonly lay claim to particular seats in a circuit. In a single state, depending upon the jurisdiction, judges at the same level may arrive at their position through somewhat different means.[11] Some states use one method for initial selection, and a quite different process for retention.[12]

In partisan and nonpartisan election systems, vacancies are filled by the governor, and subsequent elections are required for retaining the appointee.[13] In nonpartisan systems partisanship is nonetheless an important factor in cam-paigns, as well as in gubernatorial appointments to vacancies. The nomination

---

[10] For example, Florida and Tennessee.

[11] Arizona, Kansas and Missouri.

[12] Gubernatorial appointment to fill vacancies is most common, as in Washington and Oregon. California judges begin as gubernatorial appointees, but later run in a retention election.

[13] For example, nearly two-thirds of all Washington judges were initially appointed, and because of this incumbency are most often elected to their appointed position. James Herndon, "Appoint-ment as a Means of Initial Accession to Elective State Courts of Last Resort," *North Dakota Law Review* 38 (1962): 60.

process in one-party states most often determines the outcome in partisan elections. Divisive and costly campaigns are not limited to partisan races.[14] Some states, at different times, may experience uneventful elections or appointment campaigns while later, in the same jurisdiction, they may witness hotly contested races.

Appointive methods may also vary considerably between very active and sustained efforts to catch the governor's, senator's or president's attention, a process that is all too often conducted beyond the not always watchful eyes of the press and public. Variation in intensity and publicity are evident in the federal system, at both the circuit and district court levels. Informal and "hidden" activities, long before an election is held or an appointment made, largely determine the final selection to state and federal benches in many instances.

Also, as previously noted, the judicial recruitment studies tend to focus on one or two states during one or two selection cases. Longitudinal studies are rare, and multi-state data sets are seriously lacking.[15] Even these few studies are unable to account for the different details evident in one single formal method such as in the merit plan.[16] What may be happening is an attempt to compare largely incomparable phenomena. However, despite the fact that the study of recruitment is complex, it should not be abandoned.

In fact, different selection systems have more in common than initially would appear, providing opportunities for renewed study. Nearly all recruitment studies have focused on the *formal* methods by which judges are selected.[17] The constitutional and statutory definitions of these methods provide the basis for study. For example, Oregon and Washington are viewed together because both are formally classified as non-partisan states. The assumption is

---

[14] Roy Schotland, "Elective Judges' Campaign Financing: Are State Judges' Robes the Emperor's Clothes of American Democracy?" *Journal of Law & Policy* 2 (1985): 57.

[15] For example, the composition of the nominating commission may vary. The politics of the appointing governors differ. Performance evaluations before retention elections may be absent. What appear on the surface to be similarities may in practice be differences.

[16] Some exceptions that involve multi-state and longitudinal data are: M. Hall and Larry Aspin, "What 20 Years of Judicial Retention Elections Have Told Us," *Judicature* 70 (1987): 340; Philip Dubois, *From Ballot to Bench: Judicial Elections and the Quest for Accountability* (Austin: University of Texas Press, 1980); and Bradley Canon, "The Impact of Formal Selection on the Characteristics of Judges—Reconsidered," *Law & Society Review* 6 (1972): 579.

[17] Daniel Pinello has compared formal selection systems, but from a different perspective. Using a "most similar systems" approach, he compares similar states which have different formal methods of selecting judges and focuses on specific case policy outcomes of each state. For example, particular cases decided by the Virginia Supreme Court (legislative selection) are compared with those rendered by its sister state West Virginia (popular election). Case policy differences are then attributed to selection method. Although his model may be too parsimonious, he suggests some important differences which are reported in chapters that follow. Pinello, *The Impact of Judicial Selection Method.*

that because each state has the same type of formal recruitment procedure, judges with similar perspectives will result.[18] Mississippi and Pennsylvania recruit their judges through partisan elections, and therefore like results are also expected. When the similarities do not occur, the conclusion is that recruitment doesn't really matter.[19]

It is the *informal practices* that are not factored into the research. For example, because of informal practices the appointments made by two different governors, or sometimes by the same governor, may involve different motivations, endorsements and procedures, making it difficult to isolate patterns in the overall formal appointment process. Similarly, a non-partisan election may lead to the election of a particular judge because of partisan cues from past political activity. The nomination of a set of candidates by a nominating commission in a merit plan system may be based on predictions about the governor's preferences, differing little from an appointive system. It should be recognized that the informal processes shape significantly the outcome of the formal selection methods. A different view of how judges are brought to the state and federal benches is needed to incorporate what happens throughout the full selection sequence.

The recognition of a need for a new perspective does not make an understanding of the formal process irrelevant.[20] Aspirants to the bench consider their chances, organize their campaigns and shape their behavior in terms of their appraisal of the chances for election victory, gubernatorial appointment or commission nomination. To use a horse racing analogy, what transpires between the starting gate and the finish line determines the winner even though the contestants travel the same distance, carrying roughly the same weight. At the end of the race, many have been eliminated for reasons not evident if the focus is solely on the finish line. Thus, selection processes must be examined in a

---

[18] Charles H. Sheldon and Nicholas P. Lovrich, "Knowledge and Judicial Voting: The Oregon and Washington Experience," *Judicature* 67 (1982): 235.

[19] Arlen B. Coyle, "Judicial Selection and Tenure in Mississippi," *Mississippi Law Journal* 43 (1972): 90; William J. Keefe, "Judges and Politics: The Pennsylvania Plan of Judicial Selection," *University of Pittsburg Law Review* 20 (1959): 621.

[20] For example,

> "[I]t is through the selection process that potential candidates become actual candidates for political office.... [I]t is an informal stage, however, in which different actors take different perspectives in ascribing potential candidacy to different individuals. Aspiring politicians, sponsoring groups, and recruiting agencies do not necessarily agree on who is and who is not a potential candidate. Only in the [formal] selection process does it become apparent who has been considered for nomination."

Moshe A. Czudowski, "Political Recruitment," in Fred I. Greenstein and Nelson W. Polsby (eds), *Micropolitical Theory* (Reading, MA: Addison-Wesley Publishing Company, 1975), p. 219.

new light. Instead of focusing on the culmination of the process, it must be studied from beginning to end.

If judicial recruitment is to be an important consideration for understanding courts, and if comparative analysis is to contribute to that understanding, we need to be confident that we are comparing phenomena that are comparable. The search must be for common characteristics found in all forms of judicial selection.[21] Next, we must look for variation in the common characteristics. For example, one characteristic is strongly evident in one selection system while present but barely discernible in another. Our search, then, is for explanations for the variation. What does judicial recruitment in Oregon and Washington, Mississippi and Pennsylvania, Iowa and the federal district court in Vermont— and virtually all other recruitment systems—have in common? When jurisdictions are compared, are the commonalties only weakly present in one and more strongly present in another? What accounts for this variation?

A Model for the Study of Judicial Recruitment

What definitive features all political or judicial recruitment systems—federal, state and local—do share are **range and numbers of participants** effectively involved to varying degrees throughout a **recruitment sequence**.[22] The recruitment sequence or structure remains constant throughout all selections. However, the content of the structure varies according to the number of actors effectively participating. Variation in level of involvement of interested parties provides the opportunity for fruitful comparative research. On all recruitment occasions, whether judges are elected or appointed, varying numbers of actors give shape to the selection process. The candidates, their supporters, those who endorse and those who oppose, politicians, segments of the public, lawyers' organizations, the media, and perhaps a myriad of other actors may become involved in the drawing of candidates into public office. In other jurisdictions only a few actors may participate.

The numbers and variety of actors involved and the intensity of their involvement vary over a three-step sequence. Any actor may be active in the *initiation* of candidates, the *screening* of judicial aspirants, and the *affirmation* of the winners.[23] Initiation is defined by those actors who either persuade, push or permit a judicial aspirant to step forward for consideration. Insurance interests,

---

[21] "To make a systematic comparison of...judicial recruitment processes, we must find a common denominator in the [jurisdictions] under investigation." Charles H. Sheldon and Nicholas P. Lovrich, "State Judicial Recruitment," in Gates and Johnson, *The American Courts*, p. 172.

[22] Ibid., We are indebted to Professor Nicholas P. Lovrich for our thinking on a model for judicial recruitment. For example, see Nicholas P. Lovrich and Charles H. Sheldon, "Assessing Judicial Elections: Effects upon the Electorate of High and Low Articulation Systems," *Western Political Science Quarterly* 38 (1985): 276.

[23] Richard Richardson and Kenneth Vines, *The Politics of Federal Courts* (Boston: Little Brown, 1970).

prosecutors' organizations, ethnic, racial or gender groups, segments of the bar, family members or the candidate him or herself are crucial to the initiation of a candidacy. The decision to be considered or to run may have germinated years ago, or perhaps only last week. The importance of this first stage in the recruitment sequence is largely ignored in studies that focus on formal selection processes, yet this phase of the recruitment sequence may greatly shape all that follows. For example, lawyers representing certain interests, possessing particular backgrounds, or active in party politics may not be attracted to the judiciary in certain jurisdictions. They may never step forward to be considered for a judgeship. Why this is the case would be an analytical issue concerning initiation.

Initiation takes two forms, which in turn shape what follows. Aspirants may have harbored a desire to be a judge for years and begin early in the recruitment process to gather supporters, study opportunities and develop strategies of influence. These candidates can be classified as **self-initiators**. In contrast, lawyers may not have seriously considered a drive for the bench until others press upon them their candidacy. Perhaps opportunities for funding, endorsements, delegations, and the like persuade those who might have been reluctant initially to submit their names for consideration. These candidates may be termed **other-initiators**. This contrast alone might explain to some extent the numbers of actors who get involved in the recruitment process.

The calculation of odds of success probably motivates most decisions to file for an election or appointment, although a substantial number of judicial candidates may run for office for the main purpose of getting their names before the public. Funding sources, endorsements, potential opposition, and the clout of supporters may enter into other-initiation considerations. Opportunities for advancement, ambition, prestige and personal skills and desires likely all enter into self-initiation considerations. Of course, the two forms can mesh, enhancing or impeding the decision to run depending upon the circumstances prevailing. On not too few occasions the decision to run, whether self- or other-initiated, may turn on extrinsic considerations such as salary, tenure, fringe benefits (e.g., insurance, vacation policy, retirement programs, and working conditions).

> [C]apable lawyers will not accept a judicial appointment [or run for election] unless the court structure, rules, facilities, personnel and compensation provide an attractive opportunity to demonstrate the judicial acumen of the appointee. Thus, to attract able judges, we must have good courts and to have good courts we must have able judges.[24]

Screening involves those actors who define standards for judicial office and who measure the aspirants against these standards and against one another.

---

[24] Francis C. Cady, "Court Modernization: Retrospective, Prospective and Perspective," *Suffolk University Law Review* 6 (1972): 815.

Voters in primary elections, bar associations, "good government" groups, labor unions, nominating commissions, party leaders, senators, deputy attorneys general and possibly presidents or governors may be involved in screening. Screening is primarily a process of elimination. Aspirants are winnowed down to a few or one by rating, endorsing, or rejecting. In most instances, the screening stage has been experienced by aspirants long before any formal announcement of candidacy or filing for office has been made.

Screening also takes two major forms. Those responsible for screening may compare one candidate against another—a form of **comparative screening**. One candidate is judged better than another. Others may compare each candidate against a set of criteria and rate according to how they meet these standards. The question at issue is whether candidates have the requisite qualifications—a form of **qualifying screening**. Two or more candidates could be rated "well qualified" or a list might be composed with only those declared qualified included. Again, the differences between screening processes across jurisdictions may bear directly on or be a product of the numbers and variety of effective recruitment participants.

Both the screening and initiation stages are aspects of the crucial informal recruitment process which shapes the final selection. By the time the ultimate appointment is made or the final election is held, the original field of aspirants has been considerably narrowed through initiation and screening.

Those active in <u>affirmation</u> are directly responsible for the final and formal election or appointment of judges. They determine the winner of the competition. They appoint, elect or retain the judge, thereby culminating the recruitment sequence. It is this stage that is commonly the focus of most selection studies. The formal constitutional or statutory methods of appointment or election provide the boundaries for most studies of recruitment. However, affirmation typically involves more than simply legitimating final choices. As the ultimate winners experience the sequence of events from initiation, to screening, to affirmation they learn what is expected of them as a judge in that particular judicial post. In turn, the actors participating throughout the sequence also learn what to expect from the candidates. The entire process constitutes a learning experience for both those selected and those who select. Socialization into the judicial role begins with recruitment and continues in subsequent service in the position. The recruitment sequence is in many ways the beginnings of a seamless process.

The results of the affirmation process also can take different forms. The affirmation may be near unanimous, or it may be an extremely close contest between candidates. A 49% to 51% election result has different ramifications than an election where one candidate overwhelms another. Similarly, an appointment may have been either obvious or a toss-up between several candidates. There is a demonstrable tendency for close election results to leave the winner susceptible to future challenges. Similarly, a close choice between appointees bears directly on the next appointment. Hence, it is useful to note that affirmation may be either **competitive** or **uncompetitive** in nature.

Cutting across the concern for numbers of actors involved throughout the recruitment sequence is the matter of the <u>effectiveness</u> of their involvement. Many individuals or groups may be involved to some degree, but only a few may succeed in bringing their influence to bear on the selection. The participation of these parties can range between highly effective to ineffective. Effectiveness can be said to be present when the interests of the recruitment actors are considered by the affirming authorities. This influence may have been felt early on in the initiation or screening stages, or in the later stage of affirmation.

The question of relative effectiveness of each of the recruitment actors complicates our conceptualization of the recruitment systems considerably. Conceivably, a recruitment experience could enjoy a high number of participants who share somewhat equally their influence throughout the sequence. Alternatively, out of many recruitment actors only a few might exert effective influence over the process. Similarly, one (or a few) recruitment actor(s) from among many might monopolize the process.

To repeat, the recruitment of all political figures, including judges, involves the initiation, screening and affirmation sequence. This sequence constitutes the common denominator for selection research. However, it is the number and variety of participants and the effectiveness of their recruitment efforts throughout the sequence that provide the variation to be investigated in the model of judicial recruitment to be offered here.

The focus of scholars should be to isolate the variation in the number of effective actors taking part in the process along the recruitment sequence common to all judicial selection. A high number of participants involved in all stages of the sequence, sharing broadly in the exercise of influence, result in a **high articulation** selection system. One or a few actors participating sporadically in one or two of the stages of the recruitment sequence gives rise to a **low articulation** selection system. Of course, most recruitment experiences are found between these two extremes. Figure 2.1 outlines a micro version of the recruitment model.

Figure 2.1

MICRO-MODEL OF JUDICIAL RECRUITMENT

—— **Recruitment Sequence** ——→			**Number of Participants**		**Level of Articulation**
Initiation	*Screening*	*Affirmation*	*Participants*		*Articulation*
Self	Qualifying	Uncompetitive	Few	=	Low
Other	Comparing	Competitive	Many	=	High

Likely, the self-starters who meet the qualification criteria for office in largely uncompetitive appointments or elections will engage but a few recruitment actors, resulting in low articulation recruitment experiences. In contrast, those candidates who are sponsored by others and who, upon comparison, rate higher than several other candidates in a race involving many participants, will emerge from a high articulation recruitment process.

Working the Model[25]

How do we operationalize the theory or model? First, we seek to elaborate a method for deriving a measurement of articulation level for judicial selection events. Second, we isolate measurements of the hypothesized effects of varying articulation levels. Unfortunately the gathering of data concerning all fifty-one court systems and their local counterparts remains a formidable if not an impossible task. The judicial recruitment model, as with all analytical models, is an over-simplification of reality; its purpose is to provide a parsimonious framework for collecting concrete, observable and meaningful information. Fortunately, there are a few clues that are readily available that do in fact permit a test of the contentions generated by the model, and which thereby provide some hope for gaining an understanding of that complex reality which it replicates.

The level of articulation in nonpartisan, partisan and retention election systems is hinted at by the observable levels of participation, contestedness and competition taking place. **Participation** can be estimated by observing the percentage of voters who cast their ballots in the election in question but do not cast a vote for judicial candidates. While this is not a comprehensive assessment of participation throughout the election process, the connection to overall voting participation is evident and the figures for roll-off are readily available. For a

---

[25] Earlier exploratory efforts have strongly suggested the viability of the articulation model. See, for example, Lovrich and Sheldon, "Voters in Judicial Elections: An Attentive Public or an Uninformed Electorate?" *Justice System Journal* 9 (1984): 23; "Assessing Judicial Elections: The Effects of High and Low Articulation Systems in Washington and Oregon," *Western Political Quarterly* 38 (1985): 276; "Voters in Contested, Nonpartisan Judicial Elections: A Responsible Electorate of a Problematic Public?" *Western Political Quarterly* 36 (1983): 241; "Is Voting for State Judges a Flight of Fancy or a Reflection of Policy and Value Preferences?" *Justice System Journal* 16 (1994): 57; Lovrich, Pierce and Sheldon, "Citizen Knowledge and Voting in Judicial Elections," *Judicature* 73 (1989): 28; Sheldon and Lovrich, "Accountability vs. Responsibility: Balancing the Views of Voters and Judges," *Judicature* 65 (1982): 470; "Knowledge and Judicial Voting: The Washington and Oregon Experience," *Judicature* 67 (1983): 234; "State Judicial Recruitment," in Gates and Johnson (eds.) *The American Courts: A Critical Assessment* (Washington D.C.: CQ Press, 1991); Sheldon, "The Recruitment of Judges to the Washington Supreme Court: Past and Present," *Willamette Law Review* 22 (1986): 85; and "The Role of State Bar Associations in Judicial Selection," Judicature 77 (1994): 300. For results of a 1994 survey of candidates and voters that confirms the use of the model in elections, see Appendix A and Lovrich, Mazzarra and Sheldon, "Judicial Elections: Campaigning, Voting, Knowledge and Canon 7." (Paper delivered at the 1994 Annual Meeting of the Western Political Science Association in Albuquerque, N.M.)

variety of reasons, such as location on the bottom of the ballot, scarce voting cues, little campaigning and poor media coverage, some noteworthy proportion of voters fail to vote for judges. If 1,000,000 voters participated in a general election but only 600,000 voted for a judge, the participation index would be 60%.

Contestedness is based on the number of candidates vying for a particular judicial position. This may vary from an uncontested race to a situation where several candidates contest for a single judgeship in a primary election. In a retention election when incumbents run on their record unopposed, the contested ness is low. In contrast, contestedness is high in nonpartisan primary elections wherein five aspirants filing for a judicial office is not uncommon.

Competitiveness is measured by the size of the winning margin in contested races. Theoretically, this may vary from less than 1% to nearly 100%. In retention elections the measure would be the percentage difference between the "yes" and "no" retention votes.

The particular mix of these election data provides clues as to the level of articulation present. The presence of highly contested races, close voting and high participation signals a high articulation recruitment experience. It is assumed that the presence of all three clues reflects a high degree of interest in a race, intense campaigning, relatively high level of information available to voters, and a variety of supporters being active in advocacy—all factors contributing to a broadly participative situation. We would hypothesize that judicial candidates who survive this high articulation recruitment experience would be drawn to a balanced perspective between accountability and independence.

In contrast, a more limited situation with low participation, low contestedness and low competitiveness lends itself to a low articulation experience. Judges coming out of this experience assume either a highly accountable or distinctly independent perspective. Their recruitment has involved only a few participants throughout initiation, screening and affirmation. If but a few are paying some attention to the selection process, the judge who comes to occupy the judicial post has a minimum of obligations and adopts an independent role. However, if one or a few actors dominates all three stages in the recruitment, the judge will be obligated or accountable to that participant and will tend to assume a delegate role. We are using "obligated" in a very narrow sense. A judge experiencing any particular recruitment system must confront a variety of other constraints which soften the role learned from the recruitment sequence. For example, an appellate judge must work with other members of the bench, and a trial judge must work with a jury; both must consider the arguments of attorneys as well as the dictates of the law. Nonetheless, the "judicial dilemma" remains a compelling force in a judge's decisional life, and the recruitment experience is not to be discounted in resolving the dilemma.

Appointments are also accommodated by the model. Gubernatorial, presidential, or legislative appointments involve different actors along the recruitment sequence, but their number and their effectiveness remain crucial. If the appointment results after only a few applied for the opening, if few sponsors pushed a candidate, if the competitiveness is low or nonexistent and the governor or president quickly appoints whom he or she intended to in the first place, a low articulation experience is evident. However, if the appointer has many qualified candidates from which to choose, if numerous endorsements are encountered, if ratings from bar groups are submitted, if interested parties make contacts, if interviews and considerable deliberations follow, a high articulation experience ensues. Again, as in the election process, a competitive, highly participative and broad ranging appointment process involving a number of contending actors from initiation to affirmation is hypothesized to give rise to a balanced perspective toward independence and accountability on the part of the appointee.

The determination of the characteristic of **effectiveness** also must rely heavily on indirect measurements. The approach is to relate the results of affirmation in elections to funding contributions, endorsements, bar polls and ratings, group recommendations, ethnic and gender endorsements, and political party standing. If an endorsed candidate wins, we assume the endorsers were effective.[26] In appointments, again, comparing the affirmation outcomes with endorsements, petitions, nominations, bar ratings, political party strengths, ethnicity, and gender recommendations should identify active recruitment participants. In most circumstances candidates or appointing authorities can be asked directly about who was involved in the campaign or who was active in pushing for an appointment.

If the recruitment model has analytical value, the variations in articulation levels should have important consequences. A low articulation judicial recruitment experience, whether in an appointed or an elected system, should lead to different outcomes than those associated with a high articulation experience. **The contention is that, indeed, judges who survive a high articulation process will tend to view their judicial role from a more balanced viewpoint, where both accountability and independence shape that role. In contrast, a low articulation process will elevate lawyers to the bench who tend to assume roles nearer the extremes of either independence or accountability.**

Depending upon the number of effective participants engaged throughout the recruitment sequence, four distinct **recruitment roles** are possible. A high articulation system will produce judges who tend to be drawn to "stewards" or "politicos" roles.[27] **Politicos** tend to be products of a recruitment process that involves interest groups such as bar associations, political parties, labor unions,

---

[26] The candidates' files at the state's public disclosure commission or at the county auditor's office can reveal much about those active in elections.

[27] John Wahlke, et al., *The Legislative System* (New York: John Wiley, 1962); Charles H. Sheldon, *The American Judicial Process: Models and Approaches* (New York: Dodd, Mead, 1974), pp. 73-98; and Henry Glick, *Courts, Politics and Justice* (New York: McGraw Hill, 1993), pp. 333-338.

etc. attempting to influence the selection and thereby striving for political accountability.[28] Given numerous competing political groups, a balance between
political accountability and political independence is approximated. When the
many competing actors focus their efforts on convincing voters or those officials
who appoint that their favorite should be chosen, **stewards** would result, prefer-
ring to balance the demands of public accountability and public independence.[29]
Stewards are more sensitive to jurisdictional concerns because of the many often
competing public participants in their recruitment, but they retain sufficient independence from these public demands because of the pluralistic nature of their
recruitment.

In settings where few participants remain active throughout the recruitment
sequence, and with even fewer of these effectively influencing the results,
"trustee" and "delegate" recruitment roles are likely to be forthcoming. In situations where the largely ineffective efforts of a few participants in the process are
present, a judge would tend to assume a **trustee** role, remaining aloof from both
public and political interests.[30] **Delegate** judges, on the other hand, would be
products of a recruitment sequence dominated by one or two highly effective
recruitment actors.[31] These judges are delegates of those who placed them on
the bench.

Of course, these recruitment roles are but one aspect of a broader set of
roles (or behavioral and institutional constraints) acting upon those who sit on
the state and federal benches. Even if a particular recruitment role is assumed
by a judge, he or she must reconcile this role with other demands that are placed
on a judge, such as working with other judges on an appellate court or remaining within the sentencing guidelines as a trial judge. However, the model's sole
concern is to focus on recruitment and our question remains how the recruitment
process likely affects those who go through it. We are adding but a small piece
to the larger research picture for understanding courts, but it is an important
piece.

The recruitment model permits the gathering and classification of data that
bear on judicial recruitment and its effect. The attention of the selection scholar,
then, is to look beyond the results of the formal selection proceedings and focus

---

[28] A politico is defined as a judge who would shift across the other delegate, steward and trustee
roles, depending upon the circumstances. He or she would over time tend to balance the orientation of a steward, delegate or trustee.

[29] A steward would agree that elections (appointments) should inform judges of the general feelings of the people (appointers) so that the judges and their rulings don't become too isolated from
the community.

[30] A trustee would agree that elections or appointments should support those judges who are independent, remain unaffected by the people's or appointers' demands and rule strictly according to the
law.

[31] A delegate would agree that elections or appointments should tell what the people want and
judges should follow the people's desires as much as the law permits.

on what precedes. A few cautionary comments are in order. It is possible that in any given state, depending upon the jurisdiction and depending upon the particular election or appointment involved, a high articulation election may be experienced while across a county or district line a low articulation appointment may result. Conceivably, one race for the state supreme court may be different from another under the same formal selection method and during the same election period. Again, the effort is to gather data on more than the formal selection process, but still remaining attentive to the need for comparability.

The model reflects the assumption that certain recruitment experiences shape how the products of that experience view their roles. They would be beginning their careers with a particular perspective about how to behave as a result of what they learned throughout the recruitment sequence. The model also permits considered speculations about accountability and independence—the Judges' Dilemma.

Data on results of recruitment experiences are gathered, recorded and placed within the two dimensions of the recruitment model constituting the **micro** and **macro** levels. Depending upon the details of the micro level as outlined in figure 2.1, the macro level in figure 2.2 suggests recruitment systems can range from the lower hemisphere to the higher, moving from a **low articulation** category which encourages independence or accountability to a **high articulation** experience which prompts a balanced view of the judges' dilemma. The balance may also be achieved by reaching an equilibrium between shifting responses to legal and social issues.

The macro-model can be portrayed as in figure 2.2:

Figure 2.2

THE RECRUITMENT MODEL

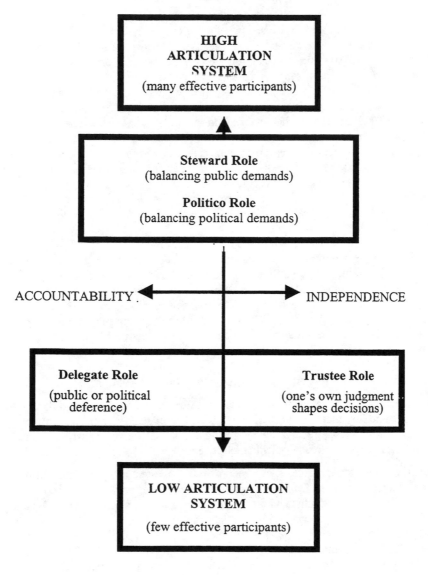

**HIGH
ARTICULATION
SYSTEM**
(many effective participants)

Steward Role
(balancing public demands)

Politico Role
(balancing political demands)

ACCOUNTABILITY ◄──────► INDEPENDENCE

Delegate Role

(public or political
deference)

Trustee Role

(one's own judgment
shapes decisions)

**LOW ARTICULATION
SYSTEM**

(few effective participants)

Formal Selection Methods

State Selection

The number of active participants involved in recruitment varies with time and with circumstances. As has been postulated, they constitute the important informal variables needed to understand judicial selection. As earlier suggested, although the informalities of selection are crucial, they are prompted by formal constitutional and statutory requirements. For example, if the constitution dictates that judges are to be elected, judicial aspirants will form campaign committees, fund voter mailings, shake hands at public events, etc.—all important activities likely affecting the final selection. However, if the formal method requires nomination by a commission, the informal process requires having sympathetic members on the commission and a receptive governor who makes the final choice. The retention election is different than a contested election under a non-partisan system. Again, as argued, the number and variety of active participants involved throughout the recruitment sequence remains crucial, although the formal methods of selection set the outer parameters for what activities occur.

The recruitment model combines the institutional factors of statutory and constitutional methods of selection with the behavioral factors of role orientations.[32] Both formal structures and rules and individual reactions to these structures are to be considered. The beginning point for any analysis of judicial selection, then, requires a listing of formal selection methods. However, as pointed out earlier, different levels of a state's court system may experience different methods, and each state has a particular system for filling vacancies on state benches.

Methods of Selecting State Judges (1996)

Alabama: All judges elected on partisan ballots, except municipal judges who are appointed by majority vote of municipal council. Governor fills temporary vacancies until next general election, and for some county court vacancies a nominating commission submits list to Governor.

Alaska: All judges of courts of record are appointed by Governor from list nominated by Judicial Council. Retention election after three or more years, except District Court judges who are retained or rejected at next general election after appointment. Vacancies filled as in initial selection.

Arizona: Supreme Court, Court of Appeals, and Superior Court judges in counties with population over 150,000 appointed by Governor from list submitted by nominating commission. Retention election at general election two

---

[32] Paul Brace and Melinda Gann Hall, "Studying Courts Comparatively: The View from the American States," *Political Research Quarterly* 48 (March, 1995): 5.

years after appointment. Superior Court judges in counties less than 250,000 population elected on nonpartisan ballots. Vacancies filled as in initial selection except Governor fills Superior Court vacancies in counties under 250,000 in population and appointees serve until next general election when judge is elected to fill remainder of term.

Arkansas: All judges elected on partisan ballots. Governor appoints to vacancies and appointees serve until next general election.

California: Supreme Court and Court of Appeals judges appointed by Governor and confirmed by Commission on Judicial Appointments. The retention elections are at next general election. Superior Court judges selected by above method or by non-partisan elections. Municipal judges appointed by Governor or county board of supervisors and retained in nonpartisan elections. Governor fills vacancies until next general election with approval of Commission on Judicial Appointments. Superior Court judges appointed by Governor and serve remainder of unexpired term. County boards appoint to vacancies on local courts, or nonpartisan elections are held.

Colorado: All judges of courts of record appointed by Governor from list submitted by nominating commissions. After two years judges run on record in retention election. Municipal judges appointed by municipal council, except Denver where mayor appoints from list submitted by nominating commission. Judges run for retention against their record. Vacancies filled as in initial selection.

Connecticut: All non-elected judges appointed by legislature from nominations submitted by Governor who must rely on list from Judicial Selection Commission. Reappointment based on recommendations by Judicial Review Council. Probate judges elected on partisan ballots. Vacancies filled as in initial selection if legislature in session, otherwise Governor appoints until next legislative session.

Delaware: All judges appointed by Governor from list submitted by nominating commissions with consent of Senate majority. Vacancies filled as in initial selection.

Florida: Appellate judges appointed by Governor from lists submitted by nominating commissions. Retention elections at next general election. Trial judges selected by nonpartisan elections. All vacancies filled by Governor from names submitted by nominating commissions.

Georgia: Judges of all courts of record elected on nonpartisan ballots. Courts of limited jurisdiction selected in partisan elections, except some county and municipal judges are appointed. Vacancies filled by Governor from list submitted by nominating commission.

Hawaii: Supreme Court, Intermediate Court of Appeals, and Circuit Court judges appointed by Governor with consent of Senate from list nominated by Judicial Selection Commission. Reappointment by Judicial Selection Commission. Chief Justice appoints district judges from list nominated by Judicial Selection Commission. Vacancies filled as in initial selection.

Idaho: Judges of courts of record elected on nonpartisan ballots.   District nominating commission appoints magistrates who run in retention elections at next general election at least 18 months later. Governor appoints to vacancies to complete unexpired term from list submitted by Judicial Council.

Illinois: Supreme Court, appellate and circuit judges selected by partisan elections.   Subsequent terms based on uncontested retention elections.   Supreme Court appoints to vacancies and appointees serve until next general elections.

Indiana: Supreme Court, Court of Appeals, and Tax Court judges appointed by Governor from list submitted by Judicial Nominating Commission.   Retention elections at next general election two years later.   Circuit, superior and most county judges selected in partisan elections.   Marion County municipal judges appointed by Governor from list submitted by nominating commission.   Appellate vacancies filled as in initial selection.   Governor fills all Circuit Court and most Superior Court vacancies, appointees who serve until next general election.

Iowa: Courts of record judges appointed by Governor from a list submitted by ad hoc nominating commissions. Retention elections after one year at next general election.   Magistrates appointed by district judges from list submitted by nominating commissions. Vacancies filled as in initial selection.

Kansas: Appeals judges and most district judges appointed by Governor from list submitted by nominating commission.   Retention election after at least one year in office at next general election. Vacancies are filled as in initial selection, except Governor fills vacancies until next general election in jurisdictions that do not have a nominating commission.

Kentucky: All judges selected on nonpartisan ballots. Governor fills vacancies from names submitted by commissions, or after 60 days, Supreme Court appoints. Appointees serve until next general election.

Louisiana: All judges elected on nonpartisan ballots. Special election if unexpired term of vacancy more than six months, otherwise Supreme Court appoints.

Maine: All judges are appointed by Governor with confirmation by Senate. Probate judges elected on partisan ballots. Vacancies filled as in initial selection.

Maryland: Judges of Court of Appeals and Court of Special Appeals appointed by Governor with consent of Senate based on nominations by Judicial Nominating Commission.   Retention elections after at least one year.   Circuit Courts and Baltimore city bench appointed by Governor from list submitted by nominating commissions, and may be challenged at next general election after appointment. District judges appointed by Governor from list submitted by nominating commissions and with confirmation by Senate. Vacancies filled as in initial selection.

Massachusetts: All judges appointed by Governor with advice and consent of Governor's Council. Nominations to Governor are submitted by nomination commission. Vacancies filled as in initial selection.

Michigan: All judges elected on nonpartisan ballots after nomination by party conventions. Municipal judges selected by various methods adopted by local governments. Vacancies on courts of record filled by Governor from list submitted by bar committees. Appointees serve until next general election. City councils fill municipal vacancies.

Minnesota: All judges selected in nonpartisan elections. Vacancies filled by Governor until next general election after serving at least one year. District Court vacancies are by gubernatorial appointment from nominating commissions' list.

Mississippi: All judges elected on partisan ballots except some municipal judges, depending upon local ordinances. Governor appoints to vacancy from names submitted by commission. Appointees serve at least seven months and until next general election.

Missouri: Appellate judges and circuit judges in larger jurisdictions appointed by Governor from list submitted by nominating commissions. Retention elections after at least one year in office. Other judges selected in partisan elections. Vacancies filled as in initial selection, except some circuit vacancies filled by special elections and municipal seats filled by mayor.

Montana: All judges are elected on nonpartisan ballots. Vacancies filled by Governor with Senate confirmation from list of names submitted by nominating commissions. Municipal vacancies filled by city councils to serve for remainder of unexpired term.

Nebraska: Governor appoints all judges from list submitted by nominating commissions. Retention elections after initial three-year term. Vacancies filled as in initial selection.

Nevada: All selected in nonpartisan elections. Governor appoints to vacancies from list of names submitted by Commission on Judicial Selection. Local vacancies filled by county commissioners or special elections.

New Hampshire: All judges are appointed by Governor with confirmation by Executive Council. Vacancies are filled as in initial selection.

New Jersey: All judges are appointed and reappointed by Governor with advice and consent of Senate. Court of Appeals judges appointed by Chief Justice from sitting Superior Court judges. Selection of municipal judges varies. Vacancies filled as in initial selection.

New Mexico: Judges of all courts appointed by Governor from list of nominating commissions. At next general election appointees run in contested partisan elections. If appointed judges win, their next elections are in uncontested retention elections. Vacancies filled by Governor from nominations by commissions.

New York: Court of Appeals judges appointed by Governor with advice and consent of Senate. Court of Claims and some appellate division judges appointed by Governor. All other judges are elected on partisan ballots, except New York City judges who are appointed by the mayor from list submitted by nominating commission. Vacancies on appeals benches filled as in initial selection. Elected vacancies filled by Governor with consent of Senate, if in session. Appointees serve until next general election.

North Carolina: Special judges of Superior Court appointed by Governor. All other judges elected in partisan elections. Governor fills vacancies and appointees serve until next general election.

North Dakota: All judges elected on nonpartisan ballots. Governor appoints to vacancies from list supplied by nominating commissions. Appointees serve until next general election. Governor can call for special election. County courts filled by county commissioners from nominating commission lists.

Ohio: All judges elected on nonpartisan ballots except Court of Claims judges appointed by Chief Justice. Vacancies filled by gubernatorial appointment, with appointees serving until next general election. If unexpired term of vacancy ends within a year, governor appoints for remainder of term.

Oklahoma: Supreme Court and Court of Criminal Appeals appointed by Governor from list of nominating commissions, with retention elections after one year. Court of Appeals, District and Associate District judges selected in nonpartisan elections. Municipal judges appointed by local governments. Supreme Court and Court of Criminal Appeals' vacancies filled as in initial selection. Other vacancies filled by Governor from list supplied by nominating commission.

Oregon: All judges elected in nonpartisan elections. Municipal judges selected by methods defined in local ordinances. Governor appoints to vacancies. Those appointed serve until next general election.

Pennsylvania: All judges initially elected on partisan ballots, and then retained in nonpartisan elections. Pittsburgh mayor appoints local magistrates. Governor appoints to vacancies with advice and consent of Senate from names submitted by nominating commissions. Appointees serve until next general election.

Rhode Island: Supreme Court justice nominated by Governor from a list submitted by a nominating commission. General Assembly appoints. Superior, District and Family Court judges appointed by Governor with advice and consent of Senate. Local authorities appoint municipal and probate judges. Vacancies on the Supreme Court filled as in initial selection. Others appointed by Governor with advice and consent of Senate.

South Carolina: Appeals, Circuit and Family Court judges elected by legislature from list submitted by nominating commission. Probate judges elected in partisan elections, magistrates appointed by Governor with advice and consent of Senate and municipal jurists appointed by local officials. Vacancies filled as in initial selection; however, if remainder of term is less than one year, Governor appoints.

South Dakota: Supreme Court judges appointed by Governor from names submitted by nominating commission. After three years in office appointees run in retention elections. Circuit judges elected in nonpartisan elections and magistrates appointed by chief judge of jurisdiction, with approval of Supreme Court. Selection to vacancies made by Governor who selects from list compiled by nominating commission. Appointees serve remainder of unexpired terms.

Tennessee: Intermediate Court of Appeals judges appointed by Governor from nominating commission's list. Retention elections at next general elections at least 30 days after appointment. All other judges selected in partisan elections, except municipal judges whose selection depends upon local ordinances. Governor fills vacancies on Supreme, Circuit, Criminal and Chancery Courts, serving until next biennial election. Court of Appeals and Court of Criminal Appeals selected to vacancies as in initial selection.

Texas: All judges elected in partisan elections. Local judges' selection depends upon local charters or ordinances. Appellate and district court vacancies filled by Governor. Appointees serve until next general election. County commissioners appoint to vacancies on county courts, and municipal vacancies filled by city officials.

Utah: All judges appointed by Governor from those names nominated by nominating commission. Retention elections after initial three-year term. Governor appoints to vacancies from list submitted by nominating commissions.

Vermont: All judges appointed by Governor from names nominated by Judicial Nominating Board and with the advice and consent of Senate. If the legislature is in session, vacancies are filled by initial means of selection. If not in session, Governor appoints from list compiled by Judicial Nominating Board.

Virginia: All judges elected by legislature. Vacancies filled as in initial selection if legislature in session. Otherwise, Governor appoints and appointees serve until 30 days after legislature in session.

Washington: All judges of courts of record and District Courts selected in nonpartisan elections. Some municipal judges are appointed by mayor or council. For courts of record, Governor appoints to vacancies. Appointees serve until next general election.

West Virginia: All judges elected in partisan elections. Vacancies filled by the Governor. Appointees serve until end of term if not less than three years; otherwise, appointees serve until next general election.

Wisconsin: All judges elected on nonpartisan ballots. Nominating commission submits names to Governor to appoint to vacancies.

Wyoming: All courts of record appointed by Governor from a list submitted by nominating commission. After at least one year retention, elections held at next general election. Municipal judges appointed by mayor with consent of council, and justices of the peace elected on nonpartisan ballots. Vacancies filled as in initial selection, except municipal and justices of peace vacancies are filled by county commissioners. Appointees serve until next general election.

> Compiled from **The Book of States, 1996-97** (Lexington: The Council of State Governments)

Federal Selection

Article II of the U.S. Constitution reads in part:

> The President...shall nominate, and by and with the Advice and Consent of the Senate, shall appoint...Judges of the Supreme Court, and all other Officers of the United States, whose Appointments are not herein otherwise provided for, and which shall be established by Law.

Article III further stipulates that "The Judges, both of the supreme and inferior Courts, shall hold their Office during good Behavior." Thus, all Article III judges are products of presidential nomination and appointment with the approval of a majority vote of the Senate. They are designated as Constitutional Courts having the protections of life-time tenure. Legislative Courts are created by Congressional action and do not possess the security of life-time tenures. Judges of Legislative Courts are appointed by the President with the advice and consent of the Senate, but commonly have terms of 15 years without the protections of "good behavior" tenure. Also, those courts exist at the mercy of Congress. The Supreme Court, Courts of Appeals, District Courts and the Court of International Trade are all constitutional courts. The Court of Appeals for the

Armed Forces, U.S. Tax Court, the Court of Veterans Appeals, and Territorial Courts are all legislative courts.

District of Columbia and all **Federal Judges**: U.S. President nominates all judges and appoints with advice and consent of U.S. Senate. Vacancies filled as in initial selection. In **District of Columbia**, if President fails to appoint within 60 days the Judicial Nominating Commission appoints with advice and consent of the U.S. Senate.

The following chapters explain in detail each of the state and federal systems of judicial selection, and provide a case study of a typical version of each.

Chapter Three

Recruitment By Nonpartisan Elections

Choosing judges through nonpartisan elections had its beginnings in the waning years of the 19th Century. Today, along with the merit plan, it remains the leading means by which persons are recruited to state benches. The patronage and corruption associated with political machines in the late 1800s had permeated the judiciary in a number of urban jurisdictions, prompting efforts to somehow protect judges from the partisan influences. Although political parties seemed necessary to elect other public officials and hold them accountable, judges needed to be isolated from party leaders and partisan voters. To the reformers, partisanship had all but destroyed the integrity of the bench—as well as greatly diminishing its quality. Political pay-offs and cronyism often had more to do with being nominated and subsequently elected judge than qualifications. For loyalty to the party organization and its most influential elements, persons were rewarded with a spot on the party ticket. Judgeships sometimes became the dumping ground for political "has-beens."[1] Because of partisan abuses, in some jurisdictions reform-minded members of the legal profession, along with some judges, urged the formation of voluntary nonpartisan slates. Under the prevailing partisan climate, these attracted little attention.[2]

Equally troublesome, the judiciary was perceived by the Populists and others as an agency for large corporations, especially the railroads, again due to the dominance of political parties. For example, in an address before a gathering of bar leaders in the state of Washington in 1894, lawyer Frank H. Graves condemned the partisan and corporate influences bearing on judicial selection.

> [A] party judiciary becomes an evil intolerable to be borne.... The second great evil of the partisan selection of judges...is the corporate influence in the courts.... Day by day, year after year, here a little and there a little, these soulless and breathless creations of the genius of modern enterprise are extending their influence, their demands and

---

[1] "The post-Civil War increase in industrialization and urbanization nurtured political 'machines' in the nation's larger cities. The Tammany Hall organization in New York epitomized the potential abuses of partisan judicial contests.... Tammany was able to run and elect its hand-picked and politically responsive slate of judicial candidates.... Elections often became rubber-stamp confirmations of the machine's slate." Sari S. Escovitz, *Judicial Selection and Tenure* (Chicago: American Judicature Society, 1975), p. 6.

[2] As early as 1873, in Cook County, Illinois, the judicial candidates themselves agreed to run on a nonpartisan ballot.

their greed. They never die; they never tire; they never sleep. [Finally], the manner in which a political nominating convention...is organized makes it impossible to secure decent judicial nominations.[3]

Under the banner of the Progressives, a not altogether compatible set of interests, including the Populists, Grangers and elements of the legal profession, coalesced to provide the momentum for significant reform. The reform-minded attorneys were drawn to nonpartisanship as an opportunity to wrest control of judgeships from political parties; the Progressives' reform package also included, from the perspective of the attorneys, the less desirable direct democracy provisions of initiative, referendum, direct primary and recall.[4] In order to gain the advantages lawyers saw in nonpartisan elections, they reluctantly accepted the entire reform package.[5] Despite the hesitation of the lawyers, nonpartisanship and the instruments of direct democracy were viewed by their advocates as a means of involving voters directly in the government without being distracted by parties and special interests. Also, voters would be prompted to study issues and candidates, resulting in rational choices and a stronger commitment to government.[6] The judiciary would also be a beneficiary of the Progressive program.

For the judiciary the Progressive reforms meant that under most circumstances judges were nominated by means of a nonpartisan direct primary election, and they were affirmed in general elections without benefit of partisan la-

---

[3] Quoted in Charles H. Sheldon, *A Century of Judging: A Political History of the Washington Supreme Court* (Seattle: University of Washington Press, 1988), p. 61.

[4] The Progressive Movement meant "democratizing" government:

> The Progressives were preoccupied with one central political problem: the rampant corruption in the political system.... To secure their political goals [they] advocated...the direct primary, Australian (secret) ballot, presidential preference primary...cross filing...non-partisan local and state elections, women's suffrage, civil service...popular election of senators, short ballot, corrupt practices act...recall, referendum and the initiative.

Charles M. Price, "The Initiative: A Comparative State Analysis and Reassessment of a Western Phenomenon," *Western Political Quarterly* 28 (June 1975): 243. In many states elected judges are still exempted from recall. For example, the Washington Constitution adopted the recall reform for elected officials but exempted judges. Section 33 of Article 1 reads: "Every elective public officer of the state of Washington except judges of courts of record is subject to recall and discharge by the legal voters of the state."

[5] In 1908 Washington became one of the earliest states to adopt nonpartisan elections with direct primaries used to nominate judicial candidates. For an account of the politics of nonpartisanship in Washington see Sheldon, *A Century of Judging*, pp. 40-50.

[6] Charles R. Adrian, "Some General Characteristics on Nonpartisan Elections," *American Political Science Review* 46 (1952): 766. "Out of the middle-class businessman's 'Efficiency and Economy Movement'...came a series of innovations designed to place government 'on a business basis' and to weaken the power of political parties."

bels. However, variations of nonpartisanship evolved. Today, some states hold judicial elections at different times than elections for partisan offices. Judicial ballots at the end of, or entirely separate from, the regular ballot are common variations. The effort in each case is to isolate judicial candidates from the advantage or stigma of political parties, although the isolation is often only symbolic. For example, in Ohio judges are placed on a nonpartisan ballot in the general election, but they are nominated in partisan primaries. In Michigan and California the political parties are permitted to endorse candidates in nonpartisan races. Candidates can campaign on those endorsements, turning them often into quasi-partisan contests. Of course, the political affiliation and activities of judicial candidates in nonpartisan elections are often known and utilized even in strictly nonpartisan election systems. Finally, in some states political party endorsements of presumably nonpartisan candidates are made quite routinely.

It is not unusual for nonpartisan judicial elections in one state to be mixed with partisan and merit plan elements for recruiting judges. In Arizona, Superior Court judges (trial court of general jurisdiction) are selected by the merit plan, but outside the populous counties they are elected on nonpartisan ballots. Some counties in California elect trial judges on nonpartisan ballots, as do Florida, Oklahoma and South Dakota, even though the merit plan is used in choosing appellate judges in these states.

Vacancies created by resignations, retirements, or deaths in nonpartisan systems are filled with appointments by governors, county commissioners, or mayors, depending upon the level of the court. These appointees are often chosen for partisan reasons, but they must face the voters in possibly contested races in the next election in order to retain their positions. Consequently, executive appointment becomes an integral part of a nonpartisan judicial election system.

The anticipated benefits from nonpartisan election of judges as argued by the early reformers were many. By banishing political parties, patronage and corruption would largely disappear. The quality of the judiciary would increase since talented and highly qualified lawyers who had gained stature at lawyering rather than politicking would be drawn to service on the bench. Elections would be a screening process based upon assessments of merit rather than the expression of partisan loyalty. These judges would be more cognizant of the needs of the community as opposed to the desires of party. By retaining popular elections, although not under the guidance of political parties, the authority or legitimacy of courts would be enhanced. Also, the influence of corporations and special interests, which in early times often controlled political parties, would diminish substantially. Finally, a more active and educated electorate would evolve as a consequence of judicial campaigns based on qualifications rather than partisanship. The benefit of hindsight makes it possible to ask: What has been the record of nonpartisan elections? Does the historical record square with the expectations of the early reformers?

If the reformers had believed that politics, partisan or otherwise, would be by-and-large banned from nonpartisan campaigns, they were indeed naive. It is quite clear that the overt control of nominations and elections by political parties has been eliminated, but it is also evident that subtle (and not so subtle) vestiges of partisanship remain. For example, without party labels voters in nonpartisan elections all too often rely on name recognition, and such familiarity with names often comes from candidates' previous partisan activity and office-holding; legislators or county prosecutors have a distinct advantage, for example.[7]

For some, the hope was that the legal profession would replace the political party as the lead player in elections.[8] At least its influence over the selection of judges would be enhanced with political parties out of the picture.[9] But then instead of partisan politics determining judicial selection, bar association politics would become a primary factor. For example, prosecutors would contest with the defense bar over who should be on the bench. Plaintiff lawyers and defense attorneys would vie for control of recruitment. Apart from the professional divisions obtaining among attorneys, the conflicting interests of those who find themselves in court—such as insurance companies, labor unions, the medical profession and oil companies—are compelled to enter recruitment politics, sometimes contributing heavily to campaign coffers. The point is that although partisanship no longer dominates, it is clear that politics remains as a driving force in the nonpartisan election of judges.

Some of the selection studies available have isolated a few tendencies which have been felt to be associated with nonpartisan elections. However, these tendencies should be viewed more as suggestions requiring further research than as confirmed effects. Many of the findings depend upon the times, places and manner—i.e., when the research was conducted, where it was conducted, and how it was conducted. Nonpartisan elections have tended to encourage newcomers to vie for the bench. This is possibly due to the business community and other groups showing a greater interest in local judicial elections.[10] In some metropolitan areas, minority candidates are more likely to be elected under a nonpartisan system when compared to appointments, although

---

[7] In Ohio the party label, although missing from the general election ballot, remains the single most important factor in the voters' choices. See Lawrence Baum, "Electing Judges," in Lee Epstein (ed.), *Contemplating Courts* (Washington D.C.: CQ Press, 1995), p. 33.

[8] "It is preposterous to think that if the bar supports a candidate in a given campaign, for a given judicial office, the people will not second them and approve their choice. The arrangement is almost ideal. A profession jealous of the standing and reputation of its judiciary deliberates on the qualifications of the candidates and submits its opinion to the people who act finally upon them." James E. Maguire, "Debates in the Massachusetts Constitutional Convention, 1917-1918," quoted in Lamar T. Beman, *Election and Appointment of Judges* (New York: H.W. Wilson, 1926), p. 107.

[9] See Charles H. Sheldon, "The Role of State Bar Associations in Judicial Selection," *Judicature* 77 (1994): 300.

[10] Herbert Jacob, "The Effect of Institutional Differences in the Recruitment Process: The Case of State Judges," *Journal of Public Law* 13 (1964): 104.

the latter depends almost wholly on the preferences of the appointing authority.[11] Elections, partisan or nonpartisan, tend to result in slightly more lawyers with prosecutorial experience being promoted to the bench.[12] It may be that prior judicial experience is encouraged as a qualification for the appellate benches in nonpartisan systems.[13] Some earlier studies suggest that elected judges tended to have attended slightly more prestigious law schools.[14] Another study, however, concluded that "no method of selection consistently selects vastly more qualified judges where quality is measured by formal education."[15] Also, there is an indication that gubernatorial appointments favor those with higher educational level and more prosecutorial experience.[16] Given the fact that many if not most nonpartisan judges were initially appointed to a vacancy, this appointment tendency may be associated with nonpartisanship.

In filling judicial vacancies governors invariably lean toward appointing judges who share their party affiliation and their political/legal philosophy. Elected jurists are less likely to dissent than their appointed counterparts in controversial cases such as death penalty appeals.[17] Bar association efforts to influence recruitment tend to be more intense in nonpartisan elections, and the lawyers supply most of the funding needed to run an election race.[18]

It is clear that nonpartisan elections attract fewer voters than partisan systems and that these races are largely of low salience, generating little excitement.[19] However, the lack of voter attention is suffered as well by other nonpartisan contests such as county commissioner, state legislator or state auditor. Judicial elections are contested far less in nonpartisan elections. When compared with partisan elections, the tendency is to have fewer incumbents de-

[11] Washington State, *Minority and Justice Task Force, Final Report* (Olympia: Office of Administrator for the Courts, 1990), p. 84.

[12] Jacob, "The Effect.of Institutional Differences,": 109-111.

[13] Bradley C. Canon, "The Impact of Formal Selection Processes on the Characteristics of Judges—Reconsidered," *Law & Society Review* 6 (May 1972): 585.

[14] Jacob, "The Effect. of Institutional Differences,": 109; and Stuart Nagel, *Comparing Elected and Appointed Judicial Systems* (Beverly Hills, CA: Sage, 1973), p. 11.

[15] Victor E. Flango and Craig R. Ducat, "What Difference Does Method of Judicial Selection Make: Selection Procedures in State Courts of Last Resort," *Justice System Journal* 5 (1979): 32.

[16] Canon, "The Impact.of Formal Selection Process,": 584-585. Even with these meager tendencies caution must be exercised as they are based on data over 20 years old.

[17] Melinda Gann Hall, "Electoral Politics and Strategic Voting in State Supreme Courts," *Journal of Politics* 54 (1992): 427.

[18] Philip L. Dubois, "Financing Trial Court Elections: Who Contributes to California Judicial Campaigns?" *Judicature* 70 (1986): 8.

[19] Summarized in Mary L. Volcansek, "The Effects of Judicial Selection Reform: What We Know and What We Do Not Know," in Philip L. Dubois (ed.), *The Analysis of Judicial Reform* (Lexington, MA: Lexington Books, 1982), pp. 81-84.

feated, to experience more appointments to vacancies, to enjoy longer terms, and to record more mid-term vacancies. It is clear that those with trial court experience are attracted to the appeals bench under nonpartisanship. Trial level nonpartisan elections tend to reinforce the power of incumbency. When challenged, incumbents nearly always win, and because of this power of incumbency less than half of the sitting judges are challenged.[20] These observations would more than suggest that public accountability has a less than anticipated impact in nonpartisan elections.

With the absence of the political party voting cue, most observers of judicial elections argue that voters in nonpartisan situations lack sufficient information to make a considered choice. As a consequence, public interest in judicial contests is low. What, then, prompts the interested citizen who casts a vote for a judicial candidate? Is it primarily name familiarity, gender, ethnicity drawn from surnames, nicknames, and incumbency—or are there other more meaningful sources of information on judicial candidates which can guide the voters taking part? A 1994 mail survey of registered voters and judicial candidates in the State of Washington's nonpartisan election provides some answers. Table 3.1 reports a list of campaign activities used by candidates compared with a list of those activities relied upon by the attentive voters in the November general election.[21]

By far the most important (87%) source for the voters was the Secretary of State's *Official Voters' Pamphlet*. All candidates had a section in the pamphlet that listed background, experience and a general statement of why they should be placed or remain on the bench. Most such statements were accompanied with a photo of the candidate. What the results displayed in Table 3.1 suggest is that despite the low salience of nonpartisan elections, some important informational sources are indeed available.

---

[20] Lawrence Baum, "The Electoral Fate on Incumbent Judges in Ohio Court of Common Pleas," in Elliot E. Slotnick (ed.), *Judicial Politics: Readings from Judicature* (Chicago: American Judicature Society, 1992), pp. 86-87.

[21] The mail survey was administered to all 86 judicial candidates at all levels of the Washington judiciary in contested races in the 1994 general election. Fifty-five responded (64%). Two-hundred and twenty-six (32%) of the voters surveyed responded to the election survey.

Table 3.1

CAMPAIGN ACTIVITIES AND VOTER SOURCES
IN NONPARTISAN ELECTIONS

(State of Washington, 1994)

Activity	*Percent Candidate Used During Campaigns*	*Percent Voter Regarded as Important*
Voters' Pamphlets	100%	87%
Newspaper Advertisements	93%	7%
Lawn Signs, Bill Boards	88%	8%
Candidate "Nights" & Fairs	80%	--
Door-to-door Campaigning	73%	50%
Speeches—Rotary, Lions, etc.	73%	--
Mailings to Voters	78%	29%
Interviews—Groups	68%	--
Shaking Hands—Malls, Sporting Events, etc.	68%	--
Soliciting Endorsements*	63%	32%
Appearances—Editorial Brds.*	53%	27%
Radio Ads	35%	9%
Neighborhood Meetings*	35%	63%
Interviews with Bar Comm.	28%	42%
Telephone Canvassing	20%	7%
Television	18%	12%

*Voters' survey wording = Group endorsements; Newspaper endorsements; Meetings with candidates.
Source: 1994 General Election Survey of Washington candidates and Spokane County voters.[22]

---

[22] Nicholas P. Lovrich, Elizabeth Mazzarra and Charles H. Sheldon, "Judicial Elections: Campaigning, Voting, Knowledge and Canon 7," paper delivered at the 1995 Annual Conference, Western Political Science Association, Portland, Oregon.

Supporters of nonpartisan judicial elections have argued that voters are not at fault for knowing little about judicial races, but rather that they are not given the information they desire or need. The culprit generally pointed to is the Code of Judicial Conduct, and specifically Canon 7 of that Code. The provisions of Canon 7 regulate the political activities of judges and set rules for judicial campaigns. Lawyers running for judicial office are placed under the same restrictions.[23]

Narrowly viewed, the Canon means that nearly all political and legal issues of any consequence are likely restricted.[24] What is permitted under the Canon and what are the voters seeking? Table 3.2 reports the views of judicial candidates in Washington concerning Canon 7. Candidates were asked what topics were permissible under the Canon and what they felt the voters were most interested in hearing from them.[25]

---

[23] Because of considerable pressure from the media, losses in court cases, and from interested voters and the candidates themselves, Canon 7 was amended in 1995 in Washington. Changes in their relevant sections (text added in the new version is in bold type) dictate that candidates and judges **"shall not:"**

  (a) act as leaders or hold any office in a political organization; (b) make speeches for a political organization or **nonjudicial** candidate or publicly endorse a nonjudicial candidate for public office; (c) solicit funds for or pay an assessment or make a contribution to a political organization or nonjudicial candidate...**(d) attend public functions sponsored by political organizations or purchase tickets for political party dinners...(e) identify themselves as members of a political party...(f) contribute to a political party....** Candidates, including an incumbent judge...(a) should maintain the dignity appropriate to judicial office...(c) should not (i) make pledges or promises of conduct in office other than the faithful and impartial performance of the duties of the office; (ii) **make statements that commit or appear to commit the candidate with respect to cases, controversies or issues that are likely to come before the court; or (iii) knowingly misrepresent... the candidate or an opponent.** (The new version deleted the dictate that they should not "announce their views on disputed legal or political issues." See Michele Radoosevich, "Toward Meaningful Judicial Elections: A Case for Reform of Canon 7," *University of Puget Sound Law Review* 17 (1993): 139.

[24] It is not clear yet what will be permitted under the new rules, but until clarifications are rendered it is likely that under actual campaigning circumstances a chilling effect will remain. The State Commission on Judicial Conduct enforces the provisions of the Canons. In order to enforce the Canons, the Commission investigates complaints and, if warranted, recommends to the State Supreme Court reprimands, censures or retirement.

[25] Lovrich, Mazarra and Sheldon, "Judicial Elections...,"

Table 3.2

CANDIDATES' VIEWS REGARDING THE CONSTRAINTS OF CANON 7

(State of Washington, 1994)

Possible Topics Discussed in General Election Campaigns	Percent of Candidates Thought:	
	Topics Impermissible	*Public Interested in*
Forbidden Topics		
Partisan affiliation	93%	41%
Political backgrounds	73%	20%
Views on affirmative action	65%	6%
Religious views-affiliation	64%	20%
Views on U.S. Supreme Court cases	58%	13%
Permissible Topics		
Attitudes on sentencing	0%	67%
Free press vs. fair trial	24%	2%
Judicial philosophy	20%	4%
Attitudes toward legal reform	20%	20%
Past court cases-decisions	10%	7%
Legal-judicial backgrounds	0%	37%

With the exception of partisan inquiries, little disparity is evident between what candidates regarded as impermissible under Canon 7 and topics they felt the voters were interested in discussing with the candidates. It is clear, however, that the partisan and political affiliation topics had been put on the forbidden list even though a significant percentage of the voters had requested such information. Nonpartisanship, along with the Code of Judicial Conduct, have succeeded in achieving to an important degree one of the original purposes brought forth for substituting nonpartisan for partisan elections.

Critics of Canon 7 in Washington not only point to the fact that even with some easing of its dictates it not only encourages the withholding of relevant information from the voters, but it also infringes on the free speech rights of the judicial candidates. Part of the electoral process formula is that not only do candidates have a First Amendment right to speech, but the voter has a companion right to be informed.[26] The paradox is that nonpartisan elections are designed to provide a balance between public accountability and judicial inde-

---

[26] Radoosevich, "Toward Meaningful.Judicial Elections,": 154.

pendence; inevitably, however, to serve the former requirement means threat-
ening the latter.[27]

Not only have concerns been expressed regarding the problem of informing the voters, but serious legal issues have been raised regarding the "representativeness" of elected state benches. In the nonpartisan system in Louisiana
an issue arose over at-large judicial election districts. In such districts, at least
two judges are elected from one large district. The complaint was that "the present method of electing two Justices to the Louisiana Supreme Court at-large
from the New Orleans area impermissibly dilutes minority voting strength."
Such a system ran into conflict with the Voting Rights Act of 1965 which pro-
hibited imposition of voting qualifications or prerequisites—in this case, at-large
districts—"in a manner resulting in denial or abridgment of right to vote on account of race or color." The U.S. Supreme Court was confronted with the issue
in **Chisom v. Romer** in 1991.[28]

The nation's high bench ruled that elected judges in the states do indeed
qualify as "representatives" under the Voting Rights Act, and consequently the
at-large judicial constituencies in which African Americans were placed in the
minority clearly diluted their vote in violation of the Act. The Court majority
opinion, written by Justice John Paul Stevens, explained:

> We think...that the better reading of the word "representatives" [in
> the Voting Rights Act] describes the winners of representative
> popular elections. If executive officers, such as prosecutors, sheriffs,
> state attorneys general, and state treasurers, can be considered "repre-
> sentatives" simply because they are chosen by popular election, then
> the same reasoning should apply to elected judges.[29]

The Court clearly recognized the tension that popular elections create between
public accountability and judicial independence.

> The fundamental tension between the ideal character of the judicial
> office and the real world of electoral politics cannot be resolved by
> crediting judges with total indifference to the popular will while si-
> multaneously requiring them to run for office.[30]

"[J]udges need not be elected at all." The state could "exclude its judiciary from
coverage of the....Act by changing to a system in which judges are appointed."[31]

---

[27] Several courts have declared Canon 7 prohibitions to be unconstitutional. E.g., **J.C.J.D. v.
R.J.C.R.**, 803 S.W.2d 953 (1991); **ACLU v. Florida Bar**, 744 F. Supp 1094 (1990); **Buckley v.
Illinois Judicial Inquiry Board**, 997 F.2d 224 (1993). See Ibid., for an analysis of the several
cases dealing with the free speech issue.

[28] 111 S.Ct. 2354 (1991).

[29] Ibid.

[30] Ibid.

[31] Ibid.

Since Louisiana had chosen otherwise, however, it must live up to the dictates of the Voting Rights Act and eliminate those questionable at-large judicial election districts.[32]

Nonpartisan election systems for placing judges on state benches are under pressure from a number of directions. Primarily, the questions at issue are whether the voters can get the information they require for assessing judicial candidates, whether they can cast knowledgeable votes, and whether the elections lead to a representative bench.

The following section of this chapter looks closely at a typical nonpartisan recruitment system: the one used in the State of Washington since 1908. An effort is made to describe the often diverse and numerous informal factors that ultimately put a particular candidate on the bench.

Nonpartisan Recruitment in Washington

The Washington judiciary enjoys four levels of courts. The court of last resort, the Supreme Court, is composed of nine justices elected to six-year terms.[33] Every two years three of the justices stand for election. The intermediate Court of Appeals is separated into three divisions, hearing most appeals in three-judge rotating panels. Division I is located in Seattle and features nine judges who hear appeals from trial courts in the northwestern part of the state. Division II is located in Tacoma and includes six judges who hear cases appealed from the southwestern trial jurisdictions. Division III, located in Spokane, is composed of five judges and hears all the appeals from the eastern part of the state. These judges are elected to six-year terms from districts within their respective sectors of the state. Vacancies are filled by gubernatorial appointments, but as with all appointees they must face the voters in a possible contested race at the next general election.

The Superior Courts are the courts of general jurisdiction, with 157 judges hearing cases in 30 jurisdictions throughout the 39 counties of the state. Some populous counties have several Superior Court judges while a few share a judge with neighboring rural counties. For example, King County (Seattle) has 49

---

[32] Earlier, the U.S. Supreme Court had approved Louisiana's judicial districts as exempt from the one person-one vote requirement of other elective offices. Three dissenters felt judges perform governmental functions and therefore should be elected from districts of comparable population. See **Wells v. Edwards**, 409 U.S. 1095 (1973).

[33] In November, 1995, the voters approved a constitutional amendment permitting the legislature to decrease the size of the Supreme Court from its present nine to not less than five. Also the amendment changed the way the Chief Justice was selected from a modified seniority system for a two-year term to a majority vote of the Justices for a four-year term. A Court Composition Committee appointed by the Chief Justice recommended that the court remain at nine. After a thorough study, the Committee agreed that a smaller Court would have narrowed the opportunity for gender, ethnic-racial and geographical diversity. See Court Composition Committee, Report of Findings and Recommendations. Olympia: Supreme Court (September 1996). In January, 1997, the Justices voted to extend Chief Justice Barbara Durham's tenure for another two years.

judges while Asotin County in southeast Washington shares its judge with neighboring Garfield County. Superior Court judges are elected from county-wide constituencies to four-year terms. Again, vacancies are filled by the governor, and as with all judicial appointees they serve until the next general election when they must be elected to retain their positions. The District Courts are courts of limited jurisdiction and, like the Superior Court judges, the larger counties have a number elected from districts within those counties or from the county at-large. Some counties have only one district judge. All District Court judges are elected to four-year terms. As county courts, District Court vacancies are filled by county commissioners. A few counties have part-time judges, and a few of the District jurists are laypersons. Municipal judges are appointed by the mayor or city councils, or in larger cities they are elected to four-year terms in nonpartisan contests. Some district court judges contract with cities to provide municipal court services. Figure 3.1 portrays the hierarchical structure and selection provisions of Washington's state and county courts.

Figure 3.1

WASHINGTON COURT SYSTEM

SUPREME COURT
9 Justices
Nonpartisan Elections
State-wide
Governor appoints to vacancies between elections
6-Year Terms

COURTS OF APPEALS

Division I	Division II	Division III
9 Judges	6 Judges	5 Judges

Nonpartisan Elections
Multi-county Districts
Governor appoints to vacancies between elections
6-Year Terms

SUPERIOR COURT
30 Judicial Divisions
168 Judges
Nonpartisan Elections
One or more counties
Governor appoints to vacancies between elections
4-Year Term

DISTRICT COURTS	**MUNICIPAL COURTS**
60 Districts	134 Courts
107 Judges	96 Judges
Nonpartisan Elections	Nonpartisan Elections
County-wide or county districts	in large cities
County Commissioners appoint	Mayor-City Council or City Manager
to vacancies	appoint in cities under 30,000
4-year term	4-year term

From statehood in 1889 until 1908 the judges in the state were elected in partisan elections, with Supreme Court justices leading the slates of their respective parties.[34] Judges were nominated in party conventions. Straight party voting prevailed throughout the initial period. Voters were urged to vote straight party tickets and the ballot form was designed to encourage it. The voters in the general election had merely to check a box at the top of the ballot to cast their votes for all the candidates on the party's list.

> The fortunes of the first judicial candidates were tied to the fate of their respective political parties.... [The] high level of [voter] interest is explained by the partisan nature of the elections and straight party voting. Thus, the political parties dominated initiation, screening and even affirmation. Although the electorate affirmed candidates, they did so because of party label.[35]

During the early years of statehood the Washington recruitment system was indeed a low articulation system with the political party in complete control of nearly all aspects of the recruitment of judges at all levels. The participation of voters in judicial elections was high, and the political parties contested nearly every court race, but the races were rarely competitive. The leading political party held a tight grip on the initiation and screening of candidates and party loyalists affirmed the results of the earlier steps in recruitment.[36] In 1908 all judges were placed on a nonpartisan system with a direct primary responsible for nominations.[37] As the organized legal profession, interested groups, the governor's office and the interested voters gained confidence in their efforts to influence the recruitment of judges in the ensuing nonpartisan years, the Washington recruitment system became more balanced.

Although in Washington gubernatorial appointments blend with nonpartisan elections when those appointed to vacancies must run for the office at the next general election, for more focused discussion and a better understanding of judicial recruitment in the Evergreen state the two processes will be analyzed separately.

---

[34] Article IV, sec. 3 of the Washington Constitution, approved in 1889 reads:
> The judges of the supreme court shall be elected by the qualified electors of the state at large at the general state election at the times and places at which state officers are elected...if a vacancy occurs in the office of a judge...the governor shall appoint a person to hold the office until the election and qualification of a judge to fill the vacancy, which election shall take place at the next succeeding general election, and the judge so elected shall hold office for the remainder of the unexpired term.

[35] Charles H. Sheldon, "The Recruitment of Judges to the Washington Supreme Court: Past and Present," *Willamette Law Review* 22 (1986): 94.

[36] The first Democrat to be elected to a full term was Stephen Chadwick in the first nonpartisan election in 1908.

[37] Because of the fear that they would lose dominance of the Supreme Court, the Republican legislature returned the election of the Justices of the high bench to the partisan system for 1912 only. Thereafter, nonpartisan elections have prevailed to the present day.

Washington Judicial Elections and Initiation

Are there any peculiar characteristics about the initiation of candidacies in Washington and in nonpartisan elections generally? Judicial candidates today are either self-starters or are urged by others to file for office. For the self-starter, all that is needed to place an aspirant's name on the primary ballot is to pay a "filing fee" of 1% of the salary of the office being sought, be a lawyer in good standing with the unified bar association, and for court of appeals candidates have been in practice for at least five years.[38] These minimum requirements encourage individuals to run for the bench who might be discouraged if a nominating petition with several hundred signatures were needed or if political activities were required to gain the confidence of the party leaders. Lawyers have paid the fee in a few cases simply to get their name on the ballot and in front of the voters, hoping name familiarity would help gain clients. A candidate responding to the 1994 survey admitted that "several lawyers said run; also as a solo practitioner it would give my practice more exposure."

Many judicial candidates are prompted to file for office because of the encouragement received from other lawyers, judges, family and friends and business leaders. One candidate in our survey wrote: "There were a group of lawyers highly unsatisfied with the incumbent. Encouragement also came from prosecutors, District court personnel and the Probation Department as well."[39] About one-third of the respondents said they decided to run on their own without any pushing from others. Although a very few mentioned encouragement from political leaders, none admitted to a political party initiating their candidacy.

Most of the incumbents plan on running to retain their judgeships, and thus as soon as elected or re-elected they anticipate another run when their terms expire. The average number of months that all aspirants to the bench, incumbents and potential candidates, decide to contest or defend their judicial positions is 14 months. Nearly 70% of all winning as well as losing candidates plan to campaign again for the bench. However, one respondent remarked that it would be "unlikely" he/she would campaign again because "too little emphasis is placed on ability and too much on kissing babies," while another warned:

> If qualified people do not run they abdicate the right to have a fair,
> and free, judiciary. It is only by running for the bench that we re-
> move it from the influence of large [law] firms that support their
> own.

---

[38] Supreme Court justices in September, 1997 earned $112,078 per year, Court of Appeals judges $106,537; Superior Court judges $100,995; and District judges $96,082.

[39] Unattributed quotes and data are from a 1994 survey of all 121 candidates campaigning in the September primary election who ran for Washington judicial positions from the state supreme court to Seattle municipal bench.

But nonpartisan elections are more strenuous than partisan races, and certainly more arduous than retention elections; this is a fact that remains a major deterrent to many highly qualified attorneys. Invariably, initiation depends much on what candidates see facing them at the screening stage of recruitment. One veteran of the campaign trail observed:

> A campaign is grueling for the whole family, not just the candidate. Most campaigning by its nature is superficial. (How meaningful can you be in 2 minutes?) Endorsers (e.g., newspapers and other organizations) have agendas which are not made public and which do not have to be fair or responsible.

In some cases, the costs of conducting a run for the state or even county bench remains another deterrent to filing for office. Raising funds for elections is viewed as the most troublesome aspect of judicial elections. Not only does this consideration bear on all candidates, it is especially pressing on women and minority candidates.[40]

Although unknowns are encouraged to file for judicial office in Washington, the successful aspirant needs to accumulate several experiences before initiating a promising candidacy. Of course, none of these experiences are absolutely necessary for success, but they are widely regarded as highly desirable. Pro-tem judicial appointments, where lawyers fill a temporary bench vacancy, enhance potential candidates' chances. Other attorneys get to know pro-tems and gain a sense for their abilities. Such an experience also looks good on candidates' election resumes. Bar association activities bring the future judicial aspirant to the attention of the bar leadership, and this attention tends to be useful in future bar polls and in additional professional appointments. Some partisan experience, essential for appointments, is also desirable for elections. Name familiarity is often gained from partisan activities such as in the state legislature or prosecutor's office.[41] Of course, for trial benches representing small jurisdictions community and civic activities are crucial. Chairing United Way, lodge membership, Boy Scout sponsorship, and membership on municipal boards, Habitat for Humanity, etc. all bring the person to the attention of the community.

---

[40] "Although both white and minority judges regarded 'raising campaign funds' as the most onerous task in the electoral process, it tends to place minorities at a greater disadvantage. Funds for elections come primarily from two sources: other attorneys and the candidates' own funds. Minority candidates frequently make less income than their white counterparts and, consequently, have fewer personal funds available." Washington State, *Minority and Justice Task Force, Final Report* (1990), p. 95.

[41] "Professional activities help to nurture support from legal colleagues for those attorneys considering a future in the judiciary. One judge admitted that his efforts in the Young Lawyers' Division and other professional assignments on behalf of the Bar brought him recognition from older, influential lawyers who, subsequently, were willing to give their endorsements. The value of political party affiliation and partisan activities may be more crucial in some counties than in others, and might be considered by the Governor in the absence of formal input from the Bar." Ibid., p. 81.

Screening

The screening phase of nonpartisan recruitment in Washington has become complicated, crowded with screeners often placing conflicting requirements on the candidates. As a consequence, nonpartisan campaigns tend to be more open and inclusive when compared with partisan and merit plan systems. The former tend to be controlled by the political party leaders and voters, the latter by the bar associations or segments thereof.

In recent elections, judicial candidates have sought out numerous supporters who would endorse their candidacy and provide campaign funding and/or inkind support. This is especially the case in the Seattle, Tacoma, Spokane and other larger metropolitan areas. These screening actors include: members of leading law firms, bar association selection committees, newspaper editorial boards, law enforcement groups, Women's Political Caucus, Washington Women Lawyers, Loren Miller Bar, Asian American Bar, Hispanic Bar, Native American Bar, Municipal League, Democratic and Republican party leaders, Washington Labor Council, Teamsters, retired persons, and leading business and political officials. Endorsements from retired or sitting judges are always available. In addition to the several statewide groups, Superior and District Court candidates are in contact with county and city versions of state organizations. For example, the Washington State Labor Council often has a county organization.

The screening actor consistently involved is the organized legal profession in the form of the Washington State Bar Association, the voluntary county bars and special segments such as ethnic or gender bars.[42] Although not always successful in determining the outcome of elections, the legal profession has regarded activities concerning judicial recruitment to be its primary responsibility. Courts and lawyers are intimately related, judges come from the legal profession, and lawyers can best judge the qualifications of prospective jurists. Who better to judge judicial temperament, legal competency and impartiality? We are led to ask: How are their efforts organized?

Which bar organization is involved is determined by which jurisdiction is the subject of the contested election.[43] Statewide Supreme Court races may draw in the state bar organization. Races for the multi-county Court of Appeals involve a number of county bar associations, while county-wide Superior and

---

[42] The unified Washington State Bar Association was active in polling its membership concerning Supreme Court candidates in elections. This practice was abandoned in 1984 with the voluntary county bars assuming polling responsibilities. The State Bar is currently considering a return to some survey efforts in statewide elections.

[43] In recent years the following county, specialized and ethnic bar associations were involved or intend to be involved in judicial preferential polls, committee investigations, evaluations or recommendations: the Washington State, King, Clark, Tacoma-Pierce, Snohomish, Grant, Spokane, Kitsap, and Cowlitz bar associations, and the Hispanic Bar, Loren Miller Bar (African American), Northwest Indian Bar, Native American Bar, Asian American Bar, Washington Women Lawyers, and Northwest Legal Foundation.

District Court contests are limited to county bar efforts. The Seattle municipal courts often rely on recommendations from the county bar.

The organized legal profession performs two screening functions. One involves submitting recommendations for appointments and the other entails giving advice to voters. Advising the voters in elections takes three forms: preferential polls, selection committee screening, and judicial evaluation surveys. The preferential polls report the results of a mail survey of bar members concerning the qualifications of candidates in contested elections. Bar selection committees interview candidates and report their findings with rankings, ratings, or a short list of approved candidates. Bar evaluation surveys, usually conducted in the interim between elections, involve questionnaires, observations, consultations, and interviews. The influence on the voters of all of these activities depends upon a receptive print media.

The Spokane County Bar's preferential poll is typical. Candidates who have filed for Superior or District Court positions fill out questionnaires that are on file at the bar office and available to bar members. A mail survey is sent to 1,000 or so lawyers in the county requesting them to rate the candidates on the basis of integrity, relevant legal experience, legal ability, and judicial temperament.[44] Approximately two-thirds of the attorneys routinely respond. A week before the September primary the results of the survey are reported to the media. The bar does not repeat the survey for the general election.[45]

The King County Bar Association, the largest voluntary bar in the state, features nearly 10,000 members and is intimately involved in elections.[46] Two separate 24-member committees (21 lawyers and 3 laypersons) are responsible for appraising candidates. One committee assumes responsibility for screening for King County Superior Court positions and for Court of Appeals Division I aspirants. The other committee screens District Court contests and county court commissioners. Their efforts involve a thorough 11-page questionnaire filled out by each applicant, an investigation of up to 46 references, and an interview of candidates by committee members. The questionnaires inquire about the applicants' current practice, court appearances, legal and educational back-

---

[44] All candidates are rated along a continuum from 1 ("lowest") to 5 ("highest") with the mean score being reported. **Integrity** is defined as "Free from impropriety and favoritism, disregard of possible public criticism, fair and open-minded, committed to equal justice under the law, and does not engage in unethical or unprofessional conduct." **Legal experience**: "Does the applicant have sufficient court room experience." **Legal ability**: "Analytical ability, an interest in legal scholarship, qualities of wisdom, intellect, common sense, knowledge of rules and procedures, and a commitment to keeping up with changes." **Judicial temperament**: "Respect for the judicial process, ability to work with others, ability to be respectful to all counsel and litigants, and the ability to treat all participants with dignity and fairness."

[45] Of the six contested races in the September 1994 primary in Spokane, the voters accepted the bar's top-rated candidate in three.

[46] The King County Bar evolved from the Seattle Bar to the Seattle/King County Bar (SKCBA) to finally the King County Bar in 1994.

ground, matters pertaining to discipline, judicial experience, health, professional and community activities, honors, and names of references. The references are contacted and inquiries made of the applicants' legal competency, integrity, diligence, and temperament.

At the end of the screening, each applicant is rated as "Exceptionally Well Qualified," "Well Qualified," "Adequate," "Not Qualified," or "Insufficient Information to Rate." Candidates may refuse to participate in the screening process, which may lead to an "insufficient information" rating. In those cases where the candidate refuses to participate but the committee feels it has enough information, the appropriate rating is assigned. The results of the committees' screening are widely distributed to the media.

The King County Bar Association also evaluates sitting judges. The Judicial Evaluation Committee, a separate committee from the two selection committees, rates judges every two years in terms of diligence, conduct, legal ability, impartiality, and administration. Attorneys who have presented cases before the judges rate each incumbent from "excellent" to "very poor." The results are released to the judges in non-election years, and to the judges and the general public in election years in order to "provide useful information to the public."

In addition to the county bar associations, other ethnic, and gender affiliates of the state bar association screen and recommend candidates. For example, Washington Women Lawyers rate candidates after questionnaires have been filled out, interviews conducted, and ratings assigned. The Loren Miller Bar Association, with about 200 African American members, screens candidates through its judicial evaluation committee. It makes its recommendations public prior to the primary elections. Also the Asian Bar Association, Hispanic Bar and Native American organization evaluate candidates in contested elections and recommend to their membership and the public their preferences.

The screening process is not a monopoly held by the legal profession, however. The Washington Women's Political Caucus, the Seattle Municipal League, Washington Labor Council, other labor groups, and newspaper editorial boards are a few among the other significant organizations that screen and recommend their findings to their members, interested voters and the public.

Of course, the important question is whether these many organizations' efforts are effective? A survey of registered voters in Spokane County conducted after the 1994 general election indicated the variety of sources the voters consulted in preparation for their vote on judicial candidates. Table 3.3 reports responses to the question: "Whether you voted or not, how **important** to you would each of the following sources be in preparing to vote for candidates in judicial elections?" and "indicate the...sources of information **you actually used**."

Table 3.3

VOTER SOURCES FOR JUDICIAL CANDIDATES

(State of Washington, 1994)

	% Important Source	% Actually Used Source
Voters' Pamphlet	87%	50%
Meetings with Candidates	63%	8%
Discussions Family-Friends	51%	32%
Door-to-door Candidate Contacts	50%	4%
Results of Law Enforcement Polls	48%	12%
Results of Bar Polls	42%	16%
Group Endorsements	32%	12%
Mailings from Candidates	29%	17%
Newspaper Editorials	27%	23%
Recommendations from attorney	27%	11%
TV	12%	16%
Radio Ads	9%	8%
Lawn Signs and Billboards	8%	6%
Newspaper Ads	7%	12%
Telephone Canvassing	7%	0%

The voters prefer personal contact with candidates, but it is becoming more and more problematic within the larger jurisdictions. As in other elections, the conventional campaign activities and endorsements and editorials all play important roles in providing voters with information. Although bar polls, endorsements by special groups and newspaper recommendations do not dominate the sources of information, they likely make the difference. A swing of but a few percentages in close-contested elections can spell the difference between winning and losing. The bar and special interests provide much of the difference. What is clear is that Washington enjoys a high articulation screening process, especially in the larger metropolitan jurisdictions. Does the affirmation of candidates reinforce the high articulation trends?

Affirmation

Three measurements emerging from the affirmation stage suggest whether the intensity and numbers of actors are contributing to a higher or a lower articulation election process. Contestedness, competitiveness and voter participation provide the most telling clues. First, as voter interest widens and increases, those candidates who survive the election are pulled toward the center of the judicial dilemma continuum. Second, this is especially the case if the election is competitive and extreme views tend to lose votes. Third, if a considerable number of the available judicial positions are contested, it suggests participation on the part of a high number of those groups that initiate and screen candidacies. The theory is that as participation, contestedness and competitiveness increase the higher the articulation level. As the articulation model predicts, a highly competitive election that captures the interest of voters and special groups tends to encourage a balanced perspective between accountability and independence from those surviving.

Table 3.4 reports the voting and participation percentages in Supreme Court races from 1990 through 1996.

Table 3.4

CANDIDATE CONTESTEDNESS, VOTER PARTICIPATION AND COMPETITIVENESS IN SUPREME COURT GENERAL ELECTION RACES

Year	Number Candidates per Position	Total Votes Cast	Votes Cast for Supreme Court Candidates	Percent Voter Participation	Percent Winning Vote
1990	4 uncontested	1,362,651	789,194	58%	100%
1992	2 contested 1 uncontested	2,324,907	1,600,581	69%	56%
1994	2 contested 1 uncontested	1,733,471	1,300,343	75%	53%
1995	1 contested	1,397,039	1,072,417	77%	54%
1996	1 contested	2,293,895	1,535,180	67%	62%

Table 3.4 data suggest that the 1990 races and to an extent the 1996 races were low articulation experiences as indicated by 1990 uncontested races in the general election, low voter participation in both years and either no or low competition between candidates each year. However, in 1994 and 1995 the articu-

lation levels were raised with contested seats, competitive winning margins of only 3% or 4% and fairly high voter participation.[47]

Examples drawn from a 1996 survey of trial and appellate judicial candidates are illustrative of responses to the judicial dilemma. A candidate adopting an "accountable" stance after a somewhat low articulation experience wrote that judges should be strictly accountable: "But accountable for what? And how is that communicated to the public...." Another candidate also was sensitive toward accountability: "I understand and accept the need to be accountable, but I reserve the right to act on my conscience."

Another candidate who experienced a contested race but won by a large margin in which a moderate level of voters participated felt that judges should be "strictly independent" and added "A good judge must rule based on the law and evidence as he or she sees it. While you may pay the price for rendering an unpopular decision, you must have the courage to do so or you shouldn't be on the bench."

Many of the 1996 judicial candidates adopted a balanced stance regarding the "judicial dilemma," and were evenly divided between moderately high and low articulation experiences. A typical comment: "I try to strike a balance—uphold legal principle on legal questions, but bear in mind the views of the public on matters of judicial discretion such as sentencing.

Averages can be deceptive, of course. Several of the races reported in Table 3.4 were indeed highly contested, competitive and brought out the vote. However, in the same election, low articulation may have characterized a campaign. Again, as the model stipulates, in one jurisdiction both a high and a low articulation recruitment system could be experienced. These concerns aside, these data show a tendency—namely, increases in one of the measurements are associated with increases in the others. As contestedness increases, so do participation and competitiveness—and, consequently, so does the articulation level.

Washington Judicial Appointments

Over the years, nearly two-thirds of all judges have been initially appointed to their positions by the governor or county commissioners on an interim basis. Of course, to retain their appointments they must submit themselves to the voters within a year.[48] Consequently, appointments are an integral part of the total recruitment process in Washington.

Governors have their own recruitment procedures. Announcements are made concerning a vacancy and candidates are invited to submit resumes and

---

[47] See also Charles H. Sheldon and Nicholas P. Lovrich, "State Judicial Recruitment," in John B. Gates and Charles A. Johnson (eds.), *The American Courts: A Critical Assessment* (Washington D.C.: CQ Press, 1991), pp. 176-183.

[48] Most election challenges come at the appointee's initial election when the incumbents seem more vulnerable.

complete questionnaires. These applications are accompanied or followed by endorsement letters, petitions, and phone calls from notables, attorneys, judges and political leaders. The appropriate county or state bar association is asked for recommendations, a short list is established and after interviews the appointment is announced. Although the position is nonpartisan, partisanship most commonly becomes an important factor in the governor's choice. Invariably, the appointee at the Supreme Court level is a member of the governor's party, and may have been a political activist in the cause of the chief executive. Appointments to the state's highest bench are sometimes seen as an opportunity to redress regional, gender, ethnic, or background imbalances on the court. And, as always, political or policy coincidence between the appointee and the governor is considered. Invariably the issue of accountability arises during the interview process. Candidates are asked their views on judicial activism and restraint. The "correct" response is to favor restraint.[49]

Although separately conducted, the appointment process dovetails with elections. Some of the same criteria for appointment are based on the outcome of the inevitable election that follows. For example, electability, campaigning skills, and fund-raising potential typically are all major concerns of the appointing authorities.

The Washington State Bar Association plays a major role in appointments not enjoyed in elections. Two standing committees are assigned the task of inviting judicial aspirants to submit applications, fill out questionnaires, be investigated and interviewed and, if qualified, be placed on a standing list. The process is completely separate from the governor's screening. One committee handles the Court of Appeals vacancies while the other screens for Supreme Court vacancies. When the governor has an opportunity to appoint lawyers to the appellate benches, a list of from 12 to 25 names rated as qualified is always ready. On occasion, the governor may request that a person be investigated and hopefully put on the approved list, and it is not uncommon for committee members to anticipate the governor's preference. The arrangement with the committee is strictly voluntary. Only rarely does the governor go outside the bar's recommended list for the appointment to the court of last resort, while some discretion may be exercised in lower court appointments.

For Superior Court vacancies, county bars are requested to submit recommendations to the governor. The King County Bar Association uses the same selection committees used in elections to come up with recommendations on appointment. The Spokane Bar uses the same preferential poll used in elections. A mail survey of its membership is conducted and the results are communicated to the governor and released to the media. This places some pressure on the

---

[49] Activism generally means that the judge acts independently of the legislature and precedent. Restraint means a judge will give considerable credence to legislative enactments and to judicial precedent. See Stephen C. Halpern and Charles M. Lamb, *Supreme Court Activism and Restraint* (Lexington, MA.: Lexington Books, 1982).

governor to appoint from the list of applicants, and if not the top rated then at least near the top.

District Court vacancies receive the same attention from the county bar associations, but recommendations or poll results are submitted to the county commissioners. Again, the commissioners, themselves elected on partisan ballots, are not obligated to follow the legal profession's advice. It is not uncommon for partisan and political factors to override—or supplement—the bar's ratings.

Figure 3.2

WASHINGTON RECRUITMENT ACTORS

Formal Participants   **Advisory Participants**

AFFIRMATION

VOTERS
Primary and General Election

GOVERNOR
Temporary Appointments

SCREENING

VOTERS
Primary Election

King County Bar Association
Evaluations-Recommendations

County Bar Associates
Preferential Polls

Washington State Bar Assoc.
Screening Committees

GOVERNOR'S OFFICE

INITIATION
INCUMBENTS

CANDIDATES

Level of Articulation

Considering the number of initiating, screening and affirming actors engaged in Washington's recruitment process in recent times, many, but not all, races qualify as moderately high articulation elections. Nonpartisan judicial elections clearly permit, if not encourage, the active involvement of a diverse range and substantial number of participants along the entire recruitment sequence running from initiation through screening to affirmation. However, in some races the selection is limited to but a few participants and therefore a low articulation process results. For example, in 1992, Charles W. Johnson filed for the Supreme Court against a respected Chief Justice. Neither candidate campaigned nor participated in the many electioneering opportunities. Johnson defeated his opponent. In the same year, former Superior Court Judge Richard Guy ran against former Governor John Spellman. Both candidates campaigned vigorously. Their race was indeed a high articulation race, meeting all the criteria explained in the recruitment model, with Guy as the ultimate victor. Again, it is the informal stages that shape the final selection of judges.

What nonpartisan judicial elections permit is a fairly open process that encourages participation throughout the recruitment sequence. The potential for a high articulation recruitment experience is sometimes realized.

Recently, as with other states, Washington's judicial selection system has come under close scrutiny. In 1995, the state's Chief Justice Barbara Durham announced the formation of a 24-member study commission to "review all aspects of judicial selection." What had prompted her announcement was the fear expressed in the final report of the commission (known as the Walsh Commission after its chairperson, Ruth Walsh):

> In most of our population centers and rapidly-growing rural areas, voters are less and less likely to have knowledge of [judicial] candidates.... Voter frustration seems due partly to unfamiliarity with how the judicial system works and what judges do, and partly to the lack of information about the qualifications, experience, and performance of judicial candidates [50]

After a year's study involving hearings, surveys, focus groups, expert witnesses and subcommittee studies, the commission's final report recommended replacing the existing nonpartisan-interim appointments with a modified merit commission plan. The report urged adoption of a system of appointments from a list provided by nominating commissions or by contested nonpartisan elections, followed by unopposed retention elections. A nominating commission would submit to the governor a list of candidates approved for appointment. Following the first year on the bench the appointee would be subject to a contested nonpartisan election at the September primary elections. The person

[50] Walsh Commission, *The People Shall Judge* (Olympia: Office of Administrator for the Courts, March 1996): 12.

elected, whether the incumbent or the challenger, would face an uncontested retention election at the completion of each subsequent term.

The modified plan received considerable media coverage and support from judges and politicians grew.   The recommended plan would require several statutory changes, but more importantly, a constitutional amendment.   The Walsh Commission's plan was on the agenda of the 1997 legislature, but was lost in the legislative shuffle but likely to be resurrected in subsequent sessions. The difficulty, of course, is to sustain an interest in the need for a change. Again, as others have noted, bringing about judicial reform is not for the short winded.

Chapter Four

Partisan Judicial Recruitment

A number of different explanations, each corresponding to a particular historical period, account for the acceptance of partisan elections of judges. The older states began substituting popular election of judges in place of a disappointing process that had put the legislature in control of judicial recruitment. In the wake of the Jacksonian Revolution in the mid-1800s many states adopted popular election of many previously appointed public officials, including judges. Later, many of the newer states turned to the popular election of jurists as a reaction against their unfavorable experiences with territorial judges who had been imposed on them by a far-off administration largely unconcerned with local problems.[1]

Of course, political parties and popular elections were synonymous. In order to give meaning to elections, political parties were needed to mobilize the electorate around candidates, programs and agenda. Partisan selection has simply meant that the name of each candidate on the ballot is accompanied by his or her party affiliation. Earlier, judicial candidates were nominated in party conventions but now are products of party primaries. In practice many voters cast their vote for the party's slate of candidates which included judges, knowing only the few top presidential or gubernatorial nominees on the ballot and remaining quite unfamiliar if not unconcerned with judicial candidates. Whatever the practice, partisan judicial recruitment means that political parties are responsible for initiation, screening and much of affirmation.

Partisan election of judges is used today in eight states for all judgeships (Alabama, Arkansas, Illinois, Mississippi, North Carolina, Pennsylvania, Texas, and West Virginia), while several other states use partisan recruitment for some of their judges (Indiana, Kansas, Missouri, New York, Tennessee), or for nominating or retaining judicial candidates (Ohio, New Mexico). The central argument for partisan election of judges is to assure that the judges will be accountable to the citizens for their decisions. If judges do indeed make policy, then they should be responsible for their policy decisions. Political parties help hold them responsible.

---

[1] Charles H. Sheldon, *A Century of Judging: A Political History of the Washington Supreme Court* (Seattle: University of Washington Press, 1988), p. 14. Although the territorial citizens had this view of their judges, Kermit Hall has convincingly argued that territorial judges were often well educated and experienced professionals on par with federal district judges appointed under Article III of the U.S. Constitution. Kermit Hall, "Hacks and Derelicts Revisited: American Territorial Judiciary, 1789-1959," *Western Historical Quarterly* 12 (1981): 273.

Critics argue that partisan elections too often do not bring to the bench highly qualified persons, and in some cases even marginally qualified or unqualified judges are elected to office. The judiciary can too easily become the refuge of barely competent lawyers. "Successful lawyers are said to be reluctant to set aside their lucrative law practices to pursue election to the judiciary."[2] To many, it seems wrong-headed that election to the judiciary depends upon the fortunes of the political party rather than an assessment of the candidates qualifications or record on the bench. Also, competent attorneys often disdain politics, viewing campaigning as "kissing babies" and talking inanities with uninformed people and largely uninterested voters. "[T]he uncertainty of tenure in an elective system and the demands of election campaigning combine to deter the recruitment of the most highly qualified legal professionals to sit on state courts."[3] It is also clear that in one-party states, members of the minority party have precious little chance of being elected to the bench, depriving the judiciary of a substantial pool of talent.

The most common and perhaps most telling criticism of popular elections, and especially partisan elections, is that judicial independence is sacrificed. Judges must be free from political obligations in order to settle disputes fairly and to protect minorities and unpopular individuals from the otherwise overwhelming force of the majority. State and federal Bills of Rights would, indeed, be ineffective if judges were not free to intervene between individuals and the public when good cause arises. Having to please the sometimes strident complaints of the public as well as partisan leaders and those who contribute to campaigns can keep judges from giving full attention to the rule of law.

These criticisms are countered in many cases by equating judicial elections to elections of other officials. Persons running for the state legislature, executive offices and local positions suffer the same deterrents from public service as judicial aspirants. They too must balance their practices, professions and jobs with the demands of campaigning. Why should it be so different for judges? Also, simply because the minority party may be shut out of the recruitment process doesn't mean that the quality of those ultimately selected is inevitably sacrificed; there may indeed be an abundance of able persons in the majority party.

Despite the ease of offering criticism, there is much to recommend the partisan recruitment of judges. If it is true that voters tend to know little about judicial candidates, the political party label at least gives them a significant indication of the general inclinations of the candidate. Such an indicator is certainly equal to if not better in relevance than name recognition, gender, ethnic or some other unconsidered cue having little bearing on qualifications for judging.[4] Is a

---

[2] Philip Dubois, *From Ballot to Bench: Judicial Elections and the Quest for Accountability* (Austin: University of Texas Press, 1980), p. 6.

[3] Ibid.

[4] It is true, however, that from a representational perspective, gender, ethnic and religious indicators may be as rational a choice and as important as party identity. See Charles H. Sheldon and Nicholas

name on lawn signs in nonpartisan elections a better indication of qualifications than a party label attached to a name on the ballot? Parties, under some circumstances, also serve as training grounds for candidates. The initiation and screening tasks are turned over to party officials and activist members who have an incentive to seek out talent that can carry the party to victory in elections. To have a name placed on primary or general election ballots means that the candidate has passed certain political and ideological tests. The act of filing for judicial office in order to gain name recognition to improve legal business, or to simply take a wild stab at a judicial spot, is strongly discouraged. Although the qualifications might not be the same if the bar association did the screening, the qualifications the party would look for would in most cases not be altogether alien to judging. Electability, community involvement, political experience (i.e., state legislature or prosecutor's office) and a commitment to public service are desirable attributes in any public official—including judges.

There is little evidence to support the argument that qualified lawyers are reluctant to run for a judgeship in a partisan system any more than they are reluctant to submit their names in appointive systems or to be considered for a merit plan nomination. Leaving a lucrative law practice for lawyers is involved in all formal methods of selection and for any public office. On the positive side, it is not at all uncommon to hear a judicial candidate say that although the campaign was indeed tiring, it was well worth the effort. Meeting the voter is not an altogether onerous and unpleasant enterprise. Although it has been proven otherwise in some cases, it was thought that with the party "footing the bill" for and controlling recruitment, special interests would be kept at arm's length from the process.

From the perspective of the voters, partisan elections offer a number of attractions. Judicial positions are almost always contested in competitive two-party states, giving the voter a choice at the ballot box. In general, more information is provided, more voter cues are available, more voters participate, and the ultimate winners have a broader representational mandate in partisan judicial elections than in other election formats.

Partisan elections tend to draw judges toward the public accountability end of the "judicial dilemma" continuum. However, it is not expected that the voters would control the policy decisions of the judges directly. Rather, the voters are assigned the not insignificant task of supporting or replacing those who make decisions on the bench. "The electorate does not decide policy, it accepts or rejects politicians associated with policies," and once elected—politicians, including judges—are held accountable not in terms of the party's promises, but rather in accord with the end results when those promises are carried out. "The

P. Lovrich, "State Judicial Recruitment," in John B. Gates and Charles A. Johnson (eds.) *The American Courts: A Critical Assessment* (Washington, D.C.: CQ Press, 1991), pp. 178-182.

electorate does not determine the full governmental program, but it can judge its effects later."[5]

Although accountability is indeed important, fortunately a number of protections from unwarranted public intrusion on the judiciary are available. In many states judges are not subject to voter recall. Also, removal of judges by impeachment or legislative joint resolution is exceedingly difficult to accomplish as judged from its rarity. Judges are legally immune from civil liability for their decisions. Terms of office and salaries are fixed by law. The "cult of the robe," a symbolic type of protection, isolates judges from close public scrutiny under all but extreme circumstances. The adversary process places judges in a "third-party" position, above the legal jousting. Judicial rulings are all susceptible to legislative correction, or to being overruled by higher courts, and ultimately to correction by constitutional amendment. Although in partisan campaigns judges may have to become "politicians," their legal education, practice as an attorney and professional socialization all serve to inculcate the principles of rule of law and judicial independence.

Is there empirical evidence setting partisan elections apart from the other methods of recruiting judges as being in some sense better? Does partisanship make any difference in who sits on the bench? Some evidence does exist which suggests that partisan elections tend to recruit those attached to the locality through birth. Further, and not surprising, judges selected in partisan elections tend to have previously served in political office, often as public prosecutors.[6] Partisan judges also tend to have gained their legal education in-state when compared with nonpartisan and merit plan judges.[7] Of course, the recruitment of judges in partisan elections gives emphasis to the differences between Republican and Democratic jurists. For example, Democratic judges tend to favor the weaker litigant in cases.[8] There is also evidence that judges facing reelection tend to dissent less in highly visible cases.[9] Except for a few partisan attributes (and sometimes contrary evidence exists, depending upon when, where and how

---

[5] Gerald M. Pomper, "Elections in America," quoted in Dubois, *From Ballot to Bench*, pp. 30-31.

[6] Herbert Jacob, "The Effect of Institutional Differences in the Recruitment Process: The Case of State Judges," *Journal of Politics* 13 (1964): 104.

[7] Bradley C. Canon, "The Impact of Formal Selection Processes on the Characteristics of Judges—Reconsidered," *Law & Society Review* 6 (1972): 579.

[8] Burton M. Atkins and Henry R. Glick, "Formal Judicial Recruitment and State Supreme Courts Decisions," *American Politics Quarterly* 2 (1974): 427; Martin A. Levin, "Urban Politics and Judicial Behavior," *Journal of Legal Studies* 1 (1972): 193; and Stuart Nagel, *Comparing Elected and Appointed Judicial Systems* (Beverly Hills: Sage, 1973).

[9] "[C]onstituency influence in state supreme courts is enhanced by competitive electoral conditions and experience with electoral politics." Melinda Hall, "Electoral Politics and Strategic Voting in State Supreme Courts," *Journal of Politics* 54 (May 1992): 427.

the research was done), however, scholars generally agree with Melinda Gann Hall when she observes that:

> Empirical research on the effects of judicial selection processes has been quite consistent in finding that methods of judicial recruitment do not affect either the quality of the bench or judicial outcomes.... Based on the evidence to date, the conclusion reasonably could be drawn that selection mechanisms simply do not have much of an impact on the operation of state judiciaries.[10]

Nonetheless, the formal process of partisan elections is only part of the recruitment sequence, as we have argued throughout. The final affirmation of judges by partisan elections shapes and is shaped by what precedes. But what precedes needs to be understood. Our understanding will be enhanced by looking at the Texas partisan system.

Partisan Elections and the Texas Experience

The Texas judicial system is large and complex. At the apex of the system are the Texas Supreme Court, responsible for all civil appeals, and the Criminal Court of Appeals, responsible for all final criminal appeals. Each has nine justices, elected state-wide for six-year terms. The Chief Justice and Presiding Judge are elected specifically to those positions of leadership for six-year terms. Eighty judges sit on 14 intermediate Courts of Appeals, again elected to six-year terms from multi-judge and multi-county districts. Three-hundred and eighty-six District Court judges, elected to four-year terms, sit on county trial courts of general jurisdiction. The trial courts are divided into 376 District Courts and 10 Criminal District Courts; the latter court gives preference to criminal cases. In urban counties, numerous District judges are elected county-wide. In rural counties, a single District judge may represent more than one county. County courts of limited jurisdiction number nearly 400, and they are divided into 254 constitutional court jurists, 167 judges on courts at law, and 18 probate judges. The courts at law are established by statute while the constitutional benches are authorized by the Texas Constitution. Municipal judges, numbering over 1,000 jurists, handle misdemeanors and violations of city ordinances. They may be elected or appointed, depending upon local ordinances. Elected justices of the peace, numbering over 800, hear civil claims under $1,000, hold preliminary hearings, hear small claims and decide minor misdemeanors. They need not be licensed attorneys.

---

[10] Ibid., 428. Hall, however, has attributed dissent rate to judicial elections.

Figure 4.1

TEXAS COURT SYSTEM

SUPREME COURT **9 Justices**	**COURT OF CRIMINAL APPEALS** **9 Judges**

Partisan Elections
Vacancies between elections filled by Governor
with advice and consent of Senate
6-year term

COURT OF APPEALS
14 Courts, 80 Judges
Partisan Elections
Multi-county Districts
Vacancies between elections filled by Governor
with advice and consent of Senate
6-year term

DISTRICT COURTS
386 Judges
Partisan Elections
One or more counties
Vacancies between elections filled by Governor
with advice and consent of Senate
4-year term

COUNTY COURTS

Constitutional Courts	**Statutory Courts**	**Probate Courts**
254 Judges	185 Judges	18 Judges

Partisan Elections
County-wide
County Commissioners appoint to vacancies between elections
4-year term

MUNICIPAL COURTS	**JUSTICE OF THE PEACE COURTS**
1,206 Judges	885 Judges
Elected or appointed per city	Partisan elections per precinct year
2-year term	4-year term

Although Texas has experienced a variety of methods in recruiting judges, populism has proven to be a salient force since Reconstruction, shaping how Texans view their judiciary. Some have argued that Texans are jealous of their prerogatives as citizens. After Reconstruction, Texas began a "long detailed, and exhaustive program that was nothing short of a rebellion against government itself" to wipe the slate clean of the carpetbagger judges and the restrictions of the Reconstruction constitutions.

> Judgeships...were made elective, including the bench of the supreme court. No judge who had to run for reelection regularly was expected to decide cases against the popular feeling, on some new fangled point of law.[11]

This meant, according to a Texas Supreme Court Justice, that judges were "to remain faithful to the values and sentiments of the people who elected them," and those cases should be decided on the basis of "common sense rather than new fangled legalism."[12]

Before entering the Union, the independent Republic of Texas had experimented with a nine-member Supreme Court selected by a joint ballot of both houses of the legislature. Upon statehood, the Governor appointed—with senate confirmation—three justices to six-year terms. In 1850, direct popular elections were instituted, but the process was returned to gubernatorial appointment with senate advice and consent when Texas joined the Confederacy. In 1866 five justices were elected for 10-year terms, but in 1869 gubernatorial appointment was again reinstated. Finally, in 1876 the Texas constitution adopted the present popular election system featuring a primary election for nomination and the general election for affirmation. Vacancies were to be filled by gubernatorial appointment until the next election. Judicial elections would be held at the same time and in the same manner as elections of other partisan offices. Despite a number of attempts to adopt the merit plan, Texans have held on tightly to their populist partisan election system.

However, two recent developments may challenge the populist tradition. One has developed from within, the other was imposed from without. First, judicial elections under the auspices of political parties were to relieve the judicial candidates from having to raise funds for campaigning. The party would solicit and disperse funds for judicial races. However, the costs of elections, the willingness of interested parties to contribute, and the competitive nature of many court races have clearly left behind any financial relief political parties might have supplied in the past. Second, the Voting Rights Act of 1965, as

---

[11] T.R. Fehrenbach, *Lone Star: A History of Texas and the Texans* (New York: Macmillan, 1968), quoted in John Cornyn, "Ruminations of the Nature of Texas Judging," *St. Mary's Law Journal* 25 (1993): 373.

[12] Ibid., 374.

amended and as interpreted by the U.S. Supreme Court, has brought the Texas election system, as in Louisiana's nonpartisan elections, under close scrutiny.

Of course, the campaign funding issue not only means that increasing amounts must be raised and that more pressure to contribute has to be imposed on those who have interests in court cases, but it also means that judges find it more difficult to appear to be objective, unbiased and free from conflicts of interest. Some evidence suggests that a few judges have appeared to favor large contributors in their rulings.[13]

The problem of campaign financing in Texas exists all down the judicial hierarchy, from the state supreme court to the local trial bench.[14] Between 1982 and 1994, the largest amount of money spent on a supreme court contest increased from $637,910 to $4,941,309. Winning candidates had collected an average of $272,189 in 1982, and $2,447,524 by 1994.[15] With rare exception, those candidates that spent more were the winners. This, of course, prompts candidates to raise more money. Media, especially TV, and mailing costs have increased, absorbing more campaign funds. Also, the Texas Code of Judicial Conduct features no restrictions on campaign financing and perhaps cannot do so unless voluntary limits are accepted.[16] Further, interest groups have discovered that contributions to court contests have a pay-off similar to contributions to legislative races. The effort may or may not be to "buy" a ruling in a particular set of cases, but rather to help candidates who already are sympathetic to their interests. Although most of the contributions to judicial campaigns come from attorneys, these attorneys generally represent special interests and are encouraged to contribute as a form of insurance against the time when their clients find themselves in court.

From another direction pressures have been brought to bear on the Texas selection system. In **Chisom v. Roemer** the U.S. Supreme Court ruled that Louisiana's at-large nonpartisan system of selecting supreme court justices was

---

[13] It may be that the improprieties which appear to be associated with partisan elections are simply the result of individual judges who would be tempted in any system of selection, or it may be that the large amounts of money needed for campaigning and the high stakes in court cases encourage improprieties. Nonetheless, to many the present Texas system which tolerates the view that money makes a difference needs to be reviewed anew and possibly reformed. Anthony Champagne, "Judicial Reform in Texas," in Champagne and Judith Hydel, *Judicial Reform in the States* (New York: University Press of America, 1993), pp. 93-116.

[14] Intermediate appellate judges who have won their races have increased spending over these years from an average of $34,490 to $54,941. In 1986, $118,223 was the average winning candidate's campaign bill. The winning candidates' average funding in Dallas County trial races jumped from $44,083 to $58,876. See ibid.

[15] Orrin W. Johnson and Laura Johnson Urbis, "Judicial Selection in Texas: A Gathering Storm?" *Texas Tech Law Review* 23 (1992): 545. See also Kyle K. Cheek, *"The Bench, the Bar and the Political Economy of Justice*: Texas Supreme Court Elecions, 1980-1994," (Phd dissertation, University of Texas-Dallas, 1995.)

[16] **Buckley v. Valero**, 424 U.S. 1 (1976).

covered by the Voting Rights Act of 1965. Judges were "representatives" as defined in the Act. Louisiana, as with Texas, "has decided to elect its judges and to compel judicial candidates to vie for popular support just as other candidates do."[17] Consequently, any selection design which results in a dilution of minority votes would be in violation of the law.

In a companion case, **Houston Lawyers' Ass'n v. Attorney General of Texas**, the Supreme Court applied the law to trial court races in Texas.[18] Justice John Paul Stevens, writing for a 6-3 majority, ruled that the Voting Rights Act applied to Texas trial judges who are elected from single-member districts.[19]

> It is equally clear,.. that the coverage of the Act encompasses the election of executive officers and trial judges whose responsibilities are exercised independently in an area coextensive with the districts from which they are elected. If a State decides to elect its trial judges, as Texas did in 1861, those elections must be conducted in compliance with the Voting Rights Act.

The Supreme Court remanded the case to the District Court to apply the ruling.

Subsequently, the Fifth Circuit Court of Appeals in **League of United Latin American Citizens v. Clements** relieved some of the pressure for selection reform.[20] The Fifth Circuit majority found no violation of the Voting Rights Act in the current system of partisan elections. Judge Patrick Higginbotham could discern no dilution of minority votes in the election of 172 judges in nine counties. Texas had a valid justification for the county single-district multi-judge system of representation for trial judges.

> By making coterminous the electoral and jurisdictional bases of trial courts, Texas advances the effectiveness of its courts by balancing the virtues of accountability with the need for independence.[21]

> It recognizes Texas' historic interest in having district judges remain accountable to all voters in their district.... [J]udges make choices that affect all county residents. Texas has insisted that trial judges answer to all county voters at the ballot box.[22]

---

[17] 111 S.Ct. 2354 (1991), 2367.

[18] 111 S.Ct. 2376 (1991).

[19] Minority litigants had previously pointed out that the multi-judge Court of Appeals in South Texas, representing 20 counties with a majority Hispanic population, had only one Hispanic out of the six judges on that bench. The Fifth Circuit upheld their contention. See **Rangel v. Attorney General**, 8 F 3d 242 (Fifth Cir. 1993).

[20] 999 F. 2d 831 (1993).

[21] Ibid., 869.

[22] Ibid., 873.

If any variation in dilution of voting existed, it was due to partisan elections rather than a consequence of racial or ethnic biases in the system. "Judicial elections are decided on the basis of partisan voting patterns."[23] The court noted that the alternatives to single-district venues such as cumulative and limited voting would not change the partisan system, nor the at-large aspects of the present system. Only rarely were retention and nonpartisan elections even mentioned in the opinion as viable options.

The politics of judicial selection reform in Texas has drawn to it a number of powerful but conflicting economic, political and legal figures. In virtually every legislative session in the past decade, selection reform of some kind has been introduced. Both the Governor and the Chief Justice of Texas urged a reevaluation of how judges should be elected. They and the Texas Bar Association advocated the "Texas Plan."[24] However, the plaintiff and defense lawyers, although constituting a small but active minority of the Texas bar, could not reach a consensus. The plaintiff's bar remained supportive of the current system, although with smaller districts. The defense attorneys backed the merit plan. In the legislature, the Mexican-American Caucus, the Black Caucus, and the Democratic leadership urged adoption of a single-member district system. Conservative Democrats and Republicans supported the merit plan.[25] Although most reformers would agree on a need for a change, few can agree on what that change should be. In the 1995 legislative session a version of the Texas Plan was passed by the Senate, but the bill died in the House.

However, under increased pressure to correct the flaws of the partisan system, the independent Texas Commission on Judicial Efficiency recommended two proposals to the 1997 Texas legislature for consideration as constitutional amendments. On a tie vote, the commission proposed a hybrid plan for appellate judges involving appointment by the Governor, confirmation by two thirds of a senate committee, followed by an open contested nonpartisan election. Thereafter, the incumbents run in uncontested retention elections to retain their positions. Another plan involves trial judges in nonpartisan elections initially followed by retention elections with incumbents running on their records.

The focus of the proposals is on freeing candidates from party labels. According to one member of the Texas Commission on Judicial Efficiency, reli-

---

[23] Ibid., 877.

[24] The Texas Plan has gone through a number of revisions, depending upon the compromises needed to gain sufficient support. In October, 1988 the final recommendations of the Joint Select Committee on the Judiciary reported: "A merit election system for appellate judges should be created including a review of qualified persons by a screening commission, a public hearing on three nominees submitted to the Governor by the Commission. Senate confirmation (if in session), a confirmation election after nomination by the Governor and a retention election after nomination or initial election." Nonpartisan elections were recommended for trial judges. Quoted in Anthony Champagne, "Judicial Reform in Texas," *Judicature* 72 (1988): 151.

[25] Champagne and Hydel, *Judicial Reform in the States*, pp. 111-112.

ance on party labels often "denies the public the service of those who want to serve."[26] But, again in 1997, the lack of a strong consensus on one plan spelled defeat for any change in how judges are selected. Nonetheless, recruitment reform in Texas is alive if not well.

Two explanations may account for the difficulty in bringing about reform. First, and perhaps most important, the advocates for reform have not coalesced behind one plan. Second, Texans do take their populist tradition rather seriously, and without a respected coalition of lawyers, politicians, minorities and judges to convince the citizens otherwise, the practice of partisan election of judges will remain. A close and perceptive observer of the Texas system, Anthony Champagne, has written:

> Whether a pro-merit selection coalition will develop in Texas which can carry two-thirds of the vote in both the Senate and the House and then a majority of the popular vote remains to be seen. That kind of coalition will be needed to get non-judicially imposed merit selection in Texas. Currently [1992], that kind of coalition strength does not appear to exist.[27]

Nor does it exist in 1997.

How does the present partisan system work? What role do the parties play and has their influence been overshadowed by the special interests which contribute to the high costs of financing a successful race for Texas benches?

Initiation and Screening

The primary elections held in March are the first step toward a Texas judgeship. If candidates prevail here they are permitted to carry the all-important party label with them to the general election. Texas has a closed primary in which only members of a party can vote in that party's primary. Such a primary tends to keep considerable control over initiation of candidates in the hands of the party. In rural areas, winning the Democratic District Court nomination more than likely assures victory in the general elections. However, in the urban areas District and Court of Appeals races have become competitive. Also because of the nearly overwhelming number of voters in urban areas, state-wide Supreme Court and Criminal Court of Appeals races remain competitive. The outcome is far from decided in the primaries. Turn-out at primaries is limited because of the closed primary requirements. Only about 10% of the registered voters cast votes in the primaries; however, these would be "interested" voters.[28]

---

[26] Kate Thomas, "Overhaul for Texas Vote?" *The National Law Journal* (December 30, 1996): A14.

[27] Ibid., 112.

[28] The turnout in the 1994 Republican primary was 6.2% of registered Republicans and 11.5% of the Democrats voted in their primary.

The Texas Bar Association is not a prime player in the judicial recruitment game and does not actively initiate or screen candidates. The only election function performed by the state bar is a preference poll conducted prior to primary and general elections concerning contested races for the Supreme Court, Court of Criminal Appeals, and Court of Appeals. The bar polls have not been very effective in providing guidance to voters.[29] A survey of state bar leadership in 1991 reported that the lawyers regarded their polling as only marginally effective. The diversity of interests among the over 55,000 members of the bar, the lack of full participation, and the poor dissemination of poll results account for its marginal role. One bar leader noted that

> [T]he Bar's rating polls serve an improper influence for the reason that very few people participate in the actual poll and I personally believe that it is monopolized by the large firm commercial corporate interests, and, therefore, the results are skewed toward the more conservative Republican candidates.[30]

As suspected, when political parties dominate judicial selection the bar is only a marginal participant in judicial recruitment.

Some counties have Committees for a Qualified Judiciary that evaluate the qualifications of judicial candidates and make endorsements of those deemed "qualified." The committees are non-partisan, not affiliated with bar associations, and they are composed of both lawyers and lay people. In addition, nearly all county bar associations conduct bar polls and many have evaluation committees that survey lawyers who practice before judges, soliciting attorneys' views on the judges' performance. Finally, in some counties a scattering of good-government groups such as the League of Women Voters attempts to get candidate facts out to the voter, but without specific candidate endorsements.[31]

The need to raise huge amounts of money for state-wide and urban county jurisdictions creates records which may provide clues concerning important participants in the screening processes. Most of the contributions to judicial campaigns come from lawyers. Plaintiff and defense attorneys have often competed in support of sympathetic candidates, and members of large law firms (acting as surrogates for their clients) make their contribution to the funding totals. On occasion, large contributions come from a major private citizen with interests that may be subject to litigation.[32] Recently, the Texas Medical Asso-

---

[29] The results of the poll released to the media state that the purpose of the poll "is to give citizens an opportunity to see how attorneys evaluate the candidate.... Since it is an impartial poll, the results are not intended as an endorsement of any particular candidate or candidates." *Texas Bar Journal* (March 1990): 249.

[30] See Charles H. Sheldon, "The Role of State Bar Associations in Judicial Selection," *Judicature* 77 (May/June 1994): 300.

[31] Anthony Champagne, "The Selection and Retention of Judges in Texas," *Southwestern Law Journal* 40 (May 1986): 110.

ciation has shown a strong interest in contributing to Supreme Court races. In urban jurisdictions and for appellate places in the Texas judiciary, these funds are expended on modern campaigning techniques not all that different from other political races. However, the one difference which makes a difference in campaign activities is that the Judicial Code of Conduct as well as tradition dictate that candidates do not talk about controversial legal issues nor make promises on how they will rule. Thousands to hundreds of thousands of dollars are being spent to "inform" the voters, but the content of the information remains rather shallow. For example, the 1994 Democratic primary for the Supreme Court between incumbent Justice Raul Gonzalez and challenger Rene Haas developed into a bitter name-calling affair largely absent of meaningful voter cues.[33]

Affirmation

Approximately half of the judges on the appellate and trial benches of Texas had been initially appointed to an interim vacancy. The Governor, as in nonpartisan systems, invariably appoints a member of his or her own party to the vacancy. Until 1978 this always meant a Democrat, and the real competition for judgeships was in the Democrat primary for all levels of the judiciary. Still today it is rare in rural counties for a Democrat to be challenged, and even rarer to have them defeated by Republicans. However, this pattern of outcome is no longer the case in the urban counties and for the appellate benches. Dallas County has become a Republican stronghold. Harris (Houston) and Tarrant (Ft. Worth) counties have become highly competitive, with Republicans winning more than their share of seats on the bench in recent years.

A particular characteristic of partisan elections explains to some degree judicial voting patterns. It remains true that a considerable number of District Court places have been uncontested, but less so than in the past. Nonetheless, because of the frequency of straight ticket voting, those national figures who lead the respective party's ballot pull along with them lesser positions, including court candidates. When Senator Lloyd Bentsen headed the Democratic ticket in 1982, and when the Republican ticket was headed by Ronald Reagan in 1980 and 1984, Bush in 1988 and Senator Gramm in 1990, the fortunes of their respective party court candidates followed directly. Incumbency accounts for some of the victories, and increased population density helps some Republicans. But it is the figure at the top of the ticket that explains most of the outcomes of trial court races. "Indeed, a judicial candidate may win or lose...based solely on

---

[32] Ibid., 88.

[33] Justice Gonzalez called the campaign "the most cynical, bitterest campaign he had ever been involved in. It sets a new low for judicial politics in Texas and the public deserves better than this." Quoted in Brenda Inman, "The Haas-Gonzalez Race," (unpublished paper, University of Texas, Dallas), p. 14.

the political appeal of the party's nominee at the top of the ticket."[34] The timing of when to run for the bench may well be influenced by who is going to head the party's ticket.

Perhaps the "coat-tail effect" is dictated in the urban areas by the large number of judicial spots that are on the ballot. For example, in 1994 in Harris county 84 judicial positions (including eight justices of the peace) were on the ballot, making it nearly impossible for even the interested voter to be sufficiently familiar with most of the candidates (see appendix). Indeed, an exit poll in 1986 reported that 81% of the voters in Dallas county and 77% in Harris county were unable to recognize a name of a single judicial candidate on the ballot.[35] At least the party label provided one cue. Commenting on the poll, Anthony Champagne observed that "Party affiliation just overwhelmed everything else.... [I]ncumbency and endorsements just don't matter."[36] In rural Texas, it is likely that voters have "some knowledge of judges" and "their families." The rural districts are relatively small, and "it would be possible to meet most voters in the county over a term." Church meetings, fraternal clubs, "weddings, funerals, and homecomings" bring the judge close to his or her community.[37] In some rural counties only a few thousand votes are cast in judicial contests. In contrast, in the highly populated counties nearly a 1,000,000 voters may be involved.

Traditionally, partisan elections have prompted straight party voting. Judicial elections are no different in this respect. Estimates of the percentage of straight party voting have varied between 18% to 31% of the total vote.

> The effect of straight party voting on candidate success can be considerable.... A particular strong straight party vote in favor of one party can make it almost impossible for a judicial candidate to make up the difference with independent voters.[38]

In races where the margin of victory is narrow, this straight party voting constitutes the difference between winning and losing. Using a 5% difference as the dividing line between a "close" and a noncompetitive election, "nearly three-fifths of appellate court elections and two-thirds of district court elections were close."[39] Straight ticket voting with the coat-tails effect largely determines the outcome in these close races.

---

[34] L. Douglas Kiel, Carole Funk and Anthony Champagne, "Two-party Competition and Trial Court Elections in Texas," *Judicature* 77 (1994): 293.

[35] Barbara Johnson, "Voter Survey: Judges Unknown," *The Texas Lawyer* (November 1986): 1.

[36] Ibid., 8.

[37] Champagne, "The Selection and Retention of Judges in Texas," 77.

[38] Ibid., 73.

[39] Ibid., 75.

Recently, with the development of a two-party system in at least urban Texas, the partisan lock on judicial elections has stimulated some noteworthy party switching. Decades ago no aspiring judge could hope for a judgeship without membership in the Democratic party. Now, in some urban areas a candidate needs to be Republican, prompting a number of Democrats to changing parties. In Dallas County, for example, the increased support for Republican candidates generally—along with the strong straight Republican party voting— had prompted heretofore Democrats to file as Republicans. One former Democrat admitted that his philosophy had not changed, but "[t]he reason I'm switching is that to be a judge in Dallas County you need to be a Republican."[40]

Despite the lack of voter information on candidates, and perhaps because of (1) the increased competitiveness, (2) the large amounts of money spent, (3) the straight ticket voting, and (4) the "coat-tail effect," voter participation in Texas judicial elections is relatively high. As argued, partisan elections bring out the voters.

Table 4.1

CONTESTEDNESS, PARTICIPATION AND COMPETITION IN TEXAS
JUDICIAL ELECTIONS: THE SUPREME COURT

Year	Total Votes Cast	Average Supreme Court	Participation % Vote	Average Winning %	Contested Total Positions
1990	3,892,746	3,605,997	93%	57%	3/3
1992	6,154,018	5,671,737	92%	54	3/3
1994	4,396,242	3,765,618	86%	65	3/3*

* Justice Raul A. Gonzales had only limited minority party (Libertarian) opposition in the general election.

---

[40] Ibid., 80. In 1995, the last Democratic District judge in Dallas County switched to the Republican Party.

Figure 4.2

TEXAS RECRUITMENT ACTORS

Formal Participants   **Advisory Participants**

```
┌──────────────────────────────────┐
│           AFFIRMATION            │
│             VOTERS               │
│         General Election         │
│                                  │
│            GOVERNOR              │
│        Interim Appointments      │
└──────────────────────────────────┘

┌──────────────────────────────────┐
│            SCREENING             │                ┌──────────────────────────────┐
│             VOTERS               │                │   Texas Bar Association        │
│          Primary Election        │                │     Preferential Polls         │
│        Political Party Members   │                │                                │
│                                  │                │   County Committees for        │
│                                  │                │    A Qualified Judiciary       │
│       GOVERNOR'S OFFICE          │                │    Governor's Counsel          │
│        Interim Appointments      │                │   County Political Parties     │
└──────────────────────────────────┘                └──────────────────────────────┘

┌──────────────────────────────────┐
│            INITIATION            │
│            CANDIDATES            │
│            INCUMBENTS            │
│     POLITICAL PARTY ACTIVISTS    │
└──────────────────────────────────┘
```

Level of Articulation

As reported in Table 4.1, Supreme Court races in Texas are always contested, nearly all voters cast ballots in Supreme Court races, and the fairly low winning margin suggests competitive contests.[41] The articulation model would predict that these data should result in a balance between the conflicting demands of

---

[41] The races for the Texas courts of last resort (Supreme Court and Court of Criminal Appeals) are high profile and draw the attention of both parties. However, lower in the judicial structure, attention wanes.

accountability and independence. However, a closer look at the earlier stages of the recruitment sequence indicates otherwise.

The final result of the efforts of judicial candidates is the outcome of popular partisan elections, with the voters affirming all that has previously transpired in the recruitment sequence. Explanations for nearly all that transpires between initiation and affirmation lie with the partisan nature of recruitment. The coat-tail effect, the long ballot, straight ticket voting, winning or losing, competitiveness, contestedness of races and voter participation can all be explained by the dynamics of partisan elections. Whenever these dynamics permeate the recruitment process, the prominence of public accountability increases. The struggle for campaign contributions in order to inform the voters, however inadequately, increases the political dimension of accountability. Despite what the Fifth Circuit majority argued about the value that Texans place in their selection system to balance the demands of accountability against the needs of independence, accountability is the clear winner.

Philip Dubois has concluded:

> Partisan elections maximize voter participation...structure the voting decision of the electorate in directions relevant to the resolution of political issues, reduce...appointments, and enable voters to exercise some control over appointments. Additionally, partisan elections are superior to both nonpartisan...and nonelective methods...as instruments of judicial accountability.[42]

As we originally asserted, a pluralistic high articulation recruitment system requires a competitive mix of numerous participants from the beginning to the end of the recruitment process. In Texas, the nearly single actor in initiation, screening and affirmation is the political party and its loyal voters. Despite the indicators of a highly active affirmation stage, the primary force prompting these indicators are the two major political parties, confirming Dubois' characterization. If constitutional reform is not in the immediate future, any balance in the judge's dilemma will have to be between Republican and Democrat versions of accountability.

---

[42] Dubois, *From Ballot to Bench*, p. 248.

Chapter Five

Legislative Selection

Two states, South Carolina and Virginia, rely on their legislature for the election of all judges of courts of record.[1] A number of other states bring the legislature or a part thereof into the selection process, but largely to confirm or give "advice and consent" much like is done in the federal system. In these states the legislature reacts to appointments or elections by others, while in Virginia and South Carolina the legislatures make the affirming decision.[2]

The two states instituted legislative selection for all their judges from the beginning. South Carolina has only recently made significant changes in how judges of courts of record are selected, but the legislature remains in control.[3] Virginia instituted popular elections in 1850, but returned to legislative selection in 1864 where it remains today. Resistance to change in both states can be attributed to the traditional political culture in each state, to legislative recalcitrance, to satisfaction with legislative involvement, and to the control of state politics over the years by one party. Any constitutional changes in how judges are selected must gain the approval of a super-majority of the legislature, a formidable task when involving such an important function as judicial

---

[1] In November 1994 Rhode Island changed from legislative election to a merit plan. The voters in Rhode Island passed a constitutional provision by a vote of 211,394 to 91,294. However, the legislature is still part of the process by giving its "advice and consent" on all gubernatorial appointments. The constitutional amendment reads in part:

> The governor shall fill any vacancy of any justice of the Rhode Island Supreme Court by nominating, on the basis of merit, a person from a list submitted by an independent non-partisan judicial nominating commission, and by and with the advice and consent of the senate and...of the house...shall appoint said person., R.I. Const., Art. 10, sec. 4.

[2] E.g., judges in Connecticut, Delaware, Maine, New Jersey and Vermont are reappointed or retained in office after legislative confirmation.

[3] In **South Carolina ex rel. Riley v. Commissioners of Election**, 258 S.E.2d 433 (1979) the S.C. Supreme Court reaffirmed its age old legislative selection system and specifically rejected popular elections: "It is significant...that in every instance, in specifying the manner of selecting members of the judiciary, the Constitution provides for some method other than a popular election. In fact, the Constitution of 1868 provided...for the popular election of the 'trial justices.' The 1895 revisions to the Constitution...provided for their appointment by the Governor by and with the advice and consent of the Senate. This is a plainly manifested intent of the people of this state to avoid the popular election of members of the judiciary. Any statute...which directly or by necessary implication, operates so as to defeat the purpose and intent of the foregoing constitutional provision is unconstitutional." p. 434.

selection. Also, the dominant party since the Civil War and until very recently had been the Democrats in both South Carolina and Virginia. Their control of both houses of the General Assembly permitted them to determine who became judges, and legislators were and are in the best position to become judges themselves. The power to select judges is not easily relinquished.

Historically, in South Carolina the percentage of judges who were formerly legislators had hovered around 80%. This is gradually changing with fewer lawyers in the legislature and more non-legislators showing an interest in a judgeship. Legislative election of judges provides a second but secure career opportunity for lawmakers; this, of course, can cut two ways. The judiciary could become a retirement home for burned-out legislators or a reward for political services rendered. However, the courts could attract highly competent public servants who have earned their spurs on the campaign trail and in the give-and-take of the General Assembly, which, indeed, are no mean accomplishments. Courts must construe statutes, divining legislative intent in the process. Courts often must develop a sense for the current political climate. Clearly, experience as a legislator is valuable for performing these functions.

Only a most concerned voter pays any attention to judicial candidates; and only a very few of these voters, it is argued, have an understanding of the special requirements of being a judge. At the same time, however, judges must not be isolated from the community they serve. Selection by representatives elected by the public, but who appreciate the needs of judging, provides a balance. Additionally, the competence of judicial aspirants can be measured over several sessions of the General Assembly by those having a better understanding of the judiciary. There is no evidence that former legislators are any less competent to be judges than prominent attorneys from the private or public sectors.

Under the legislative system, vacancies can be filled quickly when the legislature is in session with incumbents enjoying the security of the remainder of the term of the person being replaced. The Governor is limited to appointing persons only to short-term vacancies, keeping the General Assembly in control of the recruitment process.

No small attribute, the legislative selection of judges frees candidates from the pressures of campaigning and from reliance on contributions from narrow special interests such as the insurance industry or labor unions. The well-heeled candidate would not have a funding advantage over the aspirant with little resources; money is simply not an important factor in this system.

Of course, legislative selection has its drawbacks. The obvious problem to many is the lack of public accountability; if any exists, it is indirect at best. Being accountable to the legislature for election or to the Governor in appointments can threaten the principle of separation of powers and weaken the rule of law, both essential to a democratic system. As mentioned previously, there exists a potential that cronyism, political patronage, reward for past party loyalty, and "forced" retirement may dictate the election of judges rather than professional qualifications. Also, many of the criticisms leveled at partisan elections have been used against legislative selection because of the partisanship involved. Invariably, the majority party in the legislature selects judgeships from among its own number. Party loyalty may be poor preparation for the bench.

Selection by the legislature removes the symbolic support for courts that is evident in popular elections. Also, the educative value to the public of popular and open elections with contesting candidates sharing contending views with the voters is entirely missing. Perhaps the most telling criticism is centered on the politics that may engulf the legislature when a judgeship becomes available. Since most of the positions have been filled with legislators, unseemly and crass politics can permeate the legislative halls on the occasion of judicial elections. "[S]trong lobbying efforts, vote counting, 'horse-trading'" typify the affirmation process.[4] Votes for judicial candidates may be swapped for promises to support unrelated legislation. Despite efforts to resist legislative politics and despite rules adopted to add some dignity to the public aspects of the process, politics continue, reflecting poorly on the legislature as well as on the state's judiciary.

What evidence is available to support the pros and cons of legislative judicial recruitment? Despite the need for a closer symbolic connection between the public and courts, public views regarding the competence of, as well as level of confidence in, the state's courts remain unaffected by whether the judges are selected by the legislature or by other means.

> [L]ittle evidence is found that formal judicial selection processes affects perceptions of judicial competence or confidence in those running state and local courts. This generalization applies with equal force to the views of the general public, attentive public, community leaders, lawyers and judges.[5]

Do the judges selected by the legislature possess background characteristics not commonly found in the results of other forms of selection? There is a tendency for legislators to elect judges affiliated with high Protestant religions.[6] As already reported, the majority of judges in South Carolina and Virginia have come from the legislature, although this practice may be changing. There also is evidence that prosecutors do not fare well under the legislative system. Legislative judges tend to have a higher education level, possess more prior judicial experience as a result of promotion within the

---

[4] Steven W. Hays with David S. Mann, "South Carolina Judicial System," in Luther F. Carter and David S. Mann (eds.), *Government in the Palmetto State* (Columbia, SC: Institute of Public Affairs, University of South Carolina, 1992), p. 117.

[5] Eric Wassman, Nicholas P. Lovrich and Charles H. Sheldon, "Perceptions of State and Local Courts: A Comparison across Selection Systems," *Justice System Journal* 11 (1986): 181.

[6] Bradley C. Canon, "The Impact of Formal Selection Processes on the Characteristics of Judges—Reconsidered," *Law & Society Review* 6 (1972): 583. Many of South Carolina's judges are Southern Baptists and Methodists.

judiciary, come from an in-state background, and are affiliated with the Democratic party. As Bradley Canon has correctly pointed out, some of the background characteristics may be due to regional forces rather than selection method. For example, the legislative selection states tend to have been Democratic states; consequently, most of their judges were Democrats.[7] Cultural factors also are associated with legislative recruitment. "Justices are chosen by legislatures in densely populated, industrial, but poor states."[8] However, the characteristics of the judiciary in southern states do not vary to any great extent among partisan, nonpartisan, legislative and merit plan systems.[9]

As elsewhere, the selection reform movement in the two states has simply not gathered together the necessary coalition of lawyers, judges, legislators and interested citizens to push for drastic change. However, in recent years Rhode Island's judiciary came under close scrutiny, resulting in the end in replacing its legislative system.[10] Also, as explained below, the politics of the 1995 election of South Carolina judges led to what may in time become a significant reform.

Brief Review of Legislative Selection in Virginia

Virginia has a slightly modified version of legislative election.[11] The final vote on judges is taken separately in each house of the General Assembly. To assist the legislature, the Virginia State Bar has instituted a Judicial Nominations Committee composed of lawyers elected by its governing body, the Virginia Bar Council, and representing each of the commonwealth's ten congressional districts. The committee investigates, interviews and evaluates applicants for appellate courts. Its evaluations are submitted to the Courts of Justice Committees of each house of the General Assembly. The state bar concerns itself only with appellate positions and seeks input from other bar groups such as the voluntary Virginia Bar Association, the trial lawyers association, Virginia Women Lawyers, and Old Dominion Bar (African-American). Recently, a

---

[7] These data are from Ibid. Canon concludes, as we have, that "another look at the relationship between selection systems (**as informally modified**) and justices' background characteristics will be worthwhile." (Emphasis added), p. 589.

[8] Victor E. Flango and Craig R. Ducat, "What Difference Does Method of Judicial Selection Procedures Make: Selection Procedures in State Courts of Last Resort," *Justice System Journal 5* (1979): 37.

[9] Ronald G. Marquardt, "Judicial Politics in the South: Robed Elites and Recruitment," in James F. Lea, *Contemporary Southern Politics* (Baton Rouge: Louisiana State University Press, 1988), p. 242.

[10] R.I. Const, Art.10, sec. 4.

[11] Article VI, sec. 7 of the Virginia Constitution reads: "The justices of the Supreme Court [and judges of all other courts of record] shall be chosen by the vote of a majority of the members elected to each house of the General Assembly." The Governor fills vacancies for short terms only.

vacancy on the Virginia Supreme Court was filled with a candidate approved by the bar, but only one of the two judges elected to the Court of Appeals had been on the current bar's approved list. Local bar associations are often consulted for trial court vacancies by the legislative delegate from the particular jurisdiction, constituting a modified form of senatorial courtesy.

Once the legislative Courts of Justice Committees review the files on each applicant, the House of Delegates and Senate caucuses meet separately and decide who should be selected. The final vote in the two houses reflects nearly exactly the majority party's caucus decisions. Some campaigning exists with letters of endorsement, telephone calls to key legislators, and visits to the legislature, but campaigning is low key and limited to the legislators.

The Bar's recommendations are viewed by some as largely "window dressing," legitimating the legislative choice. A member of the Bar Council wrote these candid and revealing remarks:

> ...a person who was widely viewed by the Bar as incompetent would not be selected by either the Governor or the General Assembly regardless of political considerations.... However...the mere fact that an individual gains the recommendation of the State Bar is in my view of little influence where political decisions are made.[12]

A "dibs system" characterizes the legislative vote-swapping practice wherein a delegate or a senator regards the choice as his or hers this time around. If a serious conflict among legislatures arises, requiring negotiations and artful compromise, this occurs between the two houses of the legislature, rather than between the political parties. Of course, until recently the Democrats had dominated the legislative process.

In appointments, the Bar is invited to screen possible appointees from a list submitted by the Governor. Three to five nominees are recommended to the Governor for each judicial vacancy occurring when the General Assembly is not in session. In the past, the Bar has been given the list from the Governor's office late in the process, allowing very little time for evaluation. Consequently, Bar leaders are rather pessimistic about their role in appointments. One lawyer commented that the "recommendation is meaningful only when it coincides with someone the Governor wanted to appoint anyway, or when it gives him an out as a compromise."[13]

The Bar's Joint Judicial Review Committee is working on composing a standing list of qualified candidates based on a review of questionnaires and interviews with candidates, lawyers, and sitting judges familiar with the applicants. This list, then, will always be available for use by the legislature.

---

[12] Quoted from a national survey of state bar leadership. The Virginia State Bar efforts were rated ineffective when compared with other state bar associations. Charles H. Sheldon, "The Role of State Bar Associations in Judicial Selection," *Judicature* 77 (1994): 303.

[13] Ibid.

Unlike the situation in South Carolina, discussion of selection reform in Virginia has been muted.   What reforms have been instituted have not challenged the legislature's prerogative seriously.   For example, in the mid-1970s the legislature considered and defeated a proposal to establish a nominating commission similar to the merit plan commission, but wherein the commission's nominations would go to the legislature for the final election.

Most of the persons elected to the appellate levels are experienced judges, coming from lower courts, although all things being equal legislators or former legislators hold an important edge in the selection. Given the low key process in Virginia, especially when compared with recent South Carolina elections, for the time being a low articulation experience is evident.   However, as a competitive two-party system becomes more firmly established, more conflict over judgeships may result, in turn changing the informal recruitment process.

South Carolina and Legislative Recruitment

Unifying the courts came late to the Palmetto State.   Critics persistently observed that the state's judiciary was a "hodgepodge of courts, lacking in uniformity and consistency."[14] Historically, as courts were established piece-meal to meet local needs, variations and overlapping jurisdictions were common.   Six kinds of trial courts existed in the state, and "not one of the sixteen judicial districts had all six types."[15] The routes for appeals also varied. Clearly, reform was needed in order to rationalize South Carolina's courts. However, most of the debate over reform centered on unifying the structures of the judiciary rather than reconsidering how judges were recruited.   Popular election of judges as an option seems inconsistent with South Carolina's constitutional history. The people's intent throughout its history has been "to avoid" such elections.[16]

Although legislative selection of judges remained untouched, in 1972 the voters approved an amended judicial article to the South Carolina Constitution calling for a unified court system and eliminating the irrational mix that had previously existed. The core of the new Article V reads:

> The judicial power shall be vested in a unified judicial system, which
> shall include a Supreme Court, a Circuit Court, and such other courts
> of uniform jurisdiction as may be provided for by general law.

Illustrative of the difficulty in modernizing its courts was the struggle to implement Article V.   Until the details were worked out and implementing legislation was passed, the old system continued to operate. This permitted

---

[14] **State ex re McLeod v. Court of Probate of Colleton County**, 266 S.C. 284 (1975).

[15] Cole Blease Graham, Jr., and William V. Moore, *South Carolina Politics and Government* (Lincoln: University of Nebraska Press, 1994), pp. 182-183.

[16] **South Carolina ex rel. Riley v. Commissioners of Election**, 258 S.E. 2d 433 (1979).

delay as the judges and legislators fought over details. Although all Supreme Court Justices were products of legislative vote and many were former legislators, they declared a variety of reform bills unconstitutional, among which was an enactment setting jurisdictional boundaries to coincide with legislative districts.[17] The justices feared this would not only encourage but would assure the selection of the legislators representing those districts to the judgeships involved, leading to selection of the best and brightest only on rare occasion.[18] The issue in controversy did not center on the procedures involved in legislative selection, but rather focused on the results of those procedures.

In 1976 an agreement on details was reached and a unified court system was enacted into law. However, conflict again arose when the legislature appointed four of its own membership to the new intermediate Court of Appeals which had been created on a temporary basis in 1979. The Supreme Court declared those appointments unconstitutional under a provision that prevented legislators from benefiting from legislation they were responsible for enacting.[19] In 1985 the Court of Appeals was made permanent and the conflict between the legislature and the judges eased, with the legislature "giving up trying to dominate management of the judicial system."[20] Nonetheless, the legislature still retained the significant power of selecting judges to the state's Supreme Court, Court of Appeals and Circuit Courts.

The unified court structure involves a five-person Supreme Court serving ten-year terms with possibility for reelection by the legislature.[21] The Court of Appeals is composed of nine judges serving six-year terms. They normally sit in panels of three to hear and decide appeals and, in extreme cases, *en banc* hearings are held. They also are products of legislative elections. Sixteen Circuit Courts serve as the trial courts of general jurisdiction, involving two to four counties each. Forty-three judges are elected by the legislature, 30 represent separate districts while 13 are selected from the state at-large. They serve throughout the sixteen circuits on a rotating basis.

All vacancies on the Supreme Court, Court of Appeals and Circuit Courts may be filled by the Governor if the unexpired term does not exceed one year. The appointees, however, if wishing to be retained, must file for office and come under the provisions of the legislative selection procedures.[22] In practice

[17] **Cort Industries Corp. v. Swirl, Inc.,** 13 S.E. 2d 445 (1975).

[18] Graham and Moore, *South Carolina Politics and Government,* p. 183.

[19] **Riley v. Martin,** 262 S.E. 2d 404 (1980).

[20] Graham and Moore, *South Carolina Politics and Government,* p. 184.

[21] Article V, sec. 3 of the South Carolina Constitution reads: "The members of the Supreme Court [Court of Appeals and Circuit Courts] shall be elected by a joint public vote of the General Assembly.... In any contested election, the vote of each member of the General Assembly present and voting shall be recorded."

[22] Article V, sec. 3 continues: "All vacancies in the Supreme Court, Court of Appeals or Circuit Court shall be filled by [legislative] elections...provided that if the unexpired term does not exceed

the Governor rarely bothers to fill a vacancy. The appointed term is simply too brief, and some legislators may take affront at the Governor preempting their prerogative. Also, the Chief Justice has a legislatively approved list of retired judges to fill the vacancy on a temporary basis until the legislature can act.

The courts of limited jurisdiction tend to be products of history. A Master-in-Equity bench, composed of 20 judges, hears cases referred to it by the Circuit Courts and decides issues of equity. Where precedent and laws do not exist to guide judges, the Masters-in-Equity resolve the issues with recommendations going to the Circuit Courts for implementation. These judges are appointed by the Governor with the advice and consent of the General Assembly, meaning both houses of the legislature. The Family Court hears cases involving family issues such as marriage, divorce, child custody, juveniles, etc. Forty-six judges preside over domestic and juvenile cases. Administrative law courts handle appeals from administrative rules and regulations. Both courts are elected by the General Assembly for four-year terms. Magisterial Court judges are appointed by the Governor with the advice and consent of the Senate for four-year terms. However, a tradition of "senatorial courtesy" prevails in most appointments. Many of these judges are not lawyers. Two hundred and ninety-seven judge magistrates serve on these courts that handle misdemeanors and minor criminal matters. Civil cases of less than $2,500 are settled by the magistrates who also conduct preliminary hearings in serious criminal cases.

In 1980 the legislature established uniform Municipal Courts to hear minor infractions of law and of city ordinances. There are 201 municipal judges selected to four-year terms. Their mode of selection depends upon the ordinances of the municipality. The 21 Probate Court judges are responsible for marriage licenses, estates, commitments of mentally ill and chemically dependent persons. They are elected for four-year terms in partisan elections. In sum, except for courts of record which are products of legislative recruitment, a mix of methods is used to fill the remaining benches.

Until 1992 the South Carolina Bar Association played no role in judicial selection except in "raising of the level of consciousness of legislators through...efforts to change the system." The bar supported some limited reform put into place by the now defunct Joint Committee on the Screening of Judges. The reforms expanded the legislative screening committee, adopted some selection guidelines, and limited the pledging of votes. Individual attorneys were active, however, by "approaching their respective legislative representatives and voic[ing] their opinions concerning the qualifications of persons running for a judicial seat."[23]

---

one year such vacancy may be filled by the Governor. When a vacancy is filled by either appointment or election, the incumbent shall hold office only for the unexpired term of his predecessor."

[23] Sheldon, "The Role of State Bar Associations in Judicial Selection," 300.

Figure 5.1

SOUTH CAROLINA COURT SYSTEM

SUPREME COURT

5 Justices

Election by both Houses of Legislature
(General Assembly)
Nomination by Merit Selection Commission
Governor appoints to vacancies with less
than 1 year left in term
10-year term

COURT OF APPEALS

6 Judges

Election by General Assembly
Nomination by Merit Selection Commission
Governor appoints to vacancies
with less than 1 year left in term
6-year term

CIRCUIT COURTS	**FAMILY COURT**	**MASTERS-IN-EQUITY**
43 Judges	46 Judges	20 Judges
6-year term	**4-year term**	**4-year term**

Election by General Assembly Merit Commission nomination...Governor appoints to vacancies with less than 1 year left in term	Governor Appoints with Legislative Consent

---

MAGISTRATE COURTS	**MUNICIPAL COURTS**	**PROBATE COURTS**
297 Judges	201 Judges	21 Judges
Appointed by Governor	varies	Partisan Election
with advice and consent of		Countywide
2-4 year term	4-year term	4-year term

The Structure of South Carolina Recruitment

Initiation

The initiation process in South Carolina is predominately guided by what plays well with the state legislature. Former legislators, or those who have close ties with the senator or representative from their district, have an initial advantage. Legislators and their allies begin building support among legislative colleagues long before vacancies are formally available.[24] Candidates formally file for a judicial post, and the screening groups limit themselves to those announced candidates alone.

As with nearly all political recruitment systems, timing plays a strong role in initiation. A judicial aspirant may be reluctant to challenge an incumbent and will often wait until his or her retirement. A legislator may urge or support the promotion of a circuit judge to the appeals bench with an idea toward filing for the vacancy should the incumbent succeed. Resignations, retirements or deaths often determine when a candidacy is initiated. The final list of initiates submitted for evaluation is usually a mix of those initiating their own candidacy, those pushed forward by others and those seeking reelection.

Screening

The screening process involves primarily the new Judicial Merit Selection Commission, with some assistance from the Bar. After years of remaining out of the screening, in 1992 the South Carolina Bar began a two-phased screening process. First, all incumbent judges are evaluated and rated by members of the bar at the mid-point in the term and then at the end. The purposes are to keep some pressure on judges to perform well, and also to indicate to lawyers who among the judiciary might be successfully challenged at the next election. Second, the South Carolina Bar conducts a poll of its members, rating each candidate for judicial posts prior to legislative consideration. The results of the Bar's poll are shared with the merit commission, members of the legislature, and with the media.[25] The Bar's poll has reflected more than a popularity contest or plebiscite. Interviews are conducted and evaluations of the judge's or lawyer's record made. In general, the organized bar is not regarded as a powerful force in South Carolina politics, and in judicial screening legislative concerns dominate.[26] However, as the 1996 reforms show, the Bar had significant input

---

[24] Law prohibits candidates from seeking "pledges" of support early in the process, but announcing intent, contacting legislators about qualifications and answering requests for information are not forbidden.

[25] The 1996 legislation reads: "The chairman of the [merit] commission shall also request the South Carolina bar to offer...an assessment of each candidate's qualifications.... This assessment must specify the bar's finding as to whether each candidate is qualified or unqualified...and the reasons for that finding." Section 2-19-25, Chapter 19, Title 2 of the 1976 Code.

into the planning, not necessarily because of its clout but rather because of its expertise.

Under pressure from the Bar, the Governor, and reform groups such as the League of Women Voters, the 170-member General Assembly approved and sent to the voters a proposed constitutional amendment which was overwhelmingly approved by the electorate on November 5, 1996. In anticipation of voter approval, the General Assembly had previously enacted implementing legislation that contained the details of the new reforms.[27] Some observers felt the two measures changed the process, but did not alter the results of the process.

A ten-member Judicial Merit Selection Commission replaces the General Assembly's Joint Legislative Committee for Judicial Screening. The Speaker of the House appoints five commissioners; three must be serving members of the legislature and two from the general public. The Chair of the Senate Judiciary Committee appoints three members, and the President Pro-tem of the Senate completes the process by appointing two. Of these Senate appointees, three must be sitting members and two must be from the public. Although lawmakers constitute a majority on the commission, the editors of the *Charleston Post-Courier* were encouraged that significant improvement in public accountability had been achieved:

> That's still a major improvement over the just abandoned system where all the screeners were lawmakers, most of the judgeship candidates were legislators and legislators could—and did—elect judges who had flunked [the previous screening committee's] test.[28]

The Judicial Merit Selection Commission screens eligible applicants and provides the General Assembly with a list of three "qualified" candidates for each position. The statute dictates that "the General Assembly shall not elect a person to...judicial office who has not been nominated by the Commission." The Commission's charge is to screen applicants for all courts elected by the General Assembly (Supreme Court, Court of Appeals, Circuit Courts, administrative law courts, and family courts). Also required to be screened and nominated by the commission are all retired judges who are appointed by the Chief Justice to continued service. All incumbent judges in courts elected by the General Assembly and who seek reelection must be determined qualified by the commission to be eligible for reelection. Masters-in-Equity appointed by

---

[26] Despite the Bar's efforts, the two candidates rated "unqualified" out of the 22 who were rated in March 1995 were still elected by the General Assembly. See Robert E. Botsch, "South Carolina: The Rise of the New South," in Ronald J. Hrebenar and Clive S. Thomas (eds.), *Interest Group Politics in the Southern States* (Tuscaloosa: University of Alabama Press, 1992), p. 226.

[27] Chapter 19, as amended, Title 2, Code of Laws of South Carolina, 1976.

[28] November 12, 1996.

the Governor with the advice and consent of the Senate also must have the nod of approval of the commission to remain eligible.

As yet the details of procedures for screening are to be worked out, but the assumption is that they will adopt the procedures of the now defunct Joint Legislative Committee for Judicial Screening.[29]   The screening will be based upon appraisals of "ethical fitness," "professional and academic ability," "character," "reputation," "physical health," "mental stability," "experience," and "judicial temperament."[30]   Public statements in support or in opposition to any of the candidates are considered, and "race, gender, national origin, and other demographic factors" are to be "considered to ensure nondiscrimination to the greatest extent possible as to all segments of the population of the state." The initial phase of the investigation may take months—involving credit checks, an FBI-like clearance, confirming with the Supreme Court on possible ethical transgressions, reviewing financial statements, administering questionnaires, contacting references, surveying bar members, and analyzing cases, opinions and appellate records.   Random courtroom observations of incumbents by commission staff may also be conducted.   The South Carolina Bar is invited to submit the results of its separate survey of candidates.[31]   Finally, when all the information has been gathered each candidate is interviewed and given an opportunity to respond to questions regarding his or her record.

The final phase of screening involves hearings in which the candidates are grilled by the commission members and by attorneys for the commission with questions generated by the materials gathered in the initial phase or from information provided by witnesses.   Candidates are given the opportunity to answer any accusations that may have come before the commission.   Interviews may last longer than an hour.   Witnesses may also testify.   Serious and relevant confidential affidavits are entered in the record after an initial review by the staff, and the candidate is given an opportunity to answer any questions that might arise.   Transcripts of the hearings will be made available to the media and public.   From this thorough screening, a list of three candidates for each vacancy is formed and sent to the General Assembly for affirmation of one of three, or for rejection of all three, requiring the commission to come up with a new list of three.

---

[29]   The statute required "the immediate devolvement of the responsibilities of the Joint Committee to Review Judicial Candidates upon the Judicial Merit Selection Commission." According to a member of the commission: "It is anticipated that all of the processes of the Joint Committee and more will be adopted by the Commission." Also, five of the new ten-member commission were members of the defunct joint committee.   Letter from Senator Glenn E. McConnell, dated December 13, 1996.

[30]   Section 2-19-35(A) of Chapter 19.

[31]   "It is my understanding that the [Commission] will continue to receive input from the South Carolina Bar. We use their report as a starting point to do an investigation of potential problems that may come up on their rating and their report." McConnell letter, December 13, 1996.

In addition to the establishment of the merit commission, the age requirement was raised from 26 to 32 years for Justices of the Supreme Court, Judges of the Court of Appeals and Circuit Courts. Also, candidates must be licensed attorneys for at least eight years rather than the previous minimum of five. Candidates at all levels of the judiciary, except magistrates, are covered by the amendment. Judges now serving are considered to have been "grandfathered" in if they fail to meet the age and years of practice requirements, and can run for reelection when their terms expire. However, they still must survive the commission's screening. If the commission disapproves of a gubernatorial appointment to a masters-in-equity vacancy, the Governor must submit another name. Further, a member of the General Assembly who wishes to be considered for a judgeship must resign from the legislature at least a year before being eligible.

To understand the thrust of the 1996 changes and the urgency for the reforms, an account of the 1995 elections is crucial. Previously, the General Assembly's joint legislative committee submitted a draft report of its evaluation to the General Assembly 48 hours before the final report was issued, giving the legislators time to review the materials before the candidates began soliciting them for pledges.[32] Some candidates dropped out at this point in the recruitment sequence. If an incumbent candidate was determined to be not qualified or withdrew after filing, the election was postponed in order to give others an opportunity to file for that office and to submit to the screening process.

Upon the release of the committee's final report, but not earlier, the candidates were permitted to solicit pledges from legislators.[33] They made the rounds, meeting and greeting senators and representatives, gathering pledges for the final and decisive vote. Some pledges were conditional, some written, some verbal and some based on how the vote might proceed. When the pledges were not available, some withdrew, leaving a single candidate unopposed. Illustrative of the importance of "pledges" was a candidate's letter to the Speaker of the House, withdrawing from the Supreme Court race:

> To be a viable candidate for the Supreme Court I must have not only
> the vote of but the active support of the delegations of the Thirteenth
> Judicial Circuit. Unfortunately, for reasons that have been addressed
> in the news media, much of this support has left me. It has also
> eroded support from other districts that I expected to help. Simply

---

[32] In March 1995, the committee's final report constituted two volumes, totaling 1,016 pages with transcripts of questions and responses for all the candidates. The May report totaled 1,493 pages.

[33] "A candidate for judicial office must not directly or indirectly seek the pledge of a legislator's vote prior to the completion of the screening process regardless of whether the pledge sought is conditional upon the candidate's future favorable review by the screening committee." *Joint Legislative Committtee for Judicial Screening Manual,* p. 11.

put, I do not have sufficient pledges to make an acceptable showing.[34]

More than one ballot was necessary, permitting if not encouraging vote switching and swapping.[35] Not unexpectedly, at this juncture in the recruitment sequence, the legislators acted like legislators, negotiating trades, reaching compromises and soliciting promises. According to one observer of the process:

> Law makers traded votes like baseball cards...elevating the least qualified candidate to the state Supreme Court and re-electing a circuit judge who critics say doesn't know the law.[36]

The results in 1995 emphasized the control of the affirmation process by the legislators and illustrated the politics involved. For example, a candidate elected to the Supreme Court, a former legislator with a winning personality who "moves with ease in legislative circles," although qualified, had been rated by the screening committee the lowest among the four candidates regarding knowledge of practices and procedures. Another circuit judge was re-elected even though his rating was the lowest possible on the committee's scale. The results prompted one senator to remark that

> It's almost like the Bar and the screening committee go through a lengthy process of screening the candidates and the people [legislators] look at it and say 'Gee, gosh, isn't this nice' and throw it in the trash can.[37]

In defense of the overwhelming retention of incumbents, the Chairman of the JLCSJ defended the process: "Somebody who's been in public office, who had to go out and get votes, is more adept at handling power than someone straight out of a law office."[38]

---

[34] *South Carolina Senate Journal*, Tuesday, March 21, 1995, p. 19.

[35] For example, in March 1995, the Joint Assembly used two ballots to choose between four candidates to fill a position on the Supreme Court. One candidate withdrew before the vote because of a lack of legislative pledges. The name of the candidate with the lowest votes out of the remaining three was withdrawn after the first ballot, making an absolute majority possible on the second ballot. The "pledging" phase of affirmation remains in the new 1996 process. According to a member of the commission,

> Once the Commission has found the three nominees qualified, then the rule against seeking pledges drops, and they may go after pledges from the members [of the General Assembly].

[36] *The State*, March 22, 1995.

[37] Ibid.

[38] *Charleston Post-Courier*, February 16, 1995.

The difficulty with the old system seemed not with the initiation and screening process, but with the legislative affirmation phase. Once the process was thrown into the legislature, initiation and screening results were down-graded or ignored and politics as usual took over prompting the 1996 constitutional amendment.[39] Four significant changes are involved in the 1996 reforms. First, the commission becomes an independent agency, not a committee of the General Assembly. Second, the lawmakers must choose from only those nominated by the commission. Third, to be eligible for a judgeship, members of the legislature must be out of office for at least a year. Finally, the implementing legislation forbids vote trading during affirmation.[40]

---

[39] One critic of the March elections expressed the bitterness some had with the "politics as usual": "The system we have now is rancid. Vote trading was more rampant this year than in the 11 years I've served. And it makes me sick." In the second round, however, the JLCJS's recommendations were all accepted by the General Assembly and there was little evidence of vote trading. *The State*, March 22, 1995. Appearances are also deceiving concerning those judicial posts that are dependent upon gubernatorial appointments. Until very recently, South Carolina held partisan pre-primaries called advisory primaries, to nominate Magistrates. In **South Carolina ex rel. Riley v. Commissioners of Election** (258 S.E. 2d 433, 1979) the Supreme Court unhesitatingly declared such impediments to the Governor's power to appoint and the Senate's power to confirm unconstitutional. Until then, this partisan effort to initiate and screen candidates had been effective. Without participating in the advisory elections, a candidate had no chance to be selected by the Governor. The fear was that such advisory votes would take the affirming power away from the legislature. In reality the appointment by the Governor is based on a form of senatorial courtesy, with the Governor accepting the nominee of local county senators without question.

[40] "No member of the General Assembly may trade anything of value, including pledges to vote for legislation or for other candidates, in exchange for another member's pledge to vote for a candidate for judicial office." Section 7-11-15, Chapter 19.

Figure 5.2

SOUTH CAROLINA RECRUITMENT ACTORS

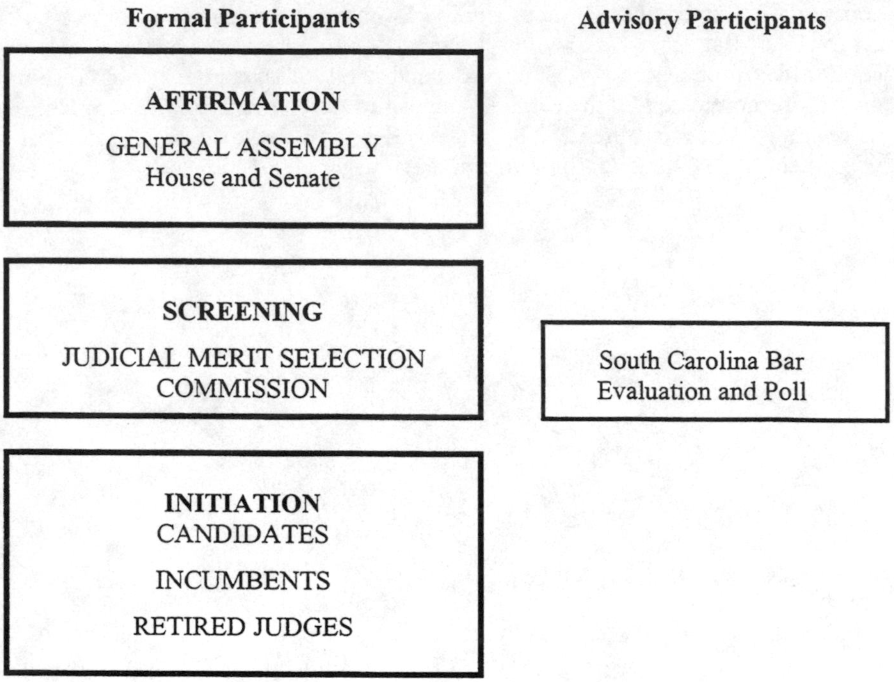

Formal Participants   **Advisory Participants**

AFFIRMATION

GENERAL ASSEMBLY
House and Senate

SCREENING

JUDICIAL MERIT SELECTION
COMMISSION

South Carolina Bar
Evaluation and Poll

INITIATION
CANDIDATES

INCUMBENTS

RETIRED JUDGES

Level of Articulation

Prior to 1996, only a few of the open judicial seats were contested. The pledging process eliminated further the number of contested races. Finally, incumbents were rarely faced with opposition. Although comparisons to popular elections are lacking, the moderate contestedness and generally low competitive results under the old system suggested that South Carolina had a fairly low articulation recruitment system. It remains to be seen how the commission plan will affect the level of articulation. One aspect of the reform may encourage more candidates to vie for the commission's favor. Qualified non-legislators will no longer hesitate to file for consideration now that the old no-win situation for outsiders has been eliminated. Even with the expansion in the initiation phase, with a thorough screening and with the elimination of the crass politics of affirmation, the General Assembly remains in control of recruitment.

One experienced legislator who chaired the old joint committee, and who is now on the commission, posed the crucial question:

> Do we agree to be an activist commission that follows leads and investigates. Or do we start off with a passive position? If so, we will have a hard time activating things in the future without risking criticism that we are treating different personalities different ways.[41]

The 1996 reforms would suggest that judges in South Carolina are accountable to the public, but indirectly through the legislature. Although elected for long terms, to retain their seats on the bench judges must not antagonize the legislature.[42] Advancement up the judicial ladder also depends upon legislative favor. Not only does the General Assembly make the final affirming choice, but the majority on the screening commission are legislators. This is not to suggest that the South Carolina judiciary is merely a puppet of the legislature, this is only to assert that those who survive recruitment may have a particular outlook to law and policy that differs little from the legislative branch. The judiciary still must confront the "judicial dilemma" as a balance seems yet to be achieved.

---

[41] *Charleston Post-Courier*, November 12, 1996.

[42] For example, the Chief Justice of the South Carolina Supreme Court was most reluctant to become involved with the legislature over the assignment of a re-elected judge to another circuit as urged by some legislators. "It's a highly political issue and I have spent the last three months...not getting involved in political issues." He had requested of the legislature more judgeships and equipment and apparently wished not to antagonize members of the General Assembly. See Sid Gaulden, "Letter Cites Problem in Martin Re-election," *Chaleston Post-Courier*, April 7, 1995.

Chapter Six

Appointments to State Courts

The appointment of judges is an integral part of nearly every judicial selection system. Besides appointments to permanent positions, Governors make tempo rary appointments to vacancies in states relying on partisan, nonpartisan, and legislative elections. In many cases, a majority of all judges in these systems were initially appointed and are able to retain their seats due, not insignificantly, to the benefit of incumbency.[1] The merit commission method also turns on Governors appointing, but from a list submitted by others. Presidential appointments fill the federal benches, although tempered with senatorial courtesy at the trial level and to some extent at the circuit court level also. Although the appointing authority has a nearly free hand in temporary appointments to vacancies, these appointments are shaped in good measure by the dynamics of the permanent affirmation. For example, Governors filling a vacancy in a nonpartisan jurisdiction are wise to consider the subsequent "electability" of the appointee. In legislative systems Governors are encouraged to pick from present or former legislators in making temporary appointments.

However, a few states have experienced a nearly pure method of appointment, much like that of the federal system. Judges in Maine, New Hampshire, and New Jersey are appointed by the Governor. California's Governor appoints appellate judges and, until recently, in Rhode Island trial judges were the product of appointments as well.

The distinction we draw between those states which fill vacancies through temporary appointments and those which enjoy pure appointments turns on the differences in the affirmation stage. In filling temporary vacancies Governors appoint judges tentatively and the final affirmation is postponed. However, in the pure systems appointments are to permanent positions for set terms far exceeding a year or two characteristic of the temporary appointments. Certainly, similar factors bear on both types of appointments. For example, partisan considerations are rarely absent from any appointment. Nonetheless, the appointments to permanent positions are not shaped by further screening or election concerns. The recruitment ends with the appointment.

The appointment of judges by Governors was a common practice prior to the Jacksonian Revolution that brought voters strongly into the process. Also, appointments were used for a short time in some Reconstruction governments.

---

[1] Lawrence Baum, "The Electoral Fates of Incumbent Judges in the Ohio Court of Common Pleas," in Elliot Slotnick (ed.), *Judicial Politics: Readings from Judicature* (Chicago: American Judicature Society, 1992), p. 81.

Twenty states have experimented off-and-on with gubernatorial appointments for some benches, and all these experiments involved confirmation by either the upper house as in the federal system or by a "council," often composed in some measure of legislators, cabinet members, or a combination of both. But in all circumstances the state Governors were responsible for final appointments even though their authority was tempered by the advice and consent provision. This legislative confirmation is still present in Maine, New Hampshire and New Jersey.

Executive appointment with legislative confirmation has several noteworthy attributes. Most observers regard appointments to provide the greatest degree of judicial independence. Once affirmed for a stated term, judges need not fear reprisals by voters or subtle threats by groups that would provide funding for election campaigns. Direct accountability to the public is absent. However, political accountability to the executive and legislative branches may substitute for the responsibility to the public, and such accountability also may impinge upon judges' independence. Constitutional provisions place in state executives the sole power to appoint, with only formality involved in confirming the choice by legislatures. Governors can ignore the results of bar polls, judicial evaluations, lawyer—or other—screening committees, and the preferences of labor, management interests, insurance companies, plaintiff's lawyers, or whatever special interest. Ignoring these other forces can, of course, threaten the political health of Governors, but ignore them they can. Lame-duck state executives are largely free of even these pressures. The only pressing consideration is the legislative confirmation requirement which plays a varying role, depending upon at what level of the judiciary the appointment is made.

It is argued that although appointees have no obligations to outside forces, they are directly accountable to the appointers. However, that accountability does not come with the appointments but rather long before appointments are made. Governors tend to appoint persons who have, through their past political, legal or social actions reflected the values, policies and preferences held by Governors. The appointments, then, are based upon the assumption that judges will continue to behave on the bench as they have in the past. For example, the political party affiliation of appointees almost invariably coincides with that of Governors, reflecting a coincidence of political views and prompting the appointments. Or appointments of former state legislators may have been prompted by their votes for the Governors' programs. The point is that the obligation to Governors is to remain consistent with the views that brought those judges to the attention of the chief executives initially. Political accountability means newly appointed judges are expected to avoid subsequent pressures to change.

Again, however, formal accountability lines may be deceiving. Chief executives have pre-existing political debts, often redeemed through judicial appointments. Geographical, diversity and gender considerations may have to be weighed as well. Friendship, or cronyism as critics would label it, can on occasion prompt an appointment. The conservative—or liberal—wing of the party may need to be placated. The favorite of a particular legislator holding a key legislative position may have to be considered in order to ease an appointment through the confirmation process. Nearly always bar associations demand a role in the appointment process. Governors are often in an awkward position of having to consider the effects of a judicial appointment on their own re-election chances. Politics is never absent from judicial recruitment of any kind, whether in appointments or elections. Consequently, appointments may have to be made that do not reflect the preferences of the appointing official.

It is these diverse demands bearing on appointments that lend a bit more balance to appointments. Governors are not wholly free from pressures to appoint a particular person. Most are deluged with endorsements, applications and petitions when an appointment is pending. E-mail and telephone lines are crowded with urgings to appoint. State chief executives commonly have a person on staff who handles appointments—judicial and otherwise—sometimes to the exclusion of other responsibilities. Although executive appointments, even with the advice and consent requirement, have been regarded as assuring a maximum of independence, consideration of the informal or political phases of the process may bring indirect accountability factors to bear.

Despite all of these possible and real forces impinging on the appointment process, Governors are the sole party responsible for affirmation. Constitutions typically dictate that: "The Governor shall nominate and appoint...." Others react to their lawfully authorized initiative. In some states Governors may have few prerogatives regarding other appointments, but judicial selections are done with great care and considered deliberation. Also, it is often the case that the term of office for these judges exceeds that of the chief executive, providing an opportunity to carry over into the next administration persons who view policy and law as did the appointing Governor. Finally, the public and the media typically pay scant attention to the judiciary and to whom the Governor may appoint. Perhaps after an initial concern, the public quickly moves on to more immediate and comprehensible events. The point is, again, that chief executives, within the numerous political constraints, have a fairly free hand to appoint and those appointees are fairly free to continue to carry forward views and policies that brought them to the attention of Governors in the first place. Nonetheless, this freedom is constrained by what the law permits and what the norms of judicial office allow.

Judges relying on appointments to fill permanent positions have an advantage not enjoyed by elected judges. Time off from judicial duties is not required to campaign for re-election. The already crowded dockets or trial calendars can be dealt with rather than postponed while the judge seeks voter attention. Further, the funding necessary for a successful run for the bench in an election system is missing in appointments. Not only is the need to raise monies, organize election committees, and conduct time-consuming campaigns absent, but the real obligations (or appearance of such) to those who contribute campaign funds are similarly absent. The "cult of the robe" and the appearance of aloofness needed by an independent and objective judiciary are kept intact. Not to be forgotten is that appointments can be accomplished without much delay. When legislative approval is needed and the solons are in recess, interim appointments are possible. There is indeed something to be said in favor of the appointment of judges.

A not altogether minor concern for appointments, however, comes from the symbolic needs of a judiciary in a democratic society. Public officials in a democracy need at the very least to appear to be a product of the people. Courts, especially, must rely on public support for compliance. Appointed judges are at a disadvantage being a product of a closed selection system, absent of any direct and obvious involvement of the public in their recruitment. Appointees do not have a constituency to give them independence from the other branches of government. Some symbolic accountability to the public is provided by the need for confirmation by the elected branch of government, but in practical terms few citizens would remember whether a legislator on the judiciary committee or on the council voted to confirm or reject the Governor's nominee.

Judicial appointments, as with any elections, can also vary between a high and low articulation system. The Governor, after consultation with a close adviser, might send a name to the Senate for confirmation. The Senate, in turn, because of party loyalty or tradition, confirms without debate. With so few participants throughout the recruitment sequence a low articulation method is the result. In contrast, a highly competitive and complicated process may have preceded the appointment, characterizing a high articulation recruitment experience. The chief executive considers a number of viable candidates suggested by the state bar association, with a number receiving endorsements from the state labor council, the trial lawyers' association, sitting and retired judges, prominent business leaders and lawyers, to name but a few of the actors sometimes involved in bringing names to the attention of the Governor. The effects attributed to a high articulation recruitment experience would be evident.

Presidential appointments of U.S. Supreme Court justices have been quite thoroughly researched, and these selection dynamics constitute a separate chapter in this monograph. However, analyses of state appointments have produced only a few published studies, and those often feature conflicting results. Most such studies have been based upon some normative assumptions. For example, county commissioners appoint a lawyer to a court of limited jurisdiction on purely partisan grounds, generating criticisms. The qualifications of the appointee may be wholly ignored. To many, when party politics is involved in any appointment, that appointment is suspect. Partisanship or politics has little to do with judicial qualifications, or it is so assumed. What have empirical studies revealed about the effects of appointments compared with other methods of selection?

Advocates of appointment argue that the executive recruitment of judges assures greater independence for those appointed. That independence, however, is not assured and depends to a significant extent on the informal activities that precede an appointment.[2] It seems clear, though, that appointments usually involve partisanship. Governors and other public officials responsible for appointing judges to permanent or temporary positions on the bench tend to appoint those with compatible party affiliations and policy values. This overall inclination may be reflected in judicial decisions. Democrats tend to make liberal decisions, e.g., giving more credence to the accused than their Republican counterparts.[3] However, contrary to some assumptions, appointed judges are not more conservative than their elected colleagues.[4] Actually, given the apparent security attached to judges that have been appointed, they tend to lean toward the individual over the state in criminal cases, and also tend to be more innovative in interpreting the law.[5] In jurisdictions that have a tradition of appointing appellate judges from the senior trial jurists tends to work against diversity on the bench.[6] Setting aside the issue of seniority, appointments tend to encourage diversity on the benches. Most of the black judges on the bench in 1973 were appointed to their posts.[7] Of course, diversifying the state benches depends on the commitment of the appointing authority.

How judges view their roles tends to vary with selection systems. Those appointed by Governors favor a "law interpreter" role, relying on precedent and strict construction of laws in contrast with merit plan judges who prefer a more activist or "adjudicator" role.[8] Appointed judges appear to have more formal education than judges involved in other selection methods, although that education tends to be at less prestigious law schools.[9] Appointed judges also tend to have been legislators, and to be a bit short on prosecutorial experience.[10] In

---

[2] David J. Danelski, *A Supreme Court Justice Is Appointed* (New York: Random House, 1964).

[3] Stuart S. Nagel, *Comparing Elected and Appointed Judicial Systems* (Beverly Hills, CA: Sage, 1973).

[4] Ronald Schneider and Ralph Maughan, "Does the Appointment of Judges Lead to a More Conservative Bench?" *Justice System Journal* 5 (1979): 45.

[5] Daniel R. Pinello, *The Impact of Judicial Selection Method on State Supreme Court Policy: Innovation, Reaction, and Atrophy* (Westport, CT: Greenwood Press, 1995), p. 135.

[6] Adomeit, "Selection by Seniority: How Much Longer Can a Custom Survive that Bars Blacks and Women from the Connecticut Supreme Court?" *Connecticut Bar Journal* 51 (1977): 295.

[7] American Judicature Society, "The Black Judges in America: A Statistical Profile," *Judicature* 57 (1973): 18.

[8] Charles H. Sheldon, "Judicial Roles: Background and Norms," *California Western Law Review* 9 (1973): 510.

[9] Victor E. Flango and Craig R. Ducat, "What Difference Does Method of Selection Procedures Make: Selection Procedures in State Courts of Last Resort," *Justice System Journal* 5 (1979): 32.

[10] Bradley C. Canon, "The Impact of Formal Selection Process on the Characteristics of Judges—Reconsidered," *Law & Society Review* 6 (1972): 584.

addition appointed judges tend to be less responsive to constituency views and dissent less frequently than elected judges.[11] States recruiting judges through appointments tend to be "densely populated, rapid growing, innovative, industrialized, and affluent."[12]

Again, despite the above tendencies found in some studies, and as with our review of the studies of other recruitment methods, little evidence is yet available to isolate appointments as resulting in some consistently unique characteristics. Stuart Nagel's conclusion of long ago is still appropriate today:

> Pulling together all the findings presented thus far leads one to conclude that elected and appointed judicial systems do not differ as much in their results or in the behavior of voters and appointers as the debate literature would have us believe.[13]

Again, it is not only the formal act of appointing that shapes the outlook of the appointee, but rather the process that has proceeded that act. What we need to know is what happens in the initiation and screening processes prior to the affirming appointment.

New Jersey's Appointment System

The innovative Article 6 of the New Jersey Constitution of 1947, largely a product of the efforts of Arthur T. Vanderbilt, sets forth one of the first unified state systems.[14] A three-level structure with Superior Courts constituting the trial courts of general jurisdiction, separated into equity and law divisions and presiding over 15 vicinages (county or multi-county jurisdictions). The intermediate court of appeals or Appellate Division of the Superior Courts is divided into eight parts, with four judges each. In each part, two- or three-judge panels hear appeals from the lower courts. The appellate division is composed of Superior Court judges, promoted to the appeals bench by the Chief Justice. A seven-member Supreme Court sits **en banc** in Trenton to hear final appeals as the court of last resort for the state. A tax court, municipal courts, and Surrogate's Offices have specialized and limited jurisdictions.

---

[11] Bradley C. Canon and Dean Jaros, "External Variables, Institutional Structure and Dissent on State Supreme Courts," *Polity* 3 (1970): 183.

[12] Flango and Ducat, "What Difference Does Method of Selection Make: Selection Procedures in State Courts of Last Resort," p. 37.

[13] Nagel, *Comparing Elected and Appointed Judicial Systems,"* p. 36.

[14] Vanderbilt had been active in Republican politics, was a highly respected professor of law and dean at New York University, President of the ABA, and later Chief Justice of the New Jersey Supreme Court. See Arthur T. Vanderbilt II, *Changing Law: A Biography of Arthur T. Vanderbilt* (New Brunswick, NJ: Rutgers University Press, 1976).

Figure 6.1

NEW JERSEY COURT SYSTEM

SUPREME COURT

7 Justices

Appointed by Governor with advice
and consent of Senate
7-year term
Reappointment by Governor with
advice and consent of Senate
Retirement at age 70

APPELLATE DIVISION (Superior Court)

32 Superior Court Judges
Districts
Appointed by Chief Justice from Superior Court
7-year term
Reappointment by C.J. until age 70

SUPERIOR COURT

421 Judges
County-wide
Appointed by Governor with advice
and consent of Senate
7-year term
Reappointed by Governor with advice
And consent of Senate
Retirement at age 70

MUNICIPAL COURT	**SURROGATES**	**TAX COURT**
363 Judges	21 Surrogates	9 Judges
Appointed by Mayor-Council or Governor	Elected County wide	Appointed and Re-appointed by Governor
3-year term	5-year term	with consent of Senate
		7-year term
		Reappointment to age 70

Article 6, sec. VI provides the broad outline for the formal process by which judges are recruited.

> The Governor shall nominate and appoint, with the advice and consent of the Senate, the Chief Justice and Associate Justices of the Supreme Court, the Judges of the Superior Court, and the judges of inferior courts with jurisdiction extending to more than one municipality.

If after an initial term of seven years judges are reappointed, they remain on the bench conditional on "good behavior" until the mandatory retirement age of 70. The selection and tenure of judges serving a single municipality are determined by its governing body.

Judicial appointments are part of New Jersey's history. In 1776 New Jersey relied on a vote by the "Council and Assembly" (or both houses of the legislature) for selecting judges. However, in 1884 appointment by the Governor with the advice and consent of the Senate was instituted and has remained to today the method for recruiting judges. According to Arthur T. Vanderbilt, the best method for selecting judges "is one which must always be determined in the light of history and local conditions."[15] New Jersey has remained true to its past. The popular election of judges has never been seriously considered and the legislature, in some way, has always been involved along with the Governor in the recruitment process.

Another tradition has a more recent beginning. The modern court system in New Jersey began in 1947, when the present constitution was adopted. An understanding was reached that judges would be selected on a bipartisan basis rather than on narrow partisanship, a practice which previously had led the courts into disrepute. The very real potential for bitter inter-party conflict over who would be placed on the state's benches was thereby largely avoided.

> In New Jersey, where the Governor is a political official with the usual party obligations, a tradition of bipartisanship has resulted in the elimination of the purely political appointment in many instances where the Governor is making his selections from the opposite political party.[16]

Partisanship remains, but it takes a bipartisanship form.

The seven-member Supreme Court reflects this bipartisan tradition with a 4/3 split between the parties, the majority party having the slight advantage. At the next vacancy readjustments are made if necessary. As appointments are made to lower courts, this tradition remains strong. Despite the competitive two-party nature of New Jersey politics, the previously highly divisive struggles for patronage advantages in the judiciary have been largely eliminated. This

---

[15] Arthur T. Vanderbilt, *Judges and Jurors* (Boston: Boston University Press, 1958), p. 47.

[16] Ibid., 48.

bipartisanship has contributed importantly to the political independence of the bench.

Initiation

The Governor's office retains control of initiating candidacies for court positions. The Supreme Court appointments have come disproportionately from the Governor's immediate staff or close advisers, suggesting this gubernatorial control. For example, five of the seven members of the 1994 court were either former counsel to the chief executive or prominent cabinet members. Another justice was a former legislator, and the seventh judge had served as president of the New Jersey Bar Association. One observer referred to the court as a "bunch of little Governors."

About one-third of the county bar associations have judicial selection committees that compile a list of names for the Governor's consideration when a vacancy in their county occurs. These county committees will attempt to narrow their lists down to only those whom they could strongly support. However, the Governor is not obligated to follow the selection committees' recommendations. Individual attorneys, the candidates themselves, and others advocating on a candidate's behalf freely contact the Governor's office to record "an interest" in the appointment. In addition, the Governor's counsel may contact other private and public officials, soliciting names for possible consideration. Important, of course, are the suggestions submitted by the Senators from the particular county involved. In the more populated counties such as Essex County, 40 or 50 names may be brought to the Governor's attention. In smaller counties often only 5 or 6 names are initiated.

Screening

Four separate efforts are pursued in the screening for all levels of the judiciary which are products of the appointment process. The Office of Governor's Counsel coordinates the selection of judges for the chief executive. A Judicial Performance Committee provides evaluations to other screeners concerned with reappointments. The organized legal profession has both state and county screening committees. Finally, the Senate's Judiciary Committee performs its screening for the "advice and consent" aspect of the formal selection process. The screening process for all levels of the New Jersey judiciary varies only in intensity and the degree of involvement of state Senators. However, by far the most crucial screening occurs in the Governor's office.

A formal application made to the Office of Governor's Counsel (lawyers attached to the Governor's office) initiates the recruitment process.[17] On occa-

---

[17] In 1984 a special Bar Association committee was formed to suggest qualified women and minority candidates for consideration by the Governor. Barbara Williams Prabbu (ed.), *Spotlight on New Jersey Government* (New Brunswick, NJ: Rutgers University Press, 1992), p. 296.

sion the Governor's office will contact potential candidates to suggest they apply. Each applicant files a resume with the office. These resumes are reviewed by the Governor's lawyers and an initial narrowing of eligible applicants is made. A 25-page questionnaire is sent to the remaining applicants, soliciting information on legal practice, civic and political activities, financial matters, state of health and other personal data. On the basis of responses on these questionnaires, not less than three and usually four or five applicants for one position are invited to an interview conducted by two or three of the Governor's counsels. Following the interview, an informal and strictly confidential investigation is conducted on the remaining viable candidate(s) involving four specific steps. The state police, under the auspices of the state Attorney General, performs a background check on criminal record, credit check, and the like. Next, the Administrative Office of the Courts is asked for an ethics review concerning violations of the Canons of Judicial Conduct or the Code of Professional Responsibility. Political party leaders and Senators in the jurisdiction involved are consulted. Finally, references and persons familiar with the qualifications of the candidates are contacted. At this point a preliminary decision is made and a name (sometimes two) is (are) submitted to the New Jersey State Bar for its evaluation. In most cases, by the time the nomination is sent to the State Bar, and certainly before the Senate Judiciary Committee receives the nomination, the informal process has assured smooth sailing for the ultimate nominee.

The Governor's counsel also screens candidates for reappointments in much the same manner as used in the initial appointments, but with considerably less intensity. Likely these judges will not be interviewed. The questionnaire sent to each candidate for reappointment is somewhat different from that used for initial appointees, and considerable reliance is placed on the report from the Supreme Court's Judicial Performance Committee (JPC). The Supreme Court appoints the members of this committee, which is composed of not less than six representatives of Superior Court judges from all divisions, not less than three attorneys, and two laypersons. The JPC evaluates the performance of a judge twice during his or her initial term; once during the first two years and then again in the fifth or sixth year. When resources are available, tenured judges may also be evaluated. Approximately 50 or 60 judges go through this program each year. On occasion, upon the urgings of the assignment or chief judge, a tenured judge may "volunteer" to be evaluated. The results of the first evaluation during the initial term are shared only between the evaluated judge, the vincinages' assignment judge, and the Judicial Evaluation Commission; the report is also made available to the Supreme Court. The results of the second evaluation are also shared with the Governor and the Senate Judiciary Committee for their screening when considering reappointments.[18]

---

[18] The Judicial Evaluation Commission is also appointed by the Supreme Court, and it is composed of at least three retired judges, serving three-year terms. The commission reviews an individual judge's evaluation report from the JPC, and its members meet with the judge to discuss the

The involvement of the State Bar in the screening process is a direct result of a specific compact negotiated between the bar leadership and the Governor in which the chief executive agrees to send the name or names of candidates being considered for appointment or reappointment to be screened by the bar's Committee on Judicial and Prosecutor Appointments (CJPA). The agreement was informally reached between the bar and Governor Alfred E. Driscoll in the 1950s, and subsequently formalized in a written compact in 1969 by Governor Richard J. Hughes who later served as Chief Justice. Governor William T. Cahill strengthened the agreement with an unbinding promise not to appoint any candidate who received an "unqualified" rating from the bar. Because of the state's constitutional provisions the Governor is not legally bound by the agreement.

The CJPA's 25 members are appointed by the Bar president for three-year terms and represent each of the state's counties. In addition, the Bar president, who serves on the committee **ex officio**, appoints a chair and two vice-chairs for one-year terms. Much like the ABA's Standing Committee on the Federal Judiciary, CJPA members are appointed because of their knowledge, interest and time available to devote to the work of the committee. The CJPA evaluates only the nominee(s) submitted by the Governor's office.

The nominee's responses to the questionnaire completed for the Governor are sent to the CJPA, and a separate screening process then ensues. The member of the state committee representing the particular county from which the prospective nominee hails is responsible for the primary investigation and evaluation. Confidential inquiries are made of the nominee's references listed on the questionnaires, and any other lawyers, judges, and persons familiar with the nominee's practice of law. The confidential report from the investigating member requires evaluations of "Integrity," "Legal Knowledge and Ability," "Temperament, Diligence and Productivity," and "Financial Responsibility and Health."[19] Detailed ratings from "good," "fair," "poor" to "unknown" under each category refine the evaluation. For example, under "Integrity" the investigating committee member rates "Reputation for personal conduct," "Reputation for propriety," "Reputation for avoiding the appearance of impropriety and unprofessional conduct," etc. Other members of the state committee often make a separate investigation of the proposed nominee.

The Bar's committee meets once a month when the legislature is in session, and it considers on the average six judicial candidates for several levels of the state bench along with a number of prosecutorial aspirants. All candidates for the initial appointments are interviewed and those being considered for reappointment are interviewed if the CJPA feels it necessary. The CJPA's rec-

---

report, answer questions, and offer guidance to assist the judge in improving future performance. See *Court Rules of General Application*, Rule 1: 35A.

[19] The member designated for undertaking the investigation for the state committee is the representative of the county from which the prospective nominee comes.

ommendations are either "qualified" or "not qualified." For reappointments to tenure, the committee simply indicates the bar's "approval" or "disapproval."

Only the CJPA's recommendations, without the supporting evidence, are communicated to the Governor; the bar's rating "shall thereafter remain absolutely confidential and not to be divulged." However, if the committee has recommended a candidate "not qualified" whom the Governor appoints nonetheless, it is free to notify the appropriate Senate committee of its reasons for the negative rating. The same opportunity arises with a "disapprove" evaluation in reappointment situations. However, it is indeed a rare occasion that would compel the bar to notify the judiciary committee.

Immediately upon the start of the CJPA's investigation a copy of the nominee's completed questionnaire is submitted to the chair of the appropriate County Judicial and Prosecutorial Appointments Committee. Each county bar organization has its separate screening committee, composed of seven to eleven members. Again, a separate investigation and evaluation are conducted during which knowledgeable lawyers, judges, and other knowledgeable persons are contacted and an interview is conducted with the prospective nominee. Interviews with judges up for reappointment are discretionary. Usually the county must complete their investigation and report to the State CJPA within 20 days.

The investigating members at both the state and county levels are urged to be thorough in their efforts:

> You certainly are encouraged not just to contact persons whom you know but also those whom you may know but who you believe (from whatever source) may shed considerable light on the candidate insofar as any of the criteria are concerned. In this respect your designated member or Chair should take care to make certain that all bases are reasonably touched. For example, and regarding original appointments, one or more members of your Committee may look into the candidate's public service activities, another into his or her writing and expressive capability, and the like. But above all: UNDISPUTED INTEGRITY and JUDICIAL TEMPERAMENT.[20]

If there is a disagreement between the county committee's evaluation and that of the state committee, the county chair is afforded an opportunity to attend and comment when the state CJPA meets for its final vote. On occasion, when requested by the Governor, the bar will "give further consideration to the qualifications of a prospective candidate after receiving the Committee's report."[21]

The importance of the county committee becomes relevant for the "advice and consent" aspect of the appointment. Likely, the candidate is the nominee of the local Senator or party organization whose turn it is under the bipartisan system. Of course, the county organization is most familiar with local candidates.

---

[20] Emphasis in original. New Jersey State Bar Association, *Manual for Judicial and Prosecutorial Appointments Committee Members* (1986), p. 6.

[21] *New Jersey LAWYER* (Summer 1984): 58.

Nonetheless, the county bar's efforts have been criticized for depending too heavily on the views of party activists rather than on those who would be more knowledgeable about the legal skills of the candidate.[22]

Reappointments remain a separate screening process which involve both the state and the county appointments committees as before. The reappointment is for a permanent position lasting until age 70, with only a "good behavior" provision as an accountability check. The review is less intense than the efforts made in the original appointment. The screening tends to be less inclusive since the committees now have seven years of bench behavior to evaluate. The CJPA members have been reluctant to withhold their support unless the incumbent has serious problems. In recent history no judge has been rejected by the bar at the reappointment stage.

Although initiation and affirmation are clearly in the hands of the Governor and the senate, screening by the New Jersey State Bar Association has had some impact on final appointments. Over the past 20 some years of the arrangement with Governors, only about six candidates out of hundreds were appointed despite a negative rating by the bar. Appointments to the Supreme Court involve "highly politically motivated positions. Unless a strong movement arises against the appointee, it will be made" despite reservations held by the legal profession. Given the realities of the politics surrounding appointments, and as long as the Governor draws predominately from those declared "qualified," the bar regards its input into the process as more than simply adequate.[23]

The Committee on Judicial and Prosecutor Appointments follows both in procedures and in screening criteria the American Bar Association's Standing Committee on the Federal Judiciary responsible for screening appointments to federal benches. For example, as with the ABA's preliminary screening, one member of the county committee is designated to do the initial screening and then to report back to the full committee. If some difficulties are encountered which might bring the qualifications of the nominee into question, informal contacts could be made. The Governor has the opportunity to withdraw a name or to substitute another candidate. Although each of the groups responsible for screening—the Governor's office, the JPC, the state bar's Judicial and Prosecutor Appointments Committee, its county counterpart, and the senate judiciary committee—all conduct separate screening efforts, opportunities are provided to negotiate and compromise in a manner not unlike what transpires with the fed-

---

[22] "It is my experience that more often the persons whose views are sought are persons active in the political parties within the counties and not necessarily persons with the expertise to make recommendations...[concerning] qualities of scholarship, objectivity, compassion, firmness, and humanity." Charles E. Ried, "Judicial Appointments in New Jersey—A Merit Plan," *New Jersey Law Journal* (February, 1973): 11.

[23] Quote from national survey of state bar leadership. See Charles H. Sheldon, "The Role of State Bar Associations in Judicial Selection," *Judicature* 77 (1994): 300.

eral recruitment process.[24]   Although lobbying on behalf of a candidate is evident, the bar committees are spared such pressures.   All lobbying is behind closed doors with special lawyers' groups and interested parties contacting the Governor's office, and if need be the Senate.

In 1988 the involvement of the bar association in the process of screening was challenged in the courts.   The plaintiff in **Loigman** v. **Trombadore** (228 N.J. Super. 437) argued that over the years the bar had "attempted to exercise a form of power of control over the decisions of the Governor...with regard to the nomination of persons to the judiciary." According to the complaint:

> [The Bar had] purposefully presented to the public the improper appearance that [it had]...attempted to exercise, such putative form of power or control [and had] led the good and honest citizens of the State of New Jersey to believe that the Governor has corruptly surrendered his constitutional authority to [the bar].....[The bar has] caused the Governor to be subject to influence by false, misleading, fraudulent and malicious statements [and had] purposely, intentionally, deliberately, and with fraudulent intent, concealed relevant and material information regarding the nomination of persons to the judiciary.[25]

The plaintiff brought suit because of the apparent lack of communication between the CJPA and the Defendants Association concerning a judicial nomination.

The trial bench and the appeals court dismissed the complaint as a nonjusticiable issue which courts could not resolve because it involved a "political question."[26]   The trial judge wrote that whom the Governor solicits for advice regarding judicial nominations "is private and is not the province of the judiciary to decide." He or she is "free to take such advice or disregard it."   The Court took notice of the fact that the Governor "accepts input from many persons and organizations" and the plaintiff's redress lies with public opinion, the legislature or within the bar itself, but not with the courts.

Armed with a "qualified" rating from the bar, the Governor files a "Notice of Intention" to nominate a specifically named person for a judgeship with the Secretary of the Senate, giving the Senate at least seven days to prepare. Next, the formal nomination is filed with presiding officers in the Senate and with the Office of Legislative Services which requests those Senators of both parties from the counties involved to "signoff" on the nominee. Senators ordinarily do not signoff on nominees for reappointments.

---

[24] Joel B. Grossman, *Lawyers and Judges: The ABA and the Politics of Judicial Selection* (New York: Wiley & Sons, 1965).

[25] **Loigman v. Trombadore,** 228 N.J. Super.427 (1988) pp. 439-440.

[26] See **Baker v. Carr,** 369 U.S. 186 (1962).

The advice and consent of the New Jersey Senate is required for all judicial appointments. New Jersey law provides that:

> If a nomination to judicial office with respect to a particular county is displeasing to one or more of the Senators from that county, then the other members of the Senate will take no action looking to the confirmation of the proposed nominee and this is quite apart from the nominee's qualifications or the lack thereof.[27]

A mix of senatorial courtesy, bipartisan tradition, and informal negotiations helps soften the threat of withholding advice and consent, although the device has been used in the past to block a judicial appointment. Most recently, the politics of the confirmation process is played out with a delaying tactic. When a package of nominees includes one judge unacceptable to a Senator, confirmation of the whole package can be delayed.[28] More common is withholding approval until a nomination is made, with his or her endorsement, to a matching vacancy in the county.[29] The outright abuse of senatorial courtesy is rare.[30] Nonetheless, the practice has its critics:

> Senatorial Courtesy is a "vice." It is a veto power which breeds compromise and bargain. Thus, it creates an unintentional equality between a single senator and the state's chief executive. The people of New Jersey have the right to demand that every member of the senate vote according to his own "conscience—not the conscience of another.[31]

The practice of senatorial courtesy has been challenged several times in the courts as a violation of the New Jersey Constitution. In **Klingerman** v. **Lynch** (1966) a lower court avoided a resolution by declaring the issue of senatorial courtesy a political question, to be decided by the political branches of government, not the courts. However, the judge did rule that the founders of the Con-

---

[27] **Passaic County Bar Association v. Hughes,** 108 N.J. Super. 161 (1969) p. 169.

[28] Recently, after months of delay, 30 or so nominations had yet to come to the Senate Judiciary Committee for a hearing. Not only has this kept one qualified lawyer off the bench, but possibly 29 others, leading to delay and resulting in an increasing backlog of cases in the jurisdictions suffering the vacancy or vacancies.

[29] In 1976 nine persons were denied appointment because of one nominee being regarded as "unacceptable" to a Senator. "During the 1974-1975 legislative session, at least eighty-one nominations were blocked either temporarily or permanently by the objections of different Senators." Michael J. Freehan, "The Role of Advice and Consent: Senatorial *Dis*courtesy," *Seton Hall Law Review* 10 (1979): 118.

[30] Senators recently involved in an apparent "misuse" of senatorial courtesy lost reelection or lost considerable voter support, not entirely unattributable to their use of the senatorial prerogative. Barbara G. Salmore and Stephen A. Salmore, *New Jersey Politics and Government: Suburban Politics Comes of Age* (Lincoln: University of Nebraska Press, 1993), pp. 189-190.

[31] Freehan, "The Role of Advice and Consent," 153.

stitution had not intended advice and consent to mean senatorial courtesy.[32]   In 1969 a similar challenge confronted the courts in **Passaic County Bar Association** v. **Hughes**.[33]   Again, the issue of whether senatorial courtesy was a distortion of the New Jersey Constitution was avoided.   The case was nonjusticiable because of the lack of judicially discoverable standards to resolve the issue.   In real terms, resolving the issue might well have brought the judiciary in direct conflict with the legislature and thereby threaten its independence.

However, the New Jersey Supreme Court came close to deciding the constitutionality of senatorial courtesy in 1993 in **De Veas** v. **Dorsey**.[34]   A Senator representing a county in a judge's jurisdiction refused to signoff on reappointment and the nomination was dropped without further consideration. Action was brought to determine whether such inaction was constitutional.   As in earlier cases, the lower court dismissed the suit as nonjusticiable.   However, the supreme court split 3-3 on the issue, thereby affirming the lower court but providing encouragement for future litigation.   Three of the Justices concluded that "[d]istressing though senatorial courtesy may be...it remains a prerogative of the Senate."   And the recourse is not with the courts, but "in the court of public opinion."   Voters can simply fail to reelect those exercising the judicial veto.[35]   The other three Justices viewed the issue as justifiable, and argued that the practice of senatorial courtesy was "unconstitutional when the ultimate effect of its exercise is to veto a gubernatorial appointment" without further action by the full Senate.

---

[32]   92 N.J. Super. 373 (1966).

[33]   108 N.J. Super. 161 (1969).

[34]   134 N.J. 420, 634 A.2d 493 (1993).

[35]   Ibid., 504.   Actually senatorial courtesy was an issue in the campaign of Senator Dorsey who had withheld his approval to the nomination.   He was turned back by the voters in his November, 1993 reelection bid.

Figure 6.2

NEW JERSEY RECRUITMENT ACTORS

Formal Participants	Advisory Participants

AFFIRMATION

SENATE
"advice and consent"

GOVERNOR
Appointments

SCREENING

SENATE JUDICIARY COMMITTEE

SUPREME COURT'S JUDICIAL
PERFORMANCE COMMITTEE
Reappointments

NEW JERSEY STATE BAR ASSOC.
Committee on Judicial and
Prosecutor Appointments

OFFICE OF GOVERNOR'S COUNSEL

County Judicial and
Prosecutor Appointments
Committees

Administrative Office
Of the Courts

INITIATION
OFFICE OF GOVERNOR'S COUNSEL

COUNTY BAR JUDICIAL
SELECTION COMMITTEES

GOVERNOR

INCUMBENTS

CANDIDATES

Affirmation

Should all the appropriate Senators signoff on the nominee, the process moves forward. The Senate Judiciary Committee has the nominee fill out a separate questionnaire and attend a public hearing before the committee to answer any inquiries arising from the Senators. Representatives from groups opposed and supportive of the nominee are permitted to testify. The report of the Supreme Court's Performance Evaluation Committee is available to the Senate Judiciary Committee for consideration in reappointments. The report of the Senate Judiciary Committee to the full senate is in writing, with the committee members' votes recorded. The vote in the full Senate is also recorded. Neither the committee members' votes nor the floor vote are accompanied by explanations. No Senator need publicly explain his or her vote. Upon the official Senate vote, the Governor makes the appointment official and the recruitment process is complete.

The model of judicial selection being tested in this monograph would predict that the New Jersey judicial recruitment process, on most occasions, possesses the attributes of a low articulation system. Governors and their close advisers control the initiation stage. Although the state and county bars assist in the screening along with the Governor, their role is clearly limited. They evaluate only those candidates the Governor gives them. Within this limited role, the leaders of the bar feel they have been somewhat effective.[36] At least it is rare when an appointment is made after a negative rating from the bar. The final affirmation is the clear responsibility of the Senate. Because of the sometimes prolonged initiation and screening stages, the advice and consent of the Senate is commonly a formality. Whatever partisan, political and personal conflicts arise are resolved by the time the formal affirmation stage arrives.

Accountable or Independent?

Two dimensions of independence are evident from our framework. First, a judicial appointee may be independent from the hue and cry of public concerns, facilitating rulings based on objective legal standards. This was one of the major motivations behind Vanderbilt's reforms:

> [T]he need of such independence seems self evident for the protection of individual and minority rights. The importance of the impartial enforcement of the law means that the judiciary should not be subject to any pressures, even those of the people.[37]

However, this independence may tempt judges to not only disregard the public but also to actively shape the law. It could permit judges to be activist in their jurisprudence. The New Jersey Supreme Court, reflecting this independ-

---

[36] See Sheldon, "The Role of State Bar Associations in Judicial Selection," 300.

[37] Vanderbilt, *Judges and Jurors*, p. 50.

ence, has been a leader in refining rights, in reaffirming and establishing public policy, and in shaping or disregarding precedent. These are all definitive attributes of an activist court.[38] The Justices of the New Jersey Supreme Court tend to drift toward a trustee role as a result of the independence the low articulation recruitment system encourages.

The other dimension of political independence concerns the degree of separation of the courts from the legislative and executive branches of government. In New Jersey judges at the trial level are obligated to the local legislator under senatorial courtesy; at the Supreme Court level they are more obligated to the Governor. However, once reappointed after the seven-year "probation" period, which most are, they have the security of life-time tenure until age 70. The recruitment process, the constitutional changes of 1947, the vigorous efforts of Chief Justice Vanderbilt and his successors, and the support of Governors, the legislature and the public have all contributed to recruiting independent minded jurists to the New Jersey benches. These political forces have New Jersey in the forefront of innovative state courts. As Tarr and Porter have correctly concluded:

> [T]he picture that emerges is of a court that has eagerly embraced opportunities to promulgate policy for the state and doctrine for the · nation, confident of its own abilities and of the legitimacy of the activist posture it has adopted.[39]

---

[38] Salmore and Salmore, *New Jersey Politics and Government,* p. 191, and G. Alan Tarr and Mary Cornelia Aldis Porter, *State Supreme Courts in State and Nation* (New Haven, CT: Yale University Press, 1988), p. 184.

[39] Ibid., pp. 185-186.

Chapter Seven

Merit Commission for the Recruitment of State Judges

At the turn of the Century, growing dissatisfaction with the politics that had taken over the selection of judges through the appointment and election processes prompted calls for reform. Appointments had too often led to extremes. Some appointments had shaped the courts into an elitist system, with only a select group of white males being elevated to state benches. Many of these judges were representatives of special interests such as the railroads. At the other extreme, in some jurisdictions political hacks, cronies and political has-beens were appointed to the refuge of state courts. In elected systems, partisanship had replaced qualifications as the overriding criterion for a judgeship. Political machines in larger metropolitan areas controlled public offices, including judgeships. Party slates were formed and subsequently confirmed by loyal party voters. A need for reform was apparent in many states.

Roscoe E. Pound, a young law professor at the University of Nebraska Law School, in an address before the 1906 convention of the American Bar Association reflected the discontent of the period. "Putting courts into politics, and compelling judges to become politicians, in many jurisdictions has almost destroyed the traditional respect for the bench."[1] In 1913, Ex-President William Howard Taft joined the reformers, condemning the practice of the election of judges and urged a return to the appointive system. The same year the American Judicature Society was established with selection reform as its primary goal. Northwestern University law professor Albert M. Kales, the Society's "director of drafting," proposed a unique system of judicial selection which combined several elements of elections and appointments. Kales initially proposed that the elected chief justice of the state's high bench be responsible for filling vacancies. The person appointed would serve a short period of probation and then go before the voters in an election where the question would be a simple "yes" or "no" concerning his or her retention. According to Kales:

> The appointment might be for a probationary period—say three years—at the end of which time the judge must submit at a popular election to a vote on the question as to whether the place which he holds shall be declared vacant. This is not a vote which puts anyone else in the judge's place, but a vote which can at most only leave the place to be filled by the appointing power.[2]

---

[1] Glenn R. Winters, "The Merit Plan for Judicial Selection and Tenure—Its Historical Development," in Glenn R. Winters (ed.), *Selected Readings: Judicial Selection and Tenure* (Chicago: American Judicature Society, 1973), p. 32.

Missing from the early version of what subsequently became known as the merit plan was a nominating commission. Composed of knowledgeable persons the commission would submit names of the best qualified candidates from which an elected official would pick the winner. However, Kales had suggested that a "judicial council" might have a "slight but reasonable control" over the appointments by the chief justice by compiling a list of eligible appointees from which the court's executive head would draw at least for every other appointment. Herbert Harley, a leader in the establishment of the American Judicature Society and its first secretary, proposed that the chief justice be required to select only from the judicial council's list of candidates. The plan was refined as the Society continued its efforts for acceptance of the reform.

In 1926 Harold J. Laski, noted lawyer and political writer, published an article in the **Michigan Law Review** proposing a version of the plan involving gubernatorial appointment of judges from a list formed by a special committee composed of sitting judges, the state attorney general, and the president of the state bar association.[3] His proposal broke the monopoly previously involving only judges in the nominating and appointing process. Later, as a compromise to gain the support of the Progressives, the idea of citizen participation in the nominating commission was integrated into the plan.

California was the first state in which reformers presented a version of the merit plan to voters. Californians rejected a form of the Kales proposal at the polls in 1934, but in the same election the state's voters accepted a scheme for recruiting appellate judges with a commission composed of the chief justice, the presiding judge of the court of appeals, and the attorney general. The Governor nominated and appointed, and the commission confirmed the appointment.[4]

In 1937 the American Bar Association joined the reform movement by endorsing the merit plan. The resolution passed by the House of Delegates outlined the modern version of the plan.

> WHEREAS, The importance of establishing methods of Judicial Selection that will be most conducive to the maintenance of the thoroughly qualified and independent judiciary and that will take the state judges out of politics as nearly as may be, is generally recognized, and
>
> WHEREAS, in many states movements are under way to find acceptable substitutes for direct election of judges, now, therefore, be it
>
> RESOLVED, By the House of Delegates of the American Bar Association, That in its judgment the following plan offers the most acceptable substitute available for direct election of judges:

---

[2] Ibid., 33.

[3] Harold J. Laski, "Techniques of Judicial Appointment," *Michigan Law Review* 24 (1926): 529.

[4] Dorothy W. Nelson, "Variations on a Theme—Selection and Tenure of Judges," *Southern California Law Review* 36 (1962): 4.

(a) The filling of vacancies by appointment by the executive or other elective official or officials, but from a list named by another agency, composed in part of high judicial officers and in part of other citizens, selected for that purpose, who will hold no other public office.

(b) If further check on appointments be desired, such check may be supplied by the requirement of confirmation by the State Senate or other legislative body of appointments made through the dual agency suggested.

(c) The appointee after a period of service should be eligible for reappointment periodically thereafter, or periodically go before the people upon his record, with no opposing candidate, the people voting upon the question "Shall Judge Blank be retained in office?"

In 1940 Missouri became the first state to adopt the Society's and ABA's three-step plan for all appeals and two trial courts.[5] Since then, Missouri has been the model for subsequent state merit plans. Missouri has three nominating commissions, one for appellate court nominations and one each for Jackson and St. Louis County circuit courts. Each county commission has five members serving overlapping six-year terms. Two lawyers are elected by bar members residing in the respective county jurisdictions. Two laypersons are appointed by the Governor and the appeals judge from the county jurisdiction serves *ex officio* as presiding officer of the commission. The appeals commission has seven members; three attorneys elected by lawyers from the three appeals court districts, three laypersons also residing in the respective appeals districts and appointed by the Governor, and the Chief Justice of the Supreme Court who presides.[6]

When vacancies occur the appropriate commission screens applicants and sends three names to the Governor, who must appoint from among the three submitted. After serving one year's probation, the appointee goes before the electorate at the next general election to retain the judgeship. The question before the voters is simply "Shall Judge ___ be retained in office?" If the response is "no," the commission meets and the process begins anew. Since 1940 thirty-five states have adopted some form of commission plans, established either by

---

[5] The definitive study of the Missouri Plan remains Richard A. Watson and Rondal G. Downing, *The Politics of the Bench and the Bar: Judicial Selection Under the Missouri Nonpartisan Court Plan* (New York: Wiley and Sons, 1969). A summary of current trends is Jona Goldschmidt, "Merit Selection: Current Status, Procedures, and Issues," *University of Miami Law Review* 49 (Fall, 1994): 1.

[6] Shortly after the 1940 adoption of the merit plan, an initiative to repeal the plan was placed on the ballot; the repeal was overwhelmingly rejected. A 1944 Constitutional Convention kept the provision, and a 1955 repeal measure was offered in the legislature but was lost in the House and never was submitted to the Senate.

constitution, statute or executive order.[7] Generally, all subsequent adoptions of the plan are similar to Missouri's.

From the beginning the purposes of the commission or merit plan were to: 1) remove the influence of political parties from the selection process; 2) improve the quality of those selected; and, 3) eliminate politics from the process. The goal was to give as much independence to judges as possible and still retain some accountability through the retention elections. In their pamphlet distributed to voters during the 1940 campaign for its adoption, the supporters of the plan in Missouri argued that:

> The Plan is designed to abolish the evils of the present primary elective system.

> Many men will be willing to serve on the bench under this Plan, who would not submit themselves to the ordeal of seeking office under the present political system.

> It will free our judges from demands upon their time from political sources.

> It should cause courts to function more efficiently.

> The Plan contains effective checks and balances. It is *not* an outright appointive system.

> It does not destroy the right of the people to have a voice in the selection of judges.

> It does, however, eliminate entirely the necessity of judges, from the courts affected, running in primary election against probably a dozen or more opponents.

> The Plan also makes it unnecessary for a judge to run against an opponent in the general election. The judge will run solely on his record, and his name will appear on a separate judicial ballot without party designation.[8]

Advocates agree that a number of benefits can be attributed to the merit plan.[9] The initiation process is enhanced through the nominating commission's efforts to assure wide-open application procedures. The screening phase is thorough with the lawyers on the commission providing expert judgment on the

---

[7] American Judicature Society, *Judicial Merit Selection: Current Status* (Chicago: American Judicature Society, 1994).

[8] For argument's favoring the merit plan see Winters, "The Merit Plan for Judicial Selection and Tenure," pp. 43-44.

[9] These arguments follow Philip L. Dubois, *From Ballot to Bench: Judicial Elections and the Quest for Accountability* (Austin, Tx.: University of Texas Press, 1980), pp. 8-20.

legal talents of prospective nominees. The laypersons serving on the committee add a citizen's view, assuring consideration of pertinent factors other than narrow legal competency. Figure 7.1 sets forth the various qualifications the commission members weigh when evaluating candidates.

Figure 7.1

COMMISSION EVALUATION CRITERIA
(Ranked in order of Importance)

Background Criteria	*Professional Skills*	*Character, and Personality Criteria*
Mental health*	Reputation for integrity	Not susceptible to influence
Physical health*	Fairness	Moral courage
Prior judicial experience	Professional reputation	Open-minded
Law school record	Prepared and thorough	Emotionally stable
Knowledge of community	Knowledge of procedure	Desire to be judge
Professional activities	Abreast legal development	Decisive
Supervising skills	Communication skills	Considerate
Prosecuting experience	Trial experience	Self-disciplined
Civic activities		Courteous
Law school		Patient
		Punctual
		Industrious
		Empathetic

* The American with Disabilities Act appears to prevent commissions from asking for documentation regarding mental and physical health. See Jona Goldschmidt, "Merit Selection: Current Status, Procedures, and Issues."

Source: Adapted from Allan Ashman and James J. Alfini, *The Key to Judicial Merit Selection: The Nominating Process.* (Chicago: American Judicature Society, 1974), pp. 62, 64, 66.

The Governor's participation serves to infuse the few political and partisan criteria that are, in any case, virtually unavoidable. The panel itself serves to diffuse the political pressure bearing on the Governor. Because of the commission's initiating and screening activities the Governor is compelled to appoint well qualified persons to the state benches, and consequently he/she can avoid the purely patronage demands that might otherwise predominate.

The retention election assures longer tenure for the judges, providing security and thereby judicial independence. Highly qualified lawyers who ordinarily would not leave a successful legal practice for an indeterminate stint on the bench may be drawn to a judgeship under these more predictable circumstances. Judges can also focus on judging and not be distracted by unseemly re-election campaigns. There will be no need for expending the time and effort to raise money to convince voters of their qualifications.

The public is still involved in the recruitment process, thereby assigning a democratic legitimacy to the process and to those selected and providing some public accountability.

> Although incapable of making an informed judgment on the professional qualifications of those seeking judicial office, the voters are said to be able to remove judges who have demonstrated inferior or unethical behavior while on the bench during their probationary period.[10]

Generally, it is argued that the merit plan pulls together all of the better aspects of all the other plans into a balanced, logical reform package; nomination by experts, appointment by an elected official, and election by the people appears to achieve the kind of balance between accountability and independence that arises from the "judge's dilemma."

Despite the attractions of the merit plan as touted by its supporters, critics remain. It is argued that it is not clear that politics has been eliminated from the selection process with the advent of the merit plan. Rather, politics has simply changed in form and comes to bear at different times in the process. Although the influence of political parties has been minimized at the nonpartisan retention election stage, partisanship is felt in the selection of members to the nominating commission and in the Governor's final appointment to the bench. The political party affiliation of appointees to the commission is often of concern to the chief executive. Having a voice in the nominating commission permits the Governor to have influence early on in the recruitment sequence. Additionally, appointments to the commission provide an opportunity for the Governor to dispense a bit of patronage. Because of the potential for partisan abuses, many states have defined the ratio between Democrats and Republicans on the nominating commission. For example, the Nebraska Supreme Court and district court commissions can have no more than two of the four members appointed by the Governor, and not more than two of the four members elected by attorneys, of the same political party. The terms for commission members are staggered and ordinarily do not coincide with the Governor's term, preventing complete dominance by one Governor in at least his or her first term. Also, a commission member cannot hold another public office and can serve only two terms.[11]

---

[10] Ibid., p. 8.

Besides the politics of partisanship, critics also argue that the politics of the organized legal profession is brought to bear on the selection of commission members. Commonly, the plaintiffs' bar competes with the civil defense bar for spots on the commission. Influence, status and a competitive edge are the rewards for attorney membership.[12] Indeed, having a sympathetic judge on the bench, or at least one that is not antagonistic toward the causes of their clients, drives the attorneys to get involved in commission politics.

Critics point out that political maneuvering is not uncommon in the commission's deliberations. Some nominating commission members have admitted that political influences permeate their deliberations, and many regard these influences as important.[13] For example, bargaining over the three names to be sent to the Governor, logrolling and vote swapping constitute the more crass aspects of the political maneuvering. Depending upon the situation, "the panel of names sent to the Governor might be 'rigged' or 'loaded'" so as "to force the Governor to choose a particular nominee" who might have been the favorite of the majority faction of the commissioners. Placing two unacceptable nominees on a list with a third that is less unacceptable to the Governor rigs the results. On the other hand, circumstances arise wherein the Governor lets it be known whom he wants to pick and those whom he has appointed to the commission may accommodate.[14]

Few deny that the Governor, although limited in his or her choice, applies political criteria in judging the three nominees submitted by the nominating commission. Assuming that the three are nearly equal in terms of qualifications, the one most politically attractive receives the Governor's nod. Geography, political party affiliation, gender, racial-ethnic criteria, and policy views are not altogether unacceptable factors to be considered by the chief executive.[15]

Balanced against the assertion that under the merit plan there is no need to take the time, effort and money for campaigning for office is another consideration especially relevant to a democratic system. The trials and tribulations of the

---

[11] Allan Ashman and James J. Alfini, *The Key to Judicial Merit Selection: The Nominating Process* (Chicago: American Judicature Society, 1974).

[12] Lawyers are either elected to the nominating commission by colleagues, appointed by bar leaders, or they are nominated by the governing board of the bar. See Charles H. Sheldon, "The Role of State Bar Associations in Judicial Selection," *Judicature* 77 (1994): 300.

[13] Alfini and Ashman found that 49% of the commissioners they surveyed recognized political considerations as part of their deliberations, but only 36% of these thought them important (*The Key to Judicial Merit Selection*, p. 76). In a more recent study, only 21% felt that political considerations were involved. When involved, 51% of the commissioners thought politics was decisive or of some importance in their deliberations. See Joanne Martin, *Merit Selection Commissions: What Do They Do? How Effective Are They?* (Chicago: American Bar Foundation, 1993).

[14] Dubois, *From Ballot to Bench*, p. 11.

[15] Glick refers to such selections as "symbolic appointments." See Henry R. Glick, *Courts, Politics and Justice* (New York: McGraw Hill, 1993), pp. 123-124.

campaign trail go "hand in hand with service to the country" and replacing these efforts with a remote and uninforming retention election does not guarantee a "dramatic improvement in public service or public servants."[16] Public officials in a democracy ought to gain office as the result of a democratic selection process. Additionally, courts and the law they symbolize depend upon voluntary compliance. People support courts and the law primarily because they have confidence in them. Having chosen the judges themselves in an elective system gives them a responsibility and a commitment to those they have had the opportunity to elect. This public sense of responsibility for those on the bench is not entirely absent, but it is greatly diminished in the merit system.

Perhaps some highly qualified lawyers are reluctant to submit themselves to the tribulations of a public campaign, but others are not. It has yet to be shown that those willing to campaign are less—or more—qualified than those who remain reluctant. Also, in rare cases merit plan judges have had to campaign vigorously to counter an organized effort to vote them out of office. These campaigns have been as expensive and hard fought as in contested partisan or nonpartisan races. The recruitment of judges is an inescapably political exercise from beginning to end no matter what the process. It cannot be expected that politics can be eliminated from the process, nor perhaps should it be. Judges make important decisions affecting public policy and political affairs. Politics, then, ought to be involved in their selection. Thus, the political maneuverings, subterranean and muted, permeating the commission plan process may not be a crippling drawback. To its credit, none of those jurisdictions that have adopted the merit plan have returned to the method it had replaced, and the extent of merit plan adoption has gradually increased over the years. Additionally, the use of nominating commissions is not unknown to the federal system. Whatever its drawbacks may be, the merit plan continues to be an attractive alternative mode of selection for recruiting judges to state benches.

Some studies are available which suggest that some tendencies can be attributed to the selection outcomes of the merit plan. Research has repeatedly confirmed that the merit system provides considerable security to judges. Incumbency virtually assures victory in retention elections. Of the over 2,000 retention elections held over the years throughout the United States, in only 1.3% of these has an incumbent been removed from office.[17] Although the need for campaign funds is not absent from some retention campaigns, comparatively speaking, far less money is needed than in other judicial election contests.[18] Background data suggest that perhaps as argued by merit plan supporters, a

---

[16] William Burnett, "Observations on the Direct Election Method of Judicial Selection," *Texas Law Review* 44 (1966): 1101; quoted in Dubois, *From Ballot to Bench*, p. 12.

[17] Robert C. Luskin, et al.; "How Minority Judges Fare in Retention Elections," *Judicature* 77 (1994): 316.

[18] Larry T. Aspin and William K. Hall, "Retention Elections and Judicial Behavior," *Judicature* 77 (1994): 306.

more "professional" lawyer is recruited to the bench. When compared with other selection systems, merit judges are "less likely to have had high levels of political activity before joining their courts." Also, fewer have held elective political office prior to the judgeship.[19] Although partially a product of the culture of the state, merit selection tends to bring more judges with Protestant religious backgrounds to state benches.[20]

Studies on diversity on the bench only recently have attributed some success to merit plans. In 1993, an American Judicature Society study found that "the largest proportion of African Americans (32%) and women (35%) attained judicial office through the merit plan."[21] However, it is the commitment of the appointing official and the diversity of the nominating commission that make the difference rather than any of the mechanics of the formal process involved.[22] Little evidence is available "that the judges' race or ethnicity played any significant part in his or her loss" in retention elections.[23]

Although most scholars conclude that, thus far, there is no "relationship between mode of judicial selection and judges' political attitudes or orientations to the judicial role," some tentative behavioral tendencies have been isolated.[24] For example, despite the remote chance of being removed from office in retention elections, judges generally agree that persons vote on the basis of the judges' performance on the bench.[25] Apparently judges can influence retention elections by striving to be open-minded, courteous, competent and emotionally stable.[26] The dissent rate of elected appellate judges tends to decrease in cases

---

[19] John M. Scheb II, "State Appellate Judges' Attitudes toward Judicial Merit Selection and Retention," *Judicature* 72 (1988): 174.

[20] Henry R. Glick and Craig F. Emmert, "Selection Systems and Judicial Characteristics: The Recruitment of State Supreme Court Justices," *Judicature* 70 (1987): 228.

[21] "African-American Judges Currently Serving on State Courts of Last Resort and Intermediate Appellate Courts," American Judicature Society study quoted in Goldschmidt, "Merit Selection: Current Status, Procedures and Issues," p. 66.

[22] In Florida "[T]he reality is that...more minorities have been appointed to the bench than have been elected, notwithstanding the composition of the commissions." Leander Shaw, Jr., "Florida's Judicial Merit Selection and Retention System: The Better Alternative," *Florida State University Law Review* 20 (1992): 287. Twenty-eight of the 39 Black or Hispanic judges on circuit and county courts were originally appointed while the remainder were elected. The Florida Bar, "Merit Selection and Retention," 1994. A 1986 study by the Fund for Modern Courts, Inc. reported that the merit system and executive appointments resulted in more women and minorities on state benches. Nonpartisan election and legislative appointment had the worse record. The membership of merit commissions is still dominated by white male lawyers, with only 25% women and, as of 1990, less than 10% minorities. Beth Henschen, Robert Moog and Steven Davis, "Judicial Nominating Commissioners: A National Profile," *Judicature* 73 (1990): 329.

[23] Luskin, "How Minority Justice Fare in Retention Elections," p. 321.

[24] Scheb, "State Appellate Judges' Attitudes toward Judicial Merit Selection and Retention," 174.

[25] Aspin and Hall, "Retention Elections and Judicial Behavior," 315.

involving high profile issues such as the death penalty, but remains low in appointed judges.[27] These tendencies would pull both ways in merit plan systems, involving as they do both elections and appointment. It would seem, given the security of the bench and the lack of time demands from campaigning, that merit plan judges would be more efficient. However, "there is no apparent distinction" between merit plan and elected judges in rate of case termination. Nor is there a difference in the time involved to reach a termination."[28]

Over the years the average affirmative vote for retention election judges has been 77%, but it has gradually declined. The decrease has been attributed to the waning trust in government generally.[29] Although roll-off is high, retention election voters stay with the list of judicial candidates rather than suffering voter fatigue as they vote for candidates near the end of the judicial ballot. Voters do not differentiate between judges running in the same district; if one receives a high retention vote, the other will also be supported at the same high rate. The difference between participation in retention elections in presidential years and off-years is negligible. Many of the tendencies in voter behavior in retention elections point toward voters having few cues to assist them in casting their judicial ballots.[30]

The original intent of the merit plan was to put together a procedure that borrowed the better aspects of existing selection methods. The result was a compromise involving nomination by experts, appointment by elected officials, and ultimate confirmation by voters. As with all workable compromises, a balance between costs and benefits is reached. The record for the merit plan is both as anticipated by its supporters and as argued by its critics. However, in an effort to account for local political and legal culture and to refine the plan, variations have been developed which make it risky to generalize from any one state's version of the merit plan or to conclude from the results of a number of states that may have subtle differences in their plans. Nonetheless, the experiences in Florida may provide clues that the merit plan may or may not provide concerning the balance between accountability and independence.

---

[26] Kenyon N. Griffin and Michael J. Horan, "Practicing Attorneys and Judicial Retention Elections: Judging the Judges in Wyoming," *Judicature* 69 (1985): 42.

[27] Paul Brace and Melinda Gann Hall, "Integrated Models of Judicial Dissent," *Journal of Politics* 55 (1993): 919.

[28] David A. Crynes, "The Electoral Connection and the Pace of Litigation in Kansas," *Judicature* 79 (1995): 246.

[29] William K. Hall and Larry T. Aspin, "What Twenty Years of Judicial Retention Elections Have Told Us," in Elliot E. Slotnick (ed.), *Judicial Politics: Readings from Judicature* (Chicago: American Judicature Society, 1992), p. 68.

[30] Ibid., See also Kenyon N. Griffin and Michael J. Horan, "Merit Retention Elections: What Influences the Voters?" *Judicature* 63 (1979): 79.

Florida and the Merit Plan

Since the ratification of the 1838 constitution, Florida has experienced a variety of judicial selection methods. Initially, the state's general assembly appointed all judges to five-year terms. After reappointment, judges served for life constrained only by a "good behavior" provision. In 1852, under pressure from the populists and reflecting the influence of Jacksonian democracy, Florida amended the constitution to require the popular election of trial judges. Reconstruction brought with it gubernatorial appointments, with legislative confirmation. For trial judges this "federal model" remained until 1942, at which time the popular election of trial judges was reinstated. However, as early as 1885 Supreme Court justices had been selected by popular elections. After nearly a century of electing judges, Florida amended its constitution in 1972, and again four years later, to institute and refine the merit plan for the recruitment of appellate judges.[31]

The Florida Supreme Court is composed of seven justices, serving six-year terms in a state-wide jurisdiction. The intermediate appeals bench, the District Court of Appeals is composed of 61 judges who sit in three-judge panels, serving six-year terms representing five district jurisdictions. All appellate jurists are recruited under the merit plan. The Circuit Courts are the trial courts of general jurisdiction, representing 20 circuits. The 421 circuit judges run in nonpartisan elections for six-year terms. However, most of them are products of gubernatorial appointments used to fill interim vacancies.[32] The Governor appoints from a list supplied by merit plan nominating commissions. To keep their trial judgeships, the appointees must run in nonpartisan elections at the next general election and possibly face a challenger. In the 67 counties, 250 judges serve four-year terms on county courts of limited jurisdiction. They, like the circuit judges, must run in nonpartisan elections, but interim appointments to vacancies are made by the Governor who picks from a list of three names submitted by a nominating commission. Thus, the trial courts enjoy only the nominating commission part of the merit plan for interim appointments when resignation, promotion, removal or death create a vacancy.

Even though most of the trial judges have been appointed after screening by a nominating commission, nearly every legislative session since 1976 has experienced an effort, as yet unsuccessful, to extend the full merit plan to cover the lower courts. The Florida Bar and its local counterparts have continued to push vigorously for extending the full merit plan to trial benches. The main problem appears to be the reluctance on the part of voters at the local level "to give up their vote." For supporters of the reform, this reluctance arises because

[31] The Florida Bar had been instrumental in the approval of the 1976 amendment. Madison B. McClellan, "Merit Appointment vs. Popular Election: A Reformer's Guide to Judicial Selection Methods in Florida," *Florida Law Review* 43 (1991): 529.

[32] For example, in 1992 60% of the circuit judges had gained their judgeships through appointments to a vacancy. Shaw, "Florida's Judicial Merit Selection and Retention System," p. 284.

the public doesn't understand how the plan works and a greater emphasis needs to be placed on public education.

Figure 7.2

FLORIDA COURT SYSTEM

Prior to the 1976 change a nominating commission assisted the Governor in appointing judges to appellate vacancies, but at the next general election all appointees had to run in competitive nonpartisan elections. Now, Article 5, secs. 10 and 11 of the Florida Constitution read:

> Any justice of the Supreme Court or any judge of a district court of appeal may qualify for retention by a vote of the electors in the general election next preceding the expiration of his term.... If a justice...or judge...is ineligible or fails to qualify for retention a vacancy shall exist....

> The Governor shall fill each vacancy on the Supreme Court or on a district Court of Appeals by appointing for a term ending...in January of the year following the next general election occurring at least one year after the date of appointment, one of not fewer than three persons nor more than six persons nominated by the appropriate judicial nominating commission.

The major reason for instituting the merit plan was explained in **Spector v. Glisson**, 305 So. 2d 777 (1974). In the opinion the Florida Supreme Court explained that the merit plan did not restrain the voters, but rather the Governor. The chief executive would no longer be able to use appointments as a "pork barrel" to make "purely political appointments" without regard for qualification and ability. "It was sometimes facetiously said in former years that the best qualification to become a judge was to be a friend of the Governor." The merit plan will do away with the "kind of selection which some people referred to as 'picking a judge merely because he was a friend or political supporter of the Governor'..."[33] However, recently some flexibility was returned to the Governor. On November 5, 1996, Florida voters approved the first amendment to Article V, section 11 and 12 requiring the appropriate nominating commission to submit to the Governor an expanded list of up to six names. The rationale for the change was to give a "Governor a better range of choices" as well as making it "harder for a nominating commission to stack the deck in favor of one candidate by nominating a favored candidate along with two marginally qualified or unpopular candidates."[34]

Each of the six Judicial Nominating Commissions (JNCs)—one for the Supreme Court and five for the various District Courts of Appeal—is composed of nine commissioners.[35] Three lawyers are appointed by the Board of Governors of the Florida Bar, three are appointed by the Governor, and these six commission members in turn elect the three non-lawyer members. Commissioners are appointed for staggered, four-year terms. The 20 circuit nominating commissions are similarly composed, and they are used only when the Governor appoints to vacancies on the circuit and county benches. By law, the Governor

---

[33] **Spector v. Glisson,** 305 So.2d 777 (1974) p. 783.

[34] *News Journal* Web Edition, October 30, 1996.

[35] The Supreme Court Nominating Commission also nominates statewide prosecutors who are appointed by the Attorney General.

must choose from among the three to six names submitted by each of the appellate and trial JNCs.

Party affiliation of commission appointees is not to be a consideration, but it is a factor in the Governor's selections. Competition for appointments to the Supreme Court and appeals court commissions is very keen. The Governor's office receives between 10 and 15 applicants for one commissioner's slot. Each applicant responds to a questionnaire, sends letters of recommendation to the Governor's office, and needs to receive a number of telephone endorsements to be competitive. Gubernatorial appointments to circuit and county commissions vary considerably in the number of willing and available applicants. Commission members must devote considerable time and effort to carrying out nominating commission responsibilities, without remuneration except for travel costs and per diem. In some counties the number of applicants gives the Governor some choice, while in others the Governor's office has to generate a name or names in order to fill a commission vacancy. Although there is no rule, the Governor usually appoints at least one attorney out of the three spots on the commissions.

On the average, lawyer applicants for appointment by the bar's governing board number around ten per Supreme Court commission vacancy. Campaigning for the appointment involves accompanying the application form with letters of endorsement, professional resumes, and extended written explanations generated by the lengthy application form. Announcements of vacancies for the additional three laypersons appointed by the six bar and gubernatorial members are widely circulated. Non-lawyer applicants have numbered as high as 25 and as low as four for an appellate JNC vacancy. Interviews of prospective members are common and each of the five references listed on the 5-page application form is contacted and questioned concerning the applicant's qualifications.

Diversity is a factor to be considered in all appointments to the JNCs. Until the provision was declared unconstitutional by a federal court, Florida law required that at least one out of three commissioners selected by the Governor as well as those selected by the bar or the commission, "must be a member of a racial or ethnic minority group or a woman."[36]

Initiation

Judicial vacancies are announced in attorney publications, in principal newspapers and in specialized publications, with notices including deadlines for applications and the address of the Judicial Nominating Commission to which formal

---

[36] Florida Statutes, 43.29. In July, 1995, a Federal district judge declared the requirement of one-third of the JNC's membership to be minorities or women unconstitutional as a race and gender based quota. The state had failed to present a compelling state interest for the quota. (**Murphy** v. **Harkness,** CIV-95-8319). However, without the requirement it was felt that "women had a slim chance of being appointed...and appointments of blacks were non-existent." Marcia Coyle, "Quotas on Judicial Panels Struck Down," *The National Law Journal* (August 7, 1995): A6.

applications are to be made. A letter of intent is accompanied by responses to a 16-page questionnaire and a waiver of confidentiality of personal records as required by the commission. Supreme Court JNC members do not solicit applicants although Court of Appeals and Circuit JNCs may request persons to apply and the Governor's office and numerous interested groups do urge preferred individuals to file applications. The process tends to encourage self-initiated applicants, however. The only requirement is that they be in good standing with the unified Florida Bar and have practiced law for at least ten years (five years for circuit and county courts). Each applicant receives copies of the rules of the particular commission and a general summary of how the commission works. Depending upon the jurisdiction involved, approximately two dozen may apply for one of the state-wide Supreme Court slots, and about a dozen for high bench positions that represent a district jurisdiction. Applicant numbers remain high for most District Court of Appeals spots but vary widely for circuit appointments.

Screening

Applicants waive confidentiality of such materials as disciplinary records with the state bar and the Florida Board of Bar Examiners, credit records, records with any law enforcement agency, records from the Judicial Qualifications Commission and, if applicable, information from the FBI. The files of the applicants are dispersed equally among the JNC members to review the records and make inquiries of references, judges and bar associations. The members of the JNCs attempt to interview as many applicants as possible, but ordinarily only about a dozen of the top applicants are invited to participate. Those dropped from consideration would be for incomplete files, failure to meet deadlines, unqualified because of years in practice, a lack of residency in appropriate jurisdiction, inadequate or questionable credentials. Applicants on the "short list" are then invited to appear before the commission "to respond to questions...designed to determine the fitness of the applicant to serve" on a particular court.[37] Any negative information a commission member may possess concerning an applicant is revealed to the entire membership prior to the interview.

In reviewing the records and in inquiries at the interview, the JNCs look at personal attributes such as "Personal integrity," "Standing in the community," "Sobriety," "Moral conduct," and the like. Also weighed in deliberation are "Competency and experience," e.g., health, intelligence, professional reputation, and knowledge of law and courts. "Judicial capabilities" are measured and involve such matters as patience, impartiality, courtesy and civility. Upon the completion of the interviews (some candidates may be asked to return for fur-

---

[37] *Supreme Court Judicial Nominating Commission Rules of Procedure* (January 9, 1995), p. 3. See also *In re Advisory Opinion to the Governor*, 600 So 2d 460 (1992).

ther questioning) the commission votes on who is to be among the list of three to six.[38] At the end of this process:

> The names of such three (3) [to six (6)]...shall be certified to the Governor in alphabetical order and a copy of all written investigative information and documents relating to each such nominees shall be delivered in person by the chair or designee.[39]

On occasion in the past some JNCs went beyond simply evaluating appli-cants. Each commission developed its own rules of procedure, some of which were not made part of the public record. One-on-one communications between applicants and commissioners existed and sometimes contacts between commis-sioners and the Governor's office during the screening process occurred. Com-missioners would "disclose, publicly or privately, [their] relative preferences" out of the three to six names submitted.[40] Lobbying was possible, and opportu-nities for informal compromises were available as well. As a consequence, the final list of names submitted to the Governor may not have been the result of the independent and objective screening by JNCs. As a result of the **ex parte** con-tacts between commissioners, interested parties, and the Governor, although admittedly rare, and upon recommendations by a special bench/bar commission, rules were recently changed.[41] Such direct contacts between commission mem-bers and applicants are now regarded as misconduct, leading to dismissal from the commission. Also, commissioners must not initiate communications with the Governor's office concerning applicants. However, if the Governor contacts members of a commission, they are permitted to respond. It remains unclear whether the Governor can inquire about relative strengths of the three to six nominees submitted by the JNCs.[42] The several JNCs are commonly under the

---

[38] The Supreme Court JNC votes in a series of balloting until the names are winnowed down to the required number. Other commissions rely on a simple majority vote.

[39] *Supreme Court Judicial Nominating Commission Rules*, p. 5. The JNCs responsible for nomi-nating judges for the District Court of Appeals and Circuit Courts follow closely the procedures of the Supreme Court's commission. Appeals court rules have added an admonition that inquiries are made concerning any membership in organizations with restrictive membership clauses. The commissions also may actively seek interested candidates for vacancies. Voting procedures vary slightly, and the circuit JNCs have a bit more flexibility in establishing local rules. Although all commission records and candidate files are deposited with the Florida Bar, a special JNC Coordi-nator with the bar is primarily concerned with Supreme Court nomination matters.

[40] Alan T. Dimond, "Judicial Merit Selection: A Legislative Odyssey," *The Florida Bar Journal*, (May 1993): 8.

[41] The Supreme Court of Florida and The Florida Bar, "The Necessities of the Times," *The Report of the Bench/Bar Commission* (January, 1993).

[42] "[N]o Commissioner shall contact the Governor...or any member of...[his or her] office or staffs for the purpose of further influencing the Governor's...ulitmate decision. However, if contacted by the Governor...or [his or her] office or staffs, a Commissioner shall be entitled to answer questions about each nominee. No attempt should be made to rank nominees or otherwise disclose prefer-

influence of attorneys. The three commissioners appointed by the bar are always attorneys, the three appointed by the Governor nearly always include attorneys, and these six elect the three lay commissioners.

The Florida Bar provides a variety of services in the screening process. It assists the nominating commissions in their reviews, and also assists the voters during retention elections. The bar is also the repository of all the records of the Supreme Court's JNC. The bar's Judicial Nominating Procedures Committee conducts educational and training seminars for commission members, publishes a handbook for each of the members of the 26 nominating commissions, and also publishes an information brochure for each applicant for judgeships. The committee also coordinates rules changes for the JNCs. Local commissions do have local rules, but they are not to be inconsistent with the state-wide uniform rules.

The Florida Bar's Judicial Evaluation Committee conducts a poll of the 42,000 in-state bar members, soliciting preferences for retention of Supreme Court and Court of Appeals incumbents. Lawyers are encouraged to respond only if they have some knowledge of the incumbents. In 1994, a total of 6,219 lawyers returned surveys in the appellate judges' retention poll.[43] Since the merit plan began, voters have followed what the bar recommends. Table 7.1 reports the average levels of support from the bar and the average retention vote.

Table 7.1

BAR POLLS AND RETENTION VOTING RATES

Year	Bar Poll % for Retention	Voter Retention %
1978	81%	64%
1980	84%	70%
1982	89%	72%
1984	90%	72%
1986	85%	76%
1988	90%	75%
1990	90%	70%
1992	86%	67%*

*1992 calculated on average range between 60% to 74%

ence of the Commission. Section VIII, "Ethical Considerations," *Supreme Court Nominating Commission Rules*, p. 8.

[43] Since 1978 all incumbent judges and justices have been supported in the polls and all the jurists were successful in the retention election. Three categories are reported in the polls. The percentage result on "retain" or "not retain" of attorney respondents who "Have Considerable Knowledge" of the candidates are separated from those who "Have Limited Knowledge." A combined grand total is also reported.

A "voters' pamphlet" with biographies of all appeals judges facing a retention election is also published by the Bar's Judicial Evaluation Committee. With encouragement and advice from the state organization, some county bars also conduct evaluations prior to the nonpartisan elections, releasing the results to the media and interested civic groups such as the League of Women Voters and PTAs.

The overall efforts of the Florida Bar are regarded as fairly effective although the retention polling is often viewed as a popularity contest which depends too heavily on how the print and electronic media publicize the results. At the trial level a poor showing in the bar poll may cause a judge to not seek reelection. Those circuit and county judges with evaluations of 70% or less favorable rating are perceived as vulnerable and may draw opposition at the next judicial race. The major influence of lawyers on recruitment comes from their participation in the JNCs and the individual efforts made in the circuit and county nonpartisan elections.[44]

The Governor's office receives from the particular nominating commission the application questionnaire containing data on personal background, professional experience, and references. Writing samples are included as well. The application is accompanied in some cases with hundreds of letters of recommendation, endorsing phone calls, and supporter appeals. The Governor's office keeps a computerized tabulation of the supporters' names, titles and relevant comments. An independent investigation is conducted, duplicating much of the JNC's screening. The data are gathered from law enforcement agencies, Florida Bar records, the Judicial Qualifications Commission, other judges, lawyers and relevant persons familiar with the nominee. The Governor's counsel schedules an appointment with the three to six nominees for Supreme Court and court of appeals appointments, the materials are summarized for the Governor, and a personal interview with the chief executive is conducted. At this point in the screening, the interview is largely a get acquainted session designed to measure the degree of rapport obtaining between the Governor and the nominee. Rarely are circuit and county court nominees interviewed.

Affirmation

Within 60 days after receiving the list of names from the relevant JNC the Governor announces the appointment. The appointee serves at least one year, then becomes subject to a retention "yes" or "no" vote at the next general election. The retention election is repeated every six years thereafter for judges on the appellate benches. Circuit and county court judges are affirmed in nonpartisan contested elections.

Voter participation in retention elections varies, of course, but in a contentious election involving Justice Leander Shaw Jr. in 1990, 85% of the voters cast

---

[44] Sheldon, "The Role of State Bar Associations in Judicial Selection," 301.

a retention ballot; the judge retained his seat by nearly a 60% favorable vote.[45] Contestedness, of course, is nonexistent in retention elections, but even the non-partisan elections for circuit and county races incumbents are rarely contested and, rarer still, are incumbents defeated. Table 7.2 summarizes retention returns for 1990, 1992 and 1994 in the uncontested races for the Supreme Court.

Table 7.2

PARTICIPATION AND COMPETITIVENESS—SUPREME COURT

Year	Total Vote	Average Supreme Court Vote	Participation %	Percent "retain"
1990	3,623,327	3,069,837	84.7%	59.6%
1992	5,438,612	4,106,687	75.5%	64.0%
1994	4,305,340	3,368,397	78.2%	66.5%

---

[45] Shaw, "Florida's Judicial Merit Selection and Retention System," 286-287.

Figure 7.3

FLORIDA RECRUITMENT ACTORS

Formal Participants   **Advisory Participants**

AFFIRMATION

GOVERNOR
Appointments

VOTERS
Retention and Nonpartisan Elections

SCREENING

OFFICE OF THE GOVERNOR
Governor's Counsel

JUDICIAL NOMINATING
COMMISSIONS

                                    Florida (and County) Bar
                                    Associations
                                    Judicial Evaluation Committees
                                    Polls-Voters' Pamphlets

INITIATION

JUDICIAL NOMINATING
COMMISSIONS

GOVERNOR
Governor's Counsel

CANDIDATES

INCUMBENTS

Level of Articulation

Despite a high participation rate, the uncontested nature of the retention elections, and the low competitive aspect as confirmed by the overwhelming favorable "yes" vote, suggest a low articulation recruitment system. As intended by its advocates, Florida's merit plan has contributed to a fairly independent judiciary. Public or political accountability pressures are felt at the screening stage, but they are limited to the considerations attorneys may express in the nominating commissions and the political concerns of the Governor in choosing among the three choices presented to him or her. Once affirmed, any accountability pressures would be only those to which the judge wishes to yield.

The Florida Bar focuses much of its effort in educating the public on how the merit plan works and pointing out its values. Perhaps the success of its efforts would be measured by whether the legislature and the voters finally accept the full merit plan for recruitment of judges on the circuit and county benches as well.

Chapter Eight

Federal Judicial Recruitment

Article II, s. 2, cl.2 of the Federal Constitution provides that the President "shall nominate, and by and with the Advice and Consent of the Senate, shall appoint" Justices to the Supreme Court and other federal judges. Over time, this apparently simple constitutional provision has evolved into an often diverse and complicated recruitment process. Similar to state recruitment, analysis of the full range of federal judicial recruitment can be used to explain the initial perceptions of newly appointed federal judges toward independence and accountability.

Although all federal appointments are governed by Article II, s. 2, variation in the recruitment process clearly exists within and among the three levels of the federal court system. For instance, one appointment at the federal trial level may show signs of a fairly moderate articulation experience while another appointment in the very same jurisdiction may engage but a few participants, resulting in a low articulation recruitment process. Arguably, those candidates who survive the two contrasting processes would likely hold different views about the proper role of federal judges in a constitutional democracy.

Despite variation in the level of articulation, the number of actors remains constant in federal recruitment whether the vacancy is on the District, Circuit, or Supreme Court level. The effectiveness and thoroughness of these actors may vary, depending upon the President's style, the partisan make-up of the Senate, and the level for which the nominee is being considered. For instance, the President may take a direct, publicly stated personal interest in a candidate for an appointment, especially to the Supreme Court. In the case of lower court vacancies, however, Presidents frequently leave initiation and screening to others in the executive branch. At the district (federal trial court) level, the home state Senator from the President's party plays a decisive role in the selection of the state's district judge, but this same Senator's vote is simply one out of 100 when the confirmation vote on a Supreme Court nominee is taken in the full Senate.

Figure 8.1

FEDERAL COURT SYSTEM

UNITED STATES SUPREME COURT

9 Justices

Appointed by President with advice and consent of Senate
Life-time tenure with "good behavior"

U.S. COURTS OF APPEALS

11 Circuit Courts   1 D C Circuit   1 Federal Circuit

179 Judges

Appointed by President with advice and consent of Senate
Life-time tenure with "good behavior"

FEDERAL DISTRICT COURTS

94 Districts   649 Judges

Appointed by President with advice and consent of Senate
(Senatorial Courtesy)
Life-time tenure with "good behavior"

U.S. Court of International Trade
7 Judges
Appointed by President with advice and consent of Senate
Life-time tenure with "good behavior"

Legislative Courts

U.S. Court of Federal Claims	U.S. Court of Appeals for Armed Forces	U.S. Tax Court	U.S. Court of Veterans Appeal
16 Judges	5 Judges	19 Judges	3-7 Judges
15-year term	15-year term	15-year term	15-year term
Legislative Courts appointed by President with advice and consent of Senate			

Although the American Bar Association's Standing Committee on the Federal Judiciary screens all federal nominations, it scrutinizes candidates for lower court vacancies somewhat less scrupulously than Supreme Court candidates. In addition, the committee is given varying levels of encouragement, depending upon its relationship with the Senate Judiciary Committee and, more importantly, the President. The Senate Judiciary Committee screens for the full Senate on all nominees, but the Committee's willingness to scrutinize nominees in depth increases exponentially at each higher court level. Moreover, the existence of divided government may further increase its willingness to investigate candidates' political and jurisprudential philosophies carefully. The Federal Bureau of Investigation screens all candidates for possible legal violations, personal indiscretions, or moral lapses. Although the FBI's clearance process remains fixed, its sensitivity increases and its investigation broadens as the jurisdiction of the vacant position enlarges. The U.S. Attorney General, usually in the person of his or her Deputy in charge of appointments, initiates and screens for the President. More recently, the White House Counsel's office has become an important player in judicial appointments.

These diverse actors in the federal recruitment process can usually be found engaged to some degree in all federal appointments, but their intensity and effectiveness varies significantly across the recruitment sequence, and it is this variance in aggregate level of engagement that characterizes each particular recruitment most sensitively. As the consistent players' involvement in federal appointments shifts, and as additional interested parties join in, the importance of analyzing highly differing recruitment experiences becomes evident. Table 8.1 identifies the key participants in the federal recruitment sequence who have a consistent presence in the process.

Table 8.1

PARTICIPANTS IN FEDERAL RECRUITMENT PROCESS

Initiation	Screening
President	President
Department of Justice	Department of Justice
Attorney General	Deputy Attorney General
Deputy Attorney General	Office of Policy Development
Office of Policy Development	Federal Bureau of Investigation
White House Staff	ABA Standing Committee
Office of Legal Counsel	Senate Judiciary Committee
Committee on Judicial Selection	White House Staff
Senators (Senatorial Courtesy)	Office of Legal Counsel
	Committee on Judicial Selection

Affirmation

Senate Judiciary Committee

Full Senate

President

Additional players may well intervene in the recruitment sequence. The number of interested parties may vary from but a few to dozens, depending upon the level of the appointment and upon the political climate. They can represent interests across the political spectrum that either support or oppose a nominee. Again, as with the habitual players, these participants contribute to the articulation level of the particular appointment. The following chapters will more fully discuss these additional players. We leave the remaining parts of this chapter, however, to a more thorough discussion of the role played by actors who consistently participate in all levels of federal judicial recruitment.

The President and White House Staff

As the Constitution dictates, the President nominates and appoints federal judges. However, others can and do advise him. They may wish that the President appoint a particular person; nevertheless, initiation ultimately rests with the Chief Executive. Others may attempt to veto or discourage, but they can not replace his choice with their own. Although the Constitution separates nomination from appointment, the final appointment by the President is awarded once the Senate has given its advice and consent. It is fair to say, however, that he who initiates the single candidate to suffer the subsequent screening endeavors clearly has the advantage in this process.

During the Carter presidency, the role of the White House staff in judicial appointments was dramatically increased. Since then, Presidents have continued to seek the advice of their White House staff—and their White House Counsel, in particular—relying upon them "to screen judicial nominees from a political perspective and to maintain communications with the Department of Justice to ensure that presidential wishes are carried out."[1] Not surprisingly, the White House staff's intermediary role frequently provokes conflict with the Attorney General over who is to have control over judicial recruitment.[2]

Individual candidates and those groups, which attempt to draw the attention of the President, often inundate the Counsel's office with letters of inquiry, petitions and self-promoting letters. Other Justices and influential judges commonly suggest names for consideration. Inquiries are often directed to the Attorney General.

Justice Department and the Attorney General

While the White House advisers tend to focus on the political criteria to be applied to candidates, the Department of Justice is more concerned with legal competency and professional qualifications. Of course there is considerable overlap in their concerns. A Deputy Attorney General specifically responsible for judicial appointments heads the search for and screening of potential nominees unless the appointment is to the Supreme Court; in the case of Supreme Court seats the Attorney General assumes the lead role. The Office of Policy Development (OPD) in the Justice Department orchestrates the screening efforts.

The head of the OPD works closely with the associate White House Counsel. An assistant attorney general attached to the OPD "chairs a judicial selection committee that meets regularly to discuss candidates and assess the progress of investigations."[3] The Justice Department lawyers who run the investigations gather and analyze relevant information as well as interview prospective candidates. Interviews focus on the candidates' professional

[1] Neil McFeeley, *Appointment of Judges: The Johnson Presidency* (Austin: University of Texas Press, 1987), p. 15.

[2] A report issued by a national bipartisan commission in 1996 noted that in recent years the judicial selection process has changed in a number of ways: "More attorneys and resources in the White House and Department of Justice are used in screening potential nominees, extensive interviews with nominees have become routine and White House staff have become more involved in selection." Marcia Coyle, "Panel Issues Report on Judicial Selection Gridlock," *The National Law Journal*, May 27, 1996, p. A10.

[3] Sheldon Goldman, "Judicial Selection under Clinton: A Midterm Examination," *Judicature* 78 (1995): 278.

experience, their experiences as practitioners of law, and their understanding of policy issues facing the courts. The Justice Department, thus, emphasizes legal norms but also policy—accountability—concerns are not neglected.[4] Following the initiation and screening efforts of the Office, the Attorney General (or his or her designee) consults with the President or President's Counsel. Disagreement invariably ensues over whether legal qualifications are more important than political qualifications. Each office recognizes that both legal and political qualifications are important. However, it is the question over the degree to which each is important that often causes disputes to arise. Potential candidates are seldom if ever equally endowed with political savvy and legal ability, often leading to difficult choices and disagreement among these powerful actors.

The President's Committee on Federal Judicial Selection

Since the 1980s, the President's Committee on Federal Judicial Selection has assisted the President by coordinating initiation and screening. The Committee's purpose is to synchronize the activities of the Justice Department and White House, keeping conflict to a minimum. The Committee is composed of nine members, five from the White House and four from the Department of Justice. If the President has a specific nominee in mind, the Committee screens the nominee to determine if he or she is qualified for the position, and to determine whether his or her political and ideological views mirror those of the administration. If the President does not identify a favored candidate, the Committee searches for individuals who stand up against presidential criteria such as party loyalty, ideological consistency, and compatible jurisprudential views.

The Committee meets weekly and compiles a list of potential candidates ready for the President's consideration should a vacancy occur. For District Court judges, the Committee screens those suggested or picked by home state Senators of the President's party. Letters of support, often numbering several score, are addressed to the President's counsel and turned over to the Committee for processing. Sheldon Goldman maintains that "the formal mechanism of the Committee has resulted in the most consistent ideological screening of judicial candidates since the first term of Franklin Roosevelt."[5]

---

[4] Goldman notes that at the initial stages, "Justice officials focus solely on the professional merits of the candidate while the White House handles the politics." Ibid. Complaints about the Justice Department's role in judicial recruitment abound. Critics maintain that the Attorney General's office is used as a stepping stone to the federal bench. Moreover, many find the Attorney General's role in initiating and screening nominees who might one day stand across from them in court to be problematic, arguing that the Attorney General, "pitches; he catches; he bats; he fields; he runs bases; and—he selects or has a great voice in selecting, the umpires." C.J. Bloch, "The Selection of Federal Judges: The Independence of the Federal Courts," *American Bar Association Journal* 41 (1955): 510.

[5] Sheldon Goldman, "Reorganizing the Judiciary: The First Term Appointments," *Judicature* 68 (1985): 315.

American Bar Association's Standing Committee on Federal Judiciary

The American Bar Association's Standing Committee on Federal Judiciary plays a legitimating role in the screening of candidates for the Supreme Court, Court of Appeals, District Court, and the Court of International Trade. Of course, depending upon the interest of other participants in the recruitment, especially the President and the Senate Judiciary Committee, the effectiveness of the Committee's participation may vary with each appointment even though its procedures and criteria remain fairly fixed.

Prior to 1948, the Committee attempted to exert influence by issuing its own ratings on an *ad hoc* basis. However, in 1948 the Senate Judiciary Committee asked the ABA committee to express an opinion on every judicial nomination—and that particular practice has persisted.[6] Beginning in 1952 the President joined the Senate Judiciary Committee in asking the ABA Committee for its advice concerning almost every federal judicial appointment. The Committee's investigation of Circuit Court and District Court candidates, however, differs somewhat from its more thorough investigation and rating of prospective nominees to the Supreme Court.

Lower Court Appointments

Once the fifteen-member Committee on Federal Judiciary receives from the Attorney General the name of the prospective lower court nominee who has survived the initial screening by the particular Senator's staff (if courtesy is involved) and the Justice Department, the evaluation process is quickly gotten underway. Normally, the Committee assigns its investigation to the member of the Standing Committee who, out of the 15 members, represents the region (circuit) where the judicial vacancy exists.[7] The investigation is based on, but not limited to, the information provided by the "Personal Data Questionnaire" sent out by the Department of Justice and completed by the candidate.[8] The entire investigation is confidential, and each person contacted by the Committee is assured anonymity.[9]

---

[6] *The ABA Standing Committee on the Federal Judiciary: What It Is and How It Works.* (Chicago: American Bar Association, 1991), p. 14.

[7] The President of the ABA appoints a committee member from each of the federal judicial circuits (not including the Federal Circuit), two from the large ninth circuit, and one at-large member, completing the membership of the fifteen. Sometimes in the initial stages another member is asked to conduct the investigation if the member representing the particular circuit is overworked, has a conflict of interest, or if the candidate's career has extended geographically over more than one circuit.

[8] The ABA-designed questionnaire seeks information relating to the fitness of the candidate for judicial service. Both the ABA's Committee on the Federal Judiciary and the Justice Department receive a copy of the completed questionnaire. See *The ABA Standing Committee on the Federal Judiciary.*

[9] See **Washington Legal Foundation** v. **US Department of Justice** (490 U.S. 1017, 1989).

The investigator "examines the legal writing of the prospective nominee and personally conducts extensive interviews with those listed by the candidate in the questionnaire and others likely to have information regarding [his or her] integrity, competence and judicial temperament."[10] Upon completion of the interviews, the Committee member meets and discusses with the candidate his or her qualifications for the position. At this time, unfavorable information is shared with the prospective nominee, who is then given the opportunity to state her or his position and add any relevant insights into the controversy. Following the interview, the Committee member may choose to conduct some additional interviews to clarify issues that remain unresolved. If after these interviews, the investigator judges the candidate as being unqualified, another Committee member is asked to reevaluate the file. This ensures that the poor rating is not due to the personal biases of the original investigator.[11]

If, however, it is determined that the candidate is at least "qualified," the investigator prepares a written informal report for the chair of the Standing Committee. The chair then discusses the report with the Attorney General, passing on the substance of the report as well as indicating the rating the candidate will likely receive if a formal request is made. Candidates may be rated "Well Qualified," "Qualified," or "Not Qualified." The investigator will prepare a formal report only if requested to do so by the Attorney General. Upon request, the full membership of the Committee discusses the report, either by phone or at a meeting, and then each member sends his or her vote to the chair. In a confidential correspondence the Committee chair advises the Attorney General of the Committee's recommendation. Only when the President officially nominates the candidate does the Senate Judiciary Committee publicly disclose the rating. Often this is when the candidate first learns how he or she was rated. For District and Circuit Court nominations, the Attorney General's office acts as the conduit between the ABA's Standing Committee and the Senate Judiciary Committee.

Supreme Court Appointments

For nominations to the U.S. Supreme Court the Standing Committee's screening varies its investigation somewhat, prompted by the importance and sensitivity of these appointments. The Committee is requested to evaluate after a nomination has been formally made by the President or a deadline is given the Committee for when the nomination will be announced, placing the Committee under a

---

[10] The member will interview, when relevant, federal and state judges, practicing lawyers in both private and government service, law school professors and deans, legal services and public interest lawyers, representatives of professional legal organizations, and community leaders and others who are in a position to evaluate the potential nominee's integrity, professional competence and judicial temperament. The committee does not evaluate the potential nominee's politics or ideology. Ibid.

[11] Henry J. Abraham, et al., *Judicial Selection: Merit, Ideology, and Politics* Washington, D.C.: (National Legal Center for Public Interest, 1990), p. 80.

strict time line. On rare occasions, the Attorney General has submitted several names for one position, asking the Committee to help narrow the choice.

All the fifteen members of the Standing Committee participate in the screening for Supreme Court nominees. The Committee's members interview hundreds of persons throughout the country who might have relevant information on the "integrity, professional competence and judicial temperament" of the nominee. They also ask groups of knowledgeable law professors, as well as attorneys and former Supreme Court law clerks, to evaluate the nominee's legal writings. Once all the relevant information is compiled, the Committee determines which of three ratings will be assigned to the candidate.

"Well Qualified" and "Qualified" are assigned those candidate nominees or potential nominees "at the top of the legal profession" who have outstanding records and wide experience. "Not Qualified" is rarely given and this rating is reserved for those who do not meet these high standards. Upon completing its investigation, the Committee Chair consults with the Attorney General, indicating the likely rating the candidates will receive and explaining how the Committee reached this particular conclusion. The ratings are reported to the Senate Judiciary Committee before whom a Standing Committee member appears and reports on the Committee's evaluation. If necessary, the Committee may conduct a follow-up screening if new information is learned from the hearings before the Senate Judiciary Committee or the full Senate. Unless the results are leaked to the press, this initial phase of screening under most circumstances remains closed to outside participants.

The Standing Committee's screening for a Supreme Court nominee is more thorough and intense because it involves the full committee engaging in a much broader search for sources of information. Also, the ABA's Committee is brought into direct communication with the Senate Judiciary Committee. By the time the ABA's Committee has completed its screening, whether for the Supreme Court or lower courts, a considerable number of persons and groups have gained some input into the process—at least regarding the legal qualifications of the nominee.[12]

---

[12] Although the Standing Committee on Judiciary presents itself as an objective screener of a potential nominee's legal qualifications, both disgruntled liberals and disaffected conservatives have accused the ABA of promoting a hidden agenda. Liberals criticize the ABA for having a minimal number of women, minorities, and noncorporate lawyers in its membership. Conservatives maintain that the Committee uses objective or neutral terms such as "judicial temperament" to remove ideologically undesirable candidates from contention, pointing to the Bork debacle where four members of the committee rated him unqualified. Moreover, critics' suspicions are enhanced by the fact that the ABA operates behind closed doors, allowing the committee to wield "unlimited and unreviewed—and hence unaccountable power." Despite attacks on the ABA's role in judicial selection, a national bipartisan commission, co-chaired by former U.S. Attorney General Nicholas Katzenbach and former U.S. District Court Judge Harold R. Tyler Jr., has endorsed its continuing role in rating the competence of judicial nominees. The commission, however, suggested the Standing Committee increase its membership to better expedite the process, and recommended that it provide a brief statement explaining why the candidate was given the rating. Coyle, "Panel Issues Report on Judicial Selection Gridlock," p. A10.

Federal Bureau of Investigation

As with the involvement of the ABA's Committee, since the Eisenhower administration the FBI has had an active role in the screening of prospective federal judicial appointments. The Bureau's role, however, is to gather information without evaluating that information and without rating candidates. Although the data gathered likely include information on a candidate's legal ability and temperament, the primary purpose is to check on the candidate's personal credibility. The candidate may be a loyalty or security risk; or personal indiscretions, conflicts of interest, financial problems, or other circumstances which give the appearance of improprieties may disqualify the candidate or embarrass the President or sponsoring Senator, and ultimately disqualify the candidate. Often a candidate finds out that he or she is a serious prospect for the nomination when an acquaintance calls to report that an FBI agent had talked with him or her concerning the judicial vacancy.

The Department of Justice evaluates the data and moves ahead with the nomination or, if some problems have come to light, consults with the President or Senator who initially recommended the candidate. In the latter case, the Attorney General usually urges that the candidate's name be withdrawn from further consideration. Upon the formal announcement of the nomination, the Attorney General or Deputy Attorney General conveys the content of the FBI report to the Chairman of the Senate Judiciary Committee. The candidate's file, with its detailed findings, remains with the Department of Justice. Although the FBI's procedures remain the same, its investigation increases in intensity and scope as the potential appointments move from the District up to the Supreme Court levels.

Senate Judiciary Committee

As the Constitution requires, the prime actor in the affirmation stage is the Senate. However, before consenting to or rejecting a judicial nominee, the Senate awaits the results of the screening by its 18-member Judiciary Committee. Membership on the Committee is usually in proportion to the partisan make-up of the Senate, with the Chairperson coming from the majority party. Partisanship explains most of the Committee's politics. All members of the Committee are attorneys reflecting a long-held tradition of the Senate.

The Committee does not begin formal consideration of a judicial candidate until a nomination has been put forth formally. Once the President officially names a candidate, the Committee determines if and when a hearing will be held, and in the case of several pending nominations a sub-committee may be assigned the screening tasks. How active a role the Committee plays during the confirmation hearings and whether it will oppose a presidential nomination depends to a significant degree upon the chair of the Committee.[13] Some

---

[13]   David M. O'Brien, *Judicial Roulette: A Report of the Twentieth Century Fund Task Force on Judicial Selection* (New York: Priority Press, 1988), p. 72.

Judiciary Committee chairs have been powerful enough to maintain complete control over appointments to federal judgeships, while most others work in concert with a President from the opposing party reflecting a commitment to confirm nominees "as long as [they] are qualified, in good health, and understand the role of judges."[14]

The Senate Judiciary Committee has no set standards for screening a nominee. When the Committee interviews a nominee it acts neither "as a court applying fixed standards, nor as a deliberative council advising the president"; instead, it acts as an investigatory committee which probes the nominee's views.[15] Members of the Committee rely upon staff reports as well as information provided by interested parties. Of course, as with other participants in the recruitment sequence, the intensity and scope of the screening depends on many factors, one of which is the level of the court under consideration.

Controversy arises on occasion over the proper role of the Committee in scrutinizing the political and legal views of nominees for the Supreme Court (and on occasion nominees for circuit) but rarely do district vacancies occasion dispute. Scholars and laypeople alike have attacked the Committee's televised confirmation hearings, maintaining that they are too visible and attract too much attention, thereby encouraging participants to use them as a political platform. Some argue that this open and public process not only politicizes judicial recruitment and threatens the independence of the candidate and the Court,[16] but that it undermines the dignity of the federal bench.[17]

However, supporters of an open confirmation process contend that "the [public] questioning of nominees at confirmation hearings enables senators to obtain useful and indeed necessary information about nominees, particularly with regard to their views on fundamental constitutional issues."[18] It also promotes the unique opportunity for dialogue between the Committee and the nominee, enabling the Committee to socialize the nominee about the appropriate role of a judge in a democratic society. Such dialogue can also send important messages about "the acceptability of decisional outcomes and justificatory norms"—not only to the judiciary and the executive, but to the public as well.[19] Public scrutiny of nominees "is consistent with the gradual but inexorable growth of popular participation in the political process in the last two

---

[14] Goldman, "Judicial Selection under Clinton: A Midterm Examination," 289.

[15] O'Brien, *Judicial Roulette*, p. 77.

[16] Ibid., 10.

[17] William G. Ross, "The Supreme Court Appointment Process: A Search for Synthesis," *Albany Law Review* 57 (1994): 1003.

[18] Ibid., 1005. See also Dennis Deconcini, "The Confirmation Process," *St. John's Legal Commentary* 7 (1991).

[19] Ibid.

centuries."[20] Open hearings not only allow the American public a chance to participate in the judicial recruitment process, they also educate the public about the process as well as underscore the important role judges play in a democratic society. And perhaps most importantly, a modicum of accountability is instilled in the nominee as a result of the highly public hearings of the Judiciary Committee.

It is at the Judiciary Committee's hearings that the often numerous and certainly varied interested parties find access to the recruitment process. Today, all nominees are invited to a Committee hearing to answer questions. Supreme Court nominees are often subjected to several days of inquiry, while most Circuit and District Court candidates may be introduced to the Committee by a home-state senator, asked several polite questions and be excused in short order. Of course, for the highly publicized Supreme Court confirmation hearing dozens of representatives testify.[21] Even for some of the lower court appointments, special groups at times express their concerns for and against the nominee. If serious allegations have been uncovered, if a poor ABA rating is revealed, or if a split on the Committee becomes evident the nomination may be withdrawn even before a formal Committee vote is taken. However, for the vast majority of nominations to the lower federal benches, the Committee's hearings are brief, positive, and deferential toward the nominee.

Senatorial Courtesy

Senatorial courtesy plays a prime role in filling District Court vacancies, but is a somewhat less important consideration in the Circuit Court recruitment process. Senatorial courtesy is a convention that dates back to the First Congress, when Senators realized that it was in their best interest to present a united front when the President nominated a political adversary of one of their peers. Even though Senators might not personally dislike the President's choice, they recognized that at a later time they might need the help of their colleagues in similar circumstances.[22]

---

[20] Ibid., 996.

[21] For example, the ACLU, NAACP, NOW, AFL/CIO, Common Cause and Sierra Club were some of the major groups opposing Robert Bork's nomination before the Committee or during the Senate debate, while the American Conservative Union, NCPAC, Fraternal Order of Police, and the National Right to Work Committee supported his nomination.

[22] During the First Session of Congress, when George Washington nominated Benjamin Fishbourn to the position of naval officer in the Port of Savannah, the efficacy of a united Senate was tested. Although the candidate was unquestionably qualified, both of Georgia's Senators opposed the nomination. Washington withdrew the nomination when it became apparent that the full Senate was prepared to oppose the nominee. He later gave his consent to a nominee proposed by the two Senators. It can be argued that if Washington had not acquiesced, the convention of "senatorial courtesy" might not have taken hold so firmly. Henry J. Abraham, *Justices and Presidents: A Political History of Appointments to the Supreme Court* (New York: Oxford University Press, 1992), p. 27.

In contemporary appointments, upon receiving the President's nominee, the Chair of the Senate Judiciary Committee sends a blue piece of paper (the "blue slip") to each of the Senators in his party from the state in which the District Court is located. If these Senators do not return their "blue slip," the chair, after consulting with the recalcitrant solon(s) concerning his or her reasons, will usually table the nomination since the full Senate may very likely refuse to confirm the nominee.[23] On rare occasions the initiation of the District Court candidate is left to the President and, if at least acceptable to the home state Senator(s), the Judiciary Committee and the full Senate will readily approve the nomination. When the two home state Senators are of the President's party, they usually take turns at choosing names to be submitted to the President in nomination. Senatorial courtesy has given Senators from the President's party a proactive role in District Court recruitment, and they remain the dominant actors in the initial stages of the recruitment process. It is important to note that their dominance early on in the judicial selection process guarantees great influence in the latter stages of recruitment.

Senatorial courtesy, in District Court appointments, also permits a variety of actors to gain access to the early phases of the recruitment process. Those same local and state political allies of U.S. Senators and legal notables either contact the Senator's office (especially if of the President's party, the senior Senator or the Senator whose turn it is to pick a candidate) in their own behalf or in support of a favored candidate. Bar associations, labor organizations, law professors, party leaders, members of the President's administration (and the list goes on) bombard the Senator to the point that a quick choice is sometimes made by the Senator in order to gain some relief from the eager aspirants and their supporters.

Even in an appointment controlled by the Senator, the recruitment sequence may include both screening and initiation by a nominating commission similar to the merit plan commissions at the state level. These commissions at the federal level are a carryover from the Carter Administration. Members of such commissions are appointed by the Senator to assist in choosing a name to be sent to the President. By 1997, the reliance on nominating commissions had been largely abandoned.

Senate

Guided by the recommendation and vote of its Judiciary Committee, the full Senate debates the issue of confirmation, and by a simple majority vote either grants or withholds its consent to the President's nomination. Controversial and troublesome nominations rarely come to a full vote of the Senate; the names of problematic candidates are diplomatically withdrawn before this final

---

[23] Since 1979, the Senate Judiciary Committee no longer blindly honors blue-slip vetoes. Elliot Slotnick, "The Changing Role of the Senate Judiciary Committee in Judicial Selection," *Judicature* 62 (May 1979).

affirmation stage. Favorable votes on District and most often Circuit Court nominees are quickly recorded. Supreme Court nominees must suffer an often-extended debate, and only rarely will the final results on the Senate floor be at variance with the Judiciary Committee's recommendation.

The broad framework for the federal recruitment process described here remains the same for all appointments, but it is within this framework that variation tends to prevail.[24] Some judicial candidates breeze through the entire process from initiation to affirmation with but a few participants actively involved, while others may be subject to an arduous, contentious and crowded ordeal. For example, the intensity of Robert Bork's nomination to the nation's high bench was in sharp contrast with David Souter's experience. Ordinarily, senatorial courtesy determines who sits on the federal district court, but on those few occasions when a Senator's choice competes with the President's preference, it's likely that a considerable number of recruitment participants are drawn into the process. As explained in the next three chapters, federal judges, as with their counterparts recruited to state benches, experience significant variations in levels of articulation of their recruitment experience.

---

[24] On rare occasions the President may make an interim appointment while the Senate is not in session. However, the appointee still must suffer the ordeal of the full process to remain on the bench.

Chapter Nine

U. S. Supreme Court Appointments

Introduction

Throughout the greater part of American history legal scholars have maintained that Supreme Court Justices, perhaps even more so than lower federal court or state judges, should be protected from the other branches of government and be insulated from the push and pull of partisan politics. Above all, they must be placed above the whims of a sometimes frivolous and often volatile citizenry. Thus, viable judicial independence has meant a strict observance of separation of powers as well as a willingness to remain removed from the pressure of public opinion and special interests. Separation from the executive and legislature prevented the concentration of power, while independence from the politics and opinions of the citizenry ensured impartiality. What this independence required was a Supreme Court that followed the Holmes-Brandeis-Frankfurter tradition of self-restraint as well as a Congress and President that respected (or more often than not, ignored) the high bench.

However, in the last several decades the Court has become less willing to exercise institutional restraint and has judicialized ever-larger areas of American public policy. As a result, some critics believe that Supreme Court decisions have come to resemble legislative enactments rather than judicial decrees.[1] The judicialization of public policy brings into question the traditional understanding of the relationship between the judiciary and the other branches of government as well as the citizenry, more generally.[2] Today critics call for judicial restraint with respect to the other branches of government. They believe the Supreme Court should revert to a more passive role. Moreover, some critics look to judicial recruitment as a means of reining in the activist Court. They demand that individuals be placed on the Supreme Court who are more accountable to the dictates of the majority.

Contemporary Presidents have responded to the Supreme Court's transformed role and subsequent pressures to rein in the Court by nominating indi-

---

[1] Cornell Clayton, *The Politics of Justice: The Attorney General and the Making of Legal Policy* (London: Oxford University Press, 1992); Mark Silverstein and Benjamin Ginsburg, "The Supreme Court and the New Politics of Judicial Powers," *Political Science Quarterly* 102 (1987): 371.

[2] The growth of interest group litigation and the acceptance of more integrative modes of political jurisprudence have led to the judicialization of public policy. See Martin Shapiro, *Who Guards the Guardians: Judicial Control of Administration* (Athens: University of Georgia Press, 1988).

viduals who share their own administration's vision. The Reagan Administration, for example, sought out individuals who would

> Respect and reflect the values of the American people, and whose judicial philosophy [would be] characterized by the highest regard for protecting the rights of law-abiding citizens...[would be] consistent with the belief in the decentralization of the federal government and efforts to return decision making power to state and local elected officials...who [would] respect traditional family values and the sanctity of innocent human life...[and who would] share our commitment to judicial restraint.[3]

Not surprisingly, presidential attempts to control the high bench have led to accusations that the executive is contravening the "independence" of the judiciary. In response to the executive's increased involvement in judicial recruitment, the Senate has become more willing to scrutinize nominees in terms of their ideological and policy beliefs.[4] Thus, in the last three decades, as frustrated conservative Presidents have attempted to place conservative ideologues on the Supreme Court, liberal Senators have relied more and more on ideological cues to obstruct nominations that, if successful, might redefine the relationship between the Court and the executive.[5]

The Senate's willingness to investigate a nominee's ideological position, of course, draws mixed responses. Some scholars contend that the Senate, whenever it is so inclined, should scrutinize the policy beliefs of a nominee.[6]

---

[3] Herman Schwartz, *Packing the Courts: The Conservative Campaign to Rewrite the Constitution* (New York: Charles Scribner's Sons, 1988), p. 5. See *Congressional Quarterly Weekly Report* 38 (1980): 2046 for a reprint of the judiciary plank of the 1980 Republican Party platform. For refutation of Schwartz's contention that the Reagan Administration was successful in its attempts to pack the federal courts, see Christopher E. Smith and Thomas R. Hensley "Unfulfilled Aspirations: The Court-Packing Efforts of Presidents Reagan and Bush," *Albany Law Review* 57 (1994): 1111.

[4] It has been contended, however, that "while the acrimony attached to the Bork hearings created the popular perception that the Senate broke new ground in strictly scrutinizing a candidate's background, qualifications and personal philosophy, that notion does not comport with the historical record." Michael Slinger, Lucy Salsbury Payne and James Lloyd Gates Jr., "The Senate Power of Advice and Consent on Judicial Appointments: An Annotated Research Bibliography," *Notre Dame Law Review* 64 (1989): 106. Freund, however, contends that the Senate in the twentieth century has moved towards "a broader conception of a nominee's essential qualifications." As a result there has been a shift away from scrutinizing the nominee's sectional and party affiliations and a movement towards focusing more seriously on his or her judicial philosophy. Paul A. Freund, "Appointment of Justices: Some Historical Perspectives," *Harvard Law Review* 101 (1990): 1146.

[5] John Felice and Herbert F. Weisberg, "The Changing Importance of Ideology, Party, and Region in Confirmation of Supreme Court Nominees, 1953-1988," *Kentucky Law Journal* 77 (1988-1989): 530.

[6] See Donald E. Lively, "The Supreme Court Nomination Process: In Search of Constitutional Roles and Responsibilities," *Southern California Law Review* 59 (1986): 551.

More often than not these scholars are concerned with the executive's overt attempts to "pack the court" with those individuals sympathetic to the President's policy agenda. Others maintain that "undue ideological scrutiny in the Senate subjects the sensitive judicial process and the third branch, itself, to unsavory and inappropriate political persuasion."[7] Thus, Senators should confine the confirmation hearings to an investigation of the nominee's professional qualifications. Many scholars are less disposed to support either extreme and advance a middle position, asserting that the Senate's role in confirmation is dependent on the role the President plays, suggesting a contextually sensitive approach to confirmation for the Upper Chamber. Simply, the Senate should concern itself only with a nominee's ideological and policy preferences when the President overtly tries to influence the policy orientation of the Court. It is safe to say, however, that as long as there is electoral dealignment and the judiciary continues to exercise progressively less institutional restraint, both the executive and the Senate will continue to scrutinize the political and jurisprudential philosophies of potential candidates.

It is not surprising that one of the most vocal critics of the Senate's increased willingness to scrutinize the ideological positions of presidential nominees is the unconfirmed judicial nominee Judge Robert H. Bork. Bork has warned that the current process of selecting federal judges directly threatens the "independence" of the Supreme Court, alleging that

> The process of confirming justices for our nation's highest court has been transformed in a way that should not and indeed must not be permitted to occur again. The tactics and techniques of national political campaigns have been unleashed on the process of confirming judges. This is not simply disturbing it is dangerous. Federal judges are not appointed to decide cases according to the latest opinion polls. They are appointed to decide cases according to law. But when judicial nominees are assessed and treated like political candidates, the effect will be to chill the climate in which judicial deliberations take place, to erode public confidence in the impartiality of the courts and to endanger the independence of the judiciary.[8]

Has the increased contentiousness of the judicial selection process endangered the "independence" of the judiciary, and made the judiciary more responsive to public opinion during an era where public policy has become increasingly judicialized? Perhaps the institutional changes in the selection process are healthy in light of the Court's current role; Mark Silverstein believes

---

[7] Bruce Fein also argues that the Senate should confine its assessment to the nominee's professional qualifications because "the Senate, simply stated, is ill-suited intellectually, morally, and politically to pass on anything more substantive than a nominee's professional fitness.... Because [S]enators tend to be intellectually shallow and result oriented, their ostensible inquiries into 'judicial philosophy' will almost invariably degenerate into partisan posturing." Fein, "A Circumscribed Senate Confirmation Role," *Harvard Law Review* 102 (1989): 677.

[8] *New York Times*, October 10, 1987, p. 13.

so. Silverstein maintains that the Senate's transformed role "from a hierarchical inner-directed chamber into a more responsive and effective institution for the articulation of group interests" has made the contemporary confirmation process a far more democratic proceeding.[9] Moreover, increased public participation and intensive media coverage of confirmation hearings has further democratized the process. Many support the democratization of judicial selection, arguing that a modern system that subjects nominees to a measure of political accountability, as well as exposure to the public at large, is to be lauded.[10]

Do those that laud the democratization, or the opening up, of the judicial selection process feel that the "independence" of the judiciary is no longer important? Surely not; they likely recognize that once on the bench, regardless of the circumstances leading up to their appointment, federal court judges continue to play a uniquely independent role in America's constitutional government. Undoubtedly, at times the demands of their office will require that they not only ignore the bidding of the executive or the legislature, but also that they turn their backs on the will of the majority. Nonetheless, those who support the democratization of the selection process see it as counterbalancing the heavier independent role Justices assume once "advice and consent" is bestowed. Again, in light of developments in the overall political landscape of American politics this may be a good thing.

Initiation and Screening of Supreme Court Candidates

Although initiation and screening are analytically distinct stages in the recruitment sequence, most of those who search for potential Supreme Court nominees also will be intimately involved in the politics of screening. Overlap, thus, necessarily occurs between the two stages. The President, the White House staff, the Attorney General, and the Deputy Attorney General are the primary actors in initiation. However, they often seek advice from home-state Senators of the President's party, public and private leaders interested in the nomination, as well as sitting Supreme Court Justices. Whereas the President's political advisers screen candidates using "political" criteria of concern to the President, the Federal Bureau of Investigation and the American Bar Association aid the President by verifying the integrity and legal competence of potential judicial candidates.

The President

---

[9] Mark Silverstein, *Judicious Choices: The New Politics of the Supreme Court Confirmations* (New York: W.W. Norton, 1994), p. 129.

[10] William G. Ross maintains that today "a clear trend exists…toward an increased public awareness of the importance of federal judicial nominations and a growing public participation in the selection process." William G. Ross, "Participation by the Public in the Federal Judicial Selection Process," *Vanderbilt Law Review* 43 (1990): 1.

Under Article II, section 2 of the Constitution, the President has the primary responsibility for the recruitment of Supreme Court Justices. However, as explained in Chapter 8, the Chief Executive has a number of advisers who can and do initiate and screen candidates for federal court appointments. But Presidents pay special attention to the selection of Justices to the nation's high bench. Unlike the parochial lower federal courts, the Supreme Court is an institution that serves the entire nation. As a consequence, Presidents will rarely defer to individual Senators when nominating Supreme Court Justices. With only nine positions in question, the President frequently fills a vacant seat with a person who has been nationally prominent. Public figures themselves, American Presidents are able to identify candidates with little outside assistance, often selecting individuals from within their administration.

Although Presidents differ greatly in their degree of involvement in judicial recruitment—some are personally involved from the beginning, while others let their Attorney General or White House Legal Counsel do all the work—it is the President who establishes the criteria, either explicit or implicit, for judicial recruitment. When determining who should fill a vacant Supreme Court position, Presidents have placed varying levels of emphasis on political patronage, professional qualifications, legal policy goals, representational characteristics and confirmability.[11] Which criterion receives greater emphasis is largely dependent upon the goals of the President and the existing socio-political environment. Presidents who are less concerned with judicial policy making tend to view vacant judgeships as patronage positions. In periods of muckraking and increasing concern over corrupt and explicitly partisan government practices, Presidents have tended to give greater weight to professionalism and merit. As the judicialization of government policy has increased, Presidents have openly pursued their legal-policy goals through the appointment of federal judges.[12]

In their search for viable candidates, all Presidents are guided by *political considerations*. They tend to appoint the party faithful to federal judgeships. The Chief Executive may nominate an individual to pacify certain political interests or to create a political climate that is receptive to their policies. Individuals who played an important role in a President's rise to prominence, as well as political or personal friends, are also often considered for a position on the high bench.

Infrequently, Presidents make "spite nominations" to retaliate against the Senate for perceived wrongs against the executive branch—specifically the Senate's rejection of the President's most favored judicial nominee. When making a "spite nomination," the President hopes to retrieve lost political capital, disci-

---

[11] David M. O'Brien, *Judicial Roulette: Report of the Twentieth Century Fund Task Force on Judicial Selection* (New York: Priority Press, 1988). See also Henry J. Abraham, *Justices and Presidents: A Political History of Appointments to the Supreme Court* (New York: Oxford University Press, 1992), pp. 3-12.

[12] O'Brien, *Judicial Roulette*, 1988, p. 49.

pline the wayward Senate, and forces the confirmation of a nominee who is likely to change the ideological direction of the Court. Most often, however, Presidents seek out candidates who will promote their social agenda long after their term in office expires. They consider only those candidates who pass an ideological litmus test, are relatively young, and whose record promises judicial performance consistent with the administration's long-term goals.[13]

Presidents not only tend to attempt to pack the Court with party faithful and candidates committed to the administration's ideological focus, they also are inclined to recruit individuals with particular ethnic characteristics to accommodate demands for a representative court. In the nineteenth century, Presidents focused on geographical *representation* because judges were at that time viewed as representing the parochial interests of the states. As the importance of a nominee's geographical representation began to recede, greater emphasis was placed on an appointee's religious background. The religious affiliation of a potential nominee, however, tends to fall secondary to other considerations such as the nominee's political or judicial ideology.[14]

In the latter part of the twentieth century, Presidents have placed greater emphasis on the racial, gender and ethnic characteristics of potential nominees. Supporters of greater *diversity* on the high bench employ a variety of arguments to defend their position; most advocate that the tenets of democratic rule clearly require a Court that is representative on its face. Simply stated, the composition of the Supreme Court should mirror the composition of the rest of society. Other advocates of diversity argue that women and minorities bring to the bench a unique perspective—that is, they have a "different voice."

Divided government and the new judicial politics have made the confirmation process more contentious and, as a result, Presidents pay more attention to the *confirmability* of a candidate. This has led in some cases to Presidents nominating "stealth" nominees whose relative anonymity and non-controversial record mask or moderate their underlying political and judicial philosophies. Presidents concerned with confirmability are inclined to avoid individuals who have strong political or judicial records that could be rigorously scrutinized by the Senate. A sparse record leaves the Senate with little tangible evidence, making it difficult for them to claim that the candidate's judicial philosophies were outside the mainstream of legal theory. In the wake of the controversial Thomas hearings, President Bush appointed David Souter as such a "stealth" nominee. Up until his appointment, Justice Souter was relatively unknown and he was perceived as being a non-extremist. Justice Souter had a scant judicial record, having served on the United States Court of Appeals for the First Circuit for only three months and having published only a single article in a law review.

---

[13] Rita Cooley, "Judicial Appointments in the Eisenhower Administration," *Social Science Review* (January 1959): 11.

[14] Approximately eighty-eight percent of Supreme Court Justices have been affiliated with the Protestant faith.

Not all Presidents, however, view a Supreme Court judgeship as a quasi-political position. Some Presidents, such as President Hoover and President Carter, promised to appoint judges based upon merit, not past political activity. When using *professional qualifications criteria,* Presidents use at least three indicators, seeking out individuals who have distinguished credentials as practitioners or scholars of the law, persons of substantial judicial experience, or those evidencing an outstanding record of public service.[15]

By determining the criteria used to initiate and screen potential nominees, the President is clearly the prime actor in Supreme Court recruitment. This said, it is important to note that a number of close advisers typically assist the Chief Executive in the process. These advisers tend to include the Attorney General, the Deputy Attorney General, the White House staff, Supreme Court Justices, the FBI and the ABA's Standing Committee on Judiciary. Although these advisers may emphasize particular aspects of the President's criteria over others, they are nonetheless the President's agents rather than competing actors in the initiation and screening stages.

Advisers to the President: Attorney General, White House Advisers and Judges

Historically, the Attorney General and the Department of Justice have played a critical role in the initiation and screening of judicial nominees. Nonetheless, how extensive a role the Attorney General or other Department of Justice officials play in the recruitment of Supreme Court justices largely depends upon the nature of the relationship between the Attorney General, the White House Legal Counsel, and the President.[16] Chief Executives also rely upon their White House staff (and their White House Counsel, in particular), to screen nominees from a political perspective and to maintain communications with the Department of Justice to ensure presidential wishes are carried out.

The White House staff's intermediary role frequently provokes conflict with the Attorney General over who is to have control over judicial recruitment. Sometimes, however, the conflict that ensues is over which criteria are to be given top priority. The Attorneys General and Department of Justice officials have objected to the role of political adviser and adopted a more legalistic conception of judicial selection. This posture has created an inherent tension

---

[15] O'Brien, *Judicial Roulette*, p.77.

[16] Although their level of involvement may vary from President to President, Attorneys General have played a role in judicial recruitment since President Washington's administration. In 1793, the first President requested that his Attorney General, Edmund Randolph, prepare a list of candidates for the bench. In preparing the list, Randolph warned Washington not to appoint incompetent men because it would give the state judiciaries a sound reason to take a stand against the national bench. In 1853, the Attorney General's role in judicial selection was institutionalized when the function of appointing judges and law officers was transferred from the Department of State to the Department of Justice. William P. Rogers, "Judicial Appointments in the Eisenhower Administration," *Journal of the American Judicature Society* 41 (August 1957): 39.

between Department of Justice lawyers who tend to focus on professional criteria and White House staff who tend to focus on policy and political considerations. However, each office recognizes that both legal and political qualifications are important when it comes to assessing judicial candidates. It is the degree to which these criteria are to be accorded importance that causes disputes to arise. Potential candidates are never equally endowed with political savvy and legal ability, often leading to hard choices and disagreement between these powerful actors.

When a pending vacancy is announced, individual aspirants, as well as private and public interest groups who wish to draw the attention of the President, often inundate the White House Counsel's office with letters of inquiry, petitions and self-promoting letters. Justices and judges also commonly suggest names for consideration. In some cases, a judge or the lawyer learns that they are under consideration only when they receive a call from the White House inviting them to apply for a vacant position. This, in turn, initiates a frantic process of filling out long and detailed questionnaires and gathering endorsements.

As explained in Chapter 8, The President's Committee on Federal Judicial Selection—sometimes called "The Judicial Selection Group"—coordinates initiation and screening between the White House and Department of Justice. Undoubtedly, contemporary Presidents rely more heavily upon White House advisers and Attorneys General than past Presidents have done. On occasion Supreme Court Justices, sitting or retired, also perform an important role in the recruitment of Supreme Court Justices by offering advice on pending nominations.[17] Thus, the White House, the Attorney General, judges and a plethora of other actors can play some role in initiating and screening Supreme Court candidates. However, absent political considerations, the President is under no obligation to follow the counsel of his many potential advisers. Moreover, in most Supreme Court appointments the President's advisers have been guided by the President's preferences or in anticipation of his desires. Although the President ultimately is responsible for making the nomination, the modern screening process is certainly more complex (if not more convoluted) than it was thirty years ago. Simply, there are more participants competing for the President's attention throughout the process.

Formal Screeners: The American Bar Association, the FBI, and the Senate Judiciary Committee

Although all of the initiation actors described above are also intimately involved in the politics of screening, there are three participants who regularly evaluate

---

[17] Justices who have lobbied the President successfully for a nominee in the nineteenth century include John Catron and Benjamin R. Curtis (for John A. Campbell, 1853); Robert C. Grier (for William Strong, 1870); Noah H. Swayne (for Joseph Bradley, 1870); Morrison R. Waite (for William B. Woods, 1880); and Henry B. Brown (for Howell E. Jackson, 1893). Abraham, *Justices and Presidents*, pp. 30-31.

all federal nominees: The American Bar Association's Standing Committee on the Federal Judiciary, the Federal Bureau of Investigation, and the Senate Judiciary Committee.

As explained in Chapter 8, the ABA's Standing Committee on the Federal Judiciary and the FBI are always involved in screening candidates for the Supreme Court, although the influence of the Bar Association's Committee may vary from case to case. For Supreme Court nominations, the President usually gives the ABA's Standing Committee on the Federal Judiciary a candidate's name before announcing the formal nomination. Upon receipt of a name or sometimes more than one, all fifteen members of the ABA's Committee interview hundreds of persons who may have information on the prospective nominee. When the candidate's file is complete, members of the Standing Committee meet, discuss, and rate the candidate on a scale of "Well Qualified," "Qualified" and "Not Qualified." The nominee who might have received a significant number of "Not Qualified" ratings usually withdraws his or her name from consideration.

Simultaneously with the ABA's Committee screening, the FBI conducts its information gathering investigation. The data the Bureau collects are not evaluated until the Justice Department receives the final FBI report. When the President's nomination is formally submitted to the Senate for its "advice and consent" it is referred to the Senate Judiciary Committee for its recommendation. At this point the Attorney General shares the file compiled by the FBI with the chair of the Judiciary Committee. The chair of the Judiciary Committee plays a key role in federal judicial appointments and especially nominees to the Supreme Court. Some Committee chairs, such as Mississippi's conservative Democratic Senator James Eastland, have been powerful enough to maintain complete control over appointments. Others, however, such as Republican chair Senator Orrin Hatch, have worked with a President from the opposing party.[18]

The degree to which the Senate Judiciary Committee scrutinizes Supreme Court candidates is much greater than the degree to which it evaluates lower federal court candidates. Reasons why past nominees have been rejected may shed some light on the types of standards the Senate Judiciary Committee tends to use to evaluate judicial candidates. The prominent reasons for rejecting candidates include: (1) opposition to the nominating President not necessarily the nominee; (2) the nominee's involvement with visible or contentious issues of public policy; (3) opposition to the record of the incumbent Court, which the nominee was presumed, rightly or wrongly, to have supported; (4) perceived political unreliability of the nominee; (5) the evident lack of qualifications or limited ability of the nominee; (6) concern about sustained opposition by interest or pressure groups; and (7) fear that the nominee will drastically alter the

---

[18] Sheldon Goldman, "Judicial Selection under Clinton: A Midterm Examination," *Judicature* 78 (May-June 1995): 289.

court's jurisprudence.[19]

Usually more than one of these reasons factor into the rejection of nominees. All these reasons, excluding an evident lack of qualifications, were implicit in the rejection of Robert Bork. Members of the Senate Judiciary Committee, then headed by Senator Biden (D-DE), not only opposed Bork's position on controversial social issues but also wanted to curtail President Reagan's attempts to alter the Court's jurisprudence and to show their disapproval of the conservative direction the current Court was taking. Moreover, interest groups such as the NAACP and NOW placed immense pressure upon the committee, as well as individual Senators, to derail Bork's candidacy. Together these factors created that political, but democratic spectacle, known as the Bork hearings.

In recent years, there has been an increase in the influence of organized groups on the Senate Judiciary Committee. This influence is an offshoot of popular participation in Supreme Court recruitment. Organized groups, even before the Bork candidacy, have attempted to influence the confirmation of presidential nominees. For example, Nixon's nomination of both Clement F. Haynsworth and G. Harrold Carswell also incited widespread public participation and organized interest group activity. Liberal groups such as the AFL-CIO, the NAACP, and Leadership Conference on Civil Rights (a group of 125 welfare, labor, religious, and civil rights groups) actively opposed the confirmation of Haynsworth because of his anti-labor decisions as a Fourth Circuit judge and because of his overt insensitivity towards African-Americans. Both groups directed their efforts at the grass roots level, building up anti-Haynsworth sentiment among constituents of influential Senators. At the Senate Judiciary Committee's hearings, an unprecedented number of persons and groups testified. Those offering testimony included a wide array of labor organizations, multiple civil rights groups, the Americans for Democratic Action; the Committee for a Fair, Honest, and Impartial Judiciary; the National Lawyers Guild, seven persons from the United States House of Representatives, an academic and a representative of a major religious denomination. Haynsworth received modest support from distinguished law school professors and leading members of the Bar.[20]

During the relatively noncontroversial appointments of John Paul Stevens and Sandra Day O'Connor a great number of groups also voiced their respective approval or disapproval of these nominees. Moreover, civil rights groups and women's groups organized the most extensive campaign to that date in opposition of William Rehnquist's ascendancy to the Chief Justiceship only to be outdone by extra-senatorial campaigns for and against the nomination of Robert Bork. Organized interests in the Bork confirmation, however, incorporated an additional feature into the public discourse by buying newspaper and television advertisements to influence public opinion. It is clear that the judicialization of

[19] Henry J. Abraham, *The Judicial Process: An Introductory Analysis of the Courts of the United States, England, and France*, 6th ed. (New York: Oxford University Press, 1993), p. 75.

[20] Ross, "Participation by the Public in the Federal Judicial Selection Process," p. 13.

policy has led to the politicization of the Supreme Court recruitment process which, in turn, has encouraged a wider and more intense participation of conflicting groups in the screening phase.

Affirmation

As the Constitution requires, the prime actor in the affirmation stage is the Senate, but that legislative body awaits the results of the screening process by its Judiciary Committee. Much like the initiation phase, affirmation involves not only formal affirmation or rejection of a nominee, but careful scrutiny of the nominee's political and judicial philosophy as well as his or her professional qualifications. The role of the full Senate in federal judicial recruitment has changed over the years, with many contending that "recent confirmation struggles have forever transformed the judicial selection process."[21] Current conditions such as divided government, the threat of intellectual homogeneity on the present Court, attacks by past Presidents on the Court, and strategic Court packing schemes by the executive branch have pushed the Senate toward a more energetic and less deferential role in the affirmation of Supreme Court nominees. The Senate, in embracing this role, has demonstrated an unwillingness to revert to the passivity it displayed before the Reagan-Bush era.[22]

After the Senate Judiciary Committee holds public hearings, it deliberates, votes on the nominee, and then sends its vote with a formal report to the full Senate. For a nominee to be confirmed, a simple majority of the Senate need only support the nomination. In noncontested confirmations, the Senate Judiciary Committee, as well as the full Senate, give their unanimous approval. In contested confirmations it is likely for both the Committee and the full Senate to be divided. Controversial confirmations also produce more floor debate.

Supreme Court Articulation

During the initiation stage of judicial recruitment, the actors involved emphasize the need for judicial independence or political accountability to varying degrees. Conceivably a nominee produced from an initiation involving all of these participants would not be excessively accountable to a single political interest or completely independent. Even in low articulation initiation and screening phases, nominees are made aware of the competing expectations of democracy and the rule of law because screening-process participants that emphasize legal

---

[21] William G. Ross, "The Supreme Court Appointment Process: A Search for Synthesis," *Albany Law Review* 57 (Fall 1994): 994. See also Silverstein, *Judicious Choices* (1994).

[22] Laurence Tribe contends that the belief that the Senate until recently merely rubber stamped the President's nominations to the Court is premised on a myth. In truth, "the Senate has vigorously exercised its power to provide 'advice and consent' on Presidents' Court nominations since the time the very first Justices were selected." Tribe, *God Save this Honorable Court: How the Choice of Supreme Court Justices Shapes Our History* (New York: Random House, 1985), p. 77.

norms, such as the Department of Justice, American Bar Association, and Judges, are never completely free of partisan concerns, nor do Presidents and their White House advisers ever fully ignore the importance of selecting legally competent judges.

The more contentious the Senate Judiciary hearings, the more likely it is that the candidate will be exposed to a variety of competing expectations. Moreover, contentious hearings may result in greater involvement by organized interests, thus pushing the candidate further in the direction of political accountability. However, in an affirmation stage free of conflict there will be little impetus for organized interests to become involved in the process, thereby hindering the assimilation of norms that emphasize public accountability.

Considering the Senate's and the general public's increased activity in Supreme Court confirmations, it can be argued that the Supreme Court recruitment stage has moved away from a low articulation system, currently at least approaching a moderate system. Presidents now are forced to consider the confirmability of their candidates quite seriously. Naming candidates is still the Chief Executive's prerogative, but an interested Senate and energized elements of the citizenry have the capability of reining in a President who has gone too far from mainstream values. Moreover, vigorous senatorial and public scrutiny ensures that candidates get a heavy dose of political and public accountability before they begin their careers as impartial arbiters of the law on the nation's high bench.

Recruitment of Ruth Bader Ginsburg

Several months into President Bill Clinton's first term, Justice Byron White announced that he would leave the bench at the end of the Court's term, making Clinton the first Democratic President in twenty-six years to make a Supreme Court appointment. In the end, after a long process of fits and starts, he appointed Ruth Bader Ginsburg, the second woman to sit on the nation's highest court. How can the recruitment process leading up to Justice Ginsburg's appointment be characterized? Which actors played a significant role in each of the stages of recruitment? How might her recruitment experience influence her behavior as a judge? These are the questions which will be addressed through an application of the articulation model featured throughout this monograph.

Initiation and Screening

From the outset, President Clinton determined the pace of the recruitment process. Unlike many past appointments in which the President named a successor within several weeks of the vacancy, President Clinton "indicated he would move deliberately and extensively consider a wide variety of candidates."[23] Observers of the process suggested that the President had specific criteria in

---

[23] Goldman, "Judicial Selection under Clinton," p. 277.

mind when searching for potential candidates. Some maintained that President Clinton wanted to nominate the first Hispanic, while others contended that he would restore the "Jewish seat." Still others speculated that he would appoint another woman to the Court. The President seemed inclined to nominate "someone schooled in high political office, thus adding some balance to a Supreme Court dominated by justices who had never held elective office."[24] President Clinton, like his Democratic predecessor President Jimmy Carter, seemed to be looking for a representational candidate who also understood the obligations of elective office.[25]

For this appointment, the President delegated the task of screening and winnowing down the large list of potential candidates to White House Counsel Bernard W. Nussbaum, and Associate White House Counsel Ronald A. Klain.[26] The Department of Justice did not screen potential nominees because the President had yet to nominate an acceptable candidate to the position of Attorney General. Although he had nominated Eleanor D. Acheson to head the Department's Office of Policy Development, she was not confirmed until August 2, 1993.[27] Thus, it was not until after Judge Ginsburg's confirmation that the Office of the White House Counsel and the Justice Department's Office of Policy Development began to work in concert.

President Clinton also relied upon the public (through organized interest groups) and the Senate Judiciary Committee to seek out candidates. Throughout the initiation process the White House strategically leaked names of potential candidates to the national press. As Sheldon Goldman notes, the leaking of names "served as trial balloons"[28] allowing the Clinton administration to forecast the degree of support or opposition candidates would receive. At the same time, these leaks tended to lure other participants into the initiation process by alerting them to potential nominees. The President also tested the murky senatorial waters by informing key members of the Senate Judiciary Committee (both Democrats and Republicans) about potential candidates. Considering the number of failed nominations to other administrative posts, this strategy is hardly surprising—President Clinton fervently wished to avoid yet another contentious confirmation battle.[29]

---

[24] Ibid., 277.

[25] See "President Clinton's Judicial Nominations," *Congressional Record--Senate Proceedings and Debates of the 103rd Congress*, Second Session (S2426), Monday, March 7, 1994.

[26] Klain was formerly the Senate Judiciary Committee's chief counsel and had worked closely with the Committee's chair, Senator Joseph Biden. Goldman, "Judicial Selection under Clinton," p. 278.

[27] Ibid.

[28] Ibid.

[29] Susan Page, *Newsday*, June 14, 1993, p. 4.

A little over two months after Justice White's announced resignation, the President narrowed his list to three candidates—two federal appeals judges (both males) and Interior Secretary Bruce Babbitt. Babbitt was "a long time Democratic politician with no judicial experience" and was at that point the President's favorite.[30] However, by the second week in June, attention shifted to Stephen Breyer, First Circuit Judge and former Senate Judiciary Committee Counsel, "reviving the old debate over the merit of politicians versus jurists for the highest court."[31] Publicly, Secretary of the Interior Bruce Babbitt was still in the running, but for all intents and purposes, he had already been screened out of the recruitment process by Republican detractors who perceived him as being too liberal and Democratic supporters who wanted him to remain in the Cabinet. Charles Cooper, Assistant Attorney General during the Reagan Administration, noted the choice between the two front runners would be exquisitely simple for President Clinton to make. He supported the point by stating:

> I haven't heard a single voice raised in opposition to Stephen Breyer's nomination should it happen. His potential nomination [has] been embraced by both sides of the political spectrum, Republicans and Democrats, whereas with respect to Mr. Babbitt, while there hasn't been serious controversy raised about his potential nomination, at the same time his greatest allies are actually his largest opponents for nomination to the court. The conservationists [and] environmentalists don't want him to leave the Interior Department. So it seems to me this is a pretty easy call for President Clinton.[32]

On Friday, June 11, 1993, Clinton summoned Stephen Breyer, who was recovering from a bicycle accident, from his hospital bed to join him for lunch.[33] After the discussion, which some have characterized as unsatisfactory, the President was unwilling to make a final decision.[34] Shortly thereafter, news broke that Breyer had failed to pay Social Security taxes for a part-time cleaning woman who had worked for him for 13 years.[35] Although the public was

---

[30] *The McNeil/Lehrer News Hour*, June 11, 1993, (Transcript 4648).

[31] Ibid.

[32] Ibid.

[33] Goldman, "Judicial Selection under Clinton," pp. 277-278.

[34] Ibid. Responding to the innuendo that Breyer was eventually dropped because the lunch did not go well, columnist Elizabeth Drew stated that "if [Breyer] was dropped, as they are saying because the lunch on Friday didn't go well—I mean, he isn't picking a fishing companion." *CNN*, June 14, 1993, (Transcript 352-4).

[35] See Bill Nichols, *USA Today*, June 14, 1993, p. 4A. "Breyer had told the White House that he did not realize until the Zoe Baird controversy in February that he was required to pay Social Security taxes for an elderly cleaning woman...who already was drawing Social Security benefits." To rectify his shortsightedness, Breyer paid $400 in 1992 back taxes and a similar amount for each of the previous years. Susan Page, *Newsday*, June 14, 1993, p. 4.

learning about the controversy for the first time, the administration had known about Breyer's situation for weeks and had already discussed whether it would be a disqualifying factor with the Senate Judiciary Committee. According to one White House official, "We did our homework, [and] it is our feeling that this does not disqualify him."[36]

Despite the admitted improprieties, Breyer's nomination continued to receive widespread bi-partisan support. Minority leader Robert Dole (R-KS) told *CNN* "I am prepared to support the nomination, and I think other Republicans are, too."[37] Majority Leader George Mitchell (D-ME) concurred, telling David Brinkley on ABC's *This Week* that "I don't think by itself, (it) is disqualifying."[38] Moreover, women's groups, from whom the Clinton administration feared a backlash, were mostly sympathetic to Breyer's predicament. Harriet Woods of the National Women's Political Caucus explained that allegations that women's groups would try to derail Breyer if he was still nominated were "nonsense," stating that: "It [is] women who would be disproportionately penalized if this became an automatic barrier."[39] Judith Lichtman of the Women's Legal Defense Fund supported this stance, maintaining that: "He ought to be judged on his qualifications for the job. I don't think this issue should become a trap door."[40]

However, on June 14, support for Breyer notwithstanding, the *Washington Post* reported that the name of Ruth Bader Ginsburg, Federal Appeals Court judge in Washington D.C., had resurfaced for consideration.[41] President Clinton had met with Judge Ginsburg two days earlier—the Saturday after his "unsatisfactory" lunch with Stephen Breyer.[42] By mid-afternoon of June 14, the White House had released letters of support for Judge Ginsburg.[43] On that same day, President Clinton made the unexpected announcement that he intended to nomi-

---

[36] Bill Nichols, *USA Today*, June 14, 1993, p. 4A.

[37] Ibid.

[38] Ibid.

[39] Ibid.

[40] Ibid.

[41] Ibid. On May 12, on a flight to New York, President Clinton had inquired of Senator Daniel Patrick Moynihan (D-NY) whom he would like to see appointed to the Court. Senator Moynihan replied that there was only one name, that being Ruth Bader Ginsburg. Later when the administration was considering Senator Moynihan's recommendation, he passed on positive remarks made by Erwin N. Griswold, former Solicitor General of the United States and Dean of the Harvard Law School, concerning Ruth Bader's involvement in representing groups interested in the rights of women. See 139 *Congressional Record*, August 2, 1993, s10094. Senator Moynihan, along with his New York colleague Senator Alfonse D'Amato (R-NY) later acted as Ginsburg's sponsors before the Senate Judiciary Committee.

[42] Goldman, "Judicial Selection under Clinton," p. 277.

[43] *U.S. Newswire*, June 14, 1993.

nate Ruth Bader Ginsburg, "the Thurgood Marshall of the women's movement" to the Supreme Court.[44]

Judge Ginsburg was clearly not a "stealth nominee." She had an extensive legal and judicial record. She had pursued her legal education, first at Harvard Law School and then at Columbia Law School, earning her Juris Doctor in 1959. After graduation, she clerked for Edmund L. Palmeri, U.S. District Court Judge for the Southern District of New York for two years. From 1961 to 1962, she served as a research associate for the Project of International Procedure at Columbia Law School. She later became the Associate Director of the program. In 1963, she left Columbia University when Rutgers, the State University School of Law, hired her as an Assistant Professor. When she returned to Columbia five years later she was brought on as a Full Professor. While at Columbia, Judge Ginsburg acted as a consultant to the U.S. Commission on Civil Rights. She was also the Director of the Women's Rights Project at the American Civil Liberties Union, and after this stint ended she served as General Counsel for the ACLU. In 1980, President Carter nominated her to the U.S. Court of Appeals for the District of Columbia. At the time President Clinton nominated her to the high court, Ginsburg had over 300 signed appellate opinions and had published more than three score articles.[45]

On the evening of her nomination, two members of the Senate Judiciary Committee—Senator Orrin Hatch of Utah, the ranking Republican, and Senator Edward Leahy, Democrat from Vermont—joined CNN's Judy Woodruff to discuss the pending confirmation hearings. When asked if Ginsburg's nomination would "fly through with little or no problem," Senator Leahy replied that

> I think that this nomination [is] going to have probably the least trouble of any nomination for the Supreme Court I [have] seen in years. It will go through. I question whether there will be anybody even [to] vote against her. She is a superb jurist. She comes, not carrying a litmus test for any one group of either the right or the left, but rather as somebody who is to represent all Americans. That [is] what the President wanted. I think that [is] what he is going to get and I think that is what the United States is going to get."[46]

Senator Hatch, who did not agree with Judge Ginsburg "on everything," suspected that "she would go through rather well." Moreover, he stressed that the Senate Judiciary Committee should proceed with "a great deal more fairness than [it had] in the past."[47] On July, 20, 1993, Judge Ginsburg appeared before the Senate Judiciary Committee. Before Ginsburg's appearance, the Chair of the Senate Judiciary Committee, Joseph Biden (D-DE), had laid out for his col-

[44] Quoted in Goldman, "Judicial Selection under Clinton," p. 277.

[45] *Senate Executive Report*, 103-6, 103d Congress, First Session, August 5, 1993.

[46] "Inside Politics," *CNN*, June 14, 1993, (Transcript 352-4).

[47] Ibid.

leagues "the process the committee would pursue in conducting [the] hearings."[48]   According to Biden, "the [confirmation] hearings...should be the crowning jewel of the evaluation process, a final chance to clear up confusion or firm up soft conclusions."[49] However, because of the disruptions experienced at Clarence Thomas's confirmation hearings, the investigatory process of the Committee required a number of changes that would be implemented in the upcoming hearing. First, any allegations against a Supreme Court nominee would be placed in the nominee's file and shared, on a confidential basis, with all U.S. Senators, not just those on the Senate Judiciary Committee. And second, the Committee would conduct a closed session with Ginsburg (and all future nominees) where no political or jurisprudential issues would be discussed, but where the nominee would be asked to discuss on the record and under oath any investigative issues that had been raised.[50]

Judge Ginsburg's confirmation hearing lasted only three days and many have characterized it as a "love fest."[51] According to Senator Howell Heflin, "Back-slapping [had] replaced back stabbing."[52] As the hearings began, both Democratic and Republican Senators rushed to endorse Ginsburg, compelling Senator Arlen Specter (R-PA) to remark that the hearings were being viewed as "pro forma."[53] The ABA's Standing Committee on the Federal Judiciary gave her its highest ranking, "well qualified," concluding that by "virtue of her academic training, her work as an appellate advocate, her academic services, her scholarly writings, and her distinguished service for thirteen years on the [D.C. Circuit] Court of Appeals Judge Ginsburg meets the highest standards of professional competence for a seat on the Supreme Court."[54]

To reach this conclusion, the Standing Committee conducted over 625 interviews. Four hundred of those interviewed were federal or state judges. Both sitting Supreme Court justices and Ginsburg's colleagues on the D.C. Circuit Court were interviewed. The remaining 225 people interviewed were practicing attorneys, former law clerks, and lawyers who had appeared before Judge Ginsburg. Besides the interviews, three reading groups chaired by Rex Lee, former Solicitor General of the U.S. and President of Brigham Young University,

---

[48] 139 *Congressional Record* S8771-01—Senate Proceedings and Debates of the 103 Congress, First Session, Thursday, July 15, 1993.

[49] Ibid.

[50] Ibid.

[51] Susan Low Bloch and Thomas G. Krattenmaker, *Supreme Court Politics: The Institution and Its Procedures* (St. Paul: West Publishing, 1994), p. 276.

[52] Ibid.

[53] *ABA Journal* 79 (September 1993): 18.

[54] Hearings before the Committee on the Judiciary, U.S. Senate, 103 Congress, First Session, July 23 at 12.

Ronald J. Allen of Northwestern University[55] and Mark G. Yodof of the University of Texas,[56] respectively, reviewed Ginsburg's opinions and legal writing.[57] Each group concluded that Ginsburg demonstrated the requisite skills for serving as a Supreme Court justice. One group wrote in their report that

> She is bright, able, sincere and apparently a hard worker. Moreover, she is committed to be an excellent jurist and is a better writer than many of her colleagues. She graces the bench with style and understanding and the confidence of one with a well-trained mind and a sense of herself.[58]

Besides testimony given by William E. Willis, chair of the ABA's Standing Committee[59] and Judah Best, the D.C. Circuit representative for the ABA's Standing Committee, the Senate Judiciary Committee considered the verbal testimony and prepared statements of eighteen other witnesses. The witnesses were divided into five panels, representing the legal community,[60] the legal academic community,[61] citizens and groups in opposition to Ginsburg's appointment,[62] individuals who had been intimately involved with Ginsburg as an activist, a lawyer and a judge,[63] and presidents of three additional bar associations.[64] Of the eighteen, only six individuals spoke out against

---

[55] Group 2 was comprised of twenty-one members.

[56] Group 3 was comprised of twelve members.

[57] Bloch and Krattenmaker, *Supreme Court Politics*, pp. 372-378.

[58] Ibid., 374.

[59] It is tradition for the chair of the ABA's Standing Committee to be the first person to testify other than the witness himself or herself on matters relating to the Supreme Court. Ibid., 372.

[60] Panel II included W.T. Coleman Jr., civil rights lawyer, chairman of the NAACP's Legal Defense Fund, and former Secretary of Transportation under President Ford; Chesterfield Smith, senior partner at Holland and Knight and former president of the ABA; Shirley Hustfelder, senior partner at Hustfelder, Kaus and Ettinger, former Ninth Circuit judge and former Secretary of Education under Carter; and Ira Milstein, senior partner at Weil, Gotshal and Manges and longtime friend of Ginsburg and her husband Marty.

[61] Gerald Gunther, William Cromwell Professor of Law at Stanford University; and Herma Hill Kay, Dean of the law school at the University of California at Berkeley, comprised the third panel.

[62] The fourth panel consisted of Paige Comstock Cunningham, president of American's United for Life; Rosa Cummare, senior partner at Hamilton and Cummare and connected to an adoption group; Nellis J. Gray, president of March for Life Education and Legal Defense Fund; Susan B. Hirschmann, executive director of Eagle Forum; Kay Cole James, representative of the Family Research Council; and Howard Philips, U.S. Taxpayer Party and the Conservative Caucus.

[63] Edith Roberts, Ginsburg's former law clerk; Stephen Weisenfield, a litigant Ginsburg represented in a landmark gender discrimination case; and Kathleen Peratis, a colleague of Ginsburg's when she headed the ACLU's Women's Rights Project, made up the fifth panel.

Ginsburg's appointment, each expressing deep concerns over the judge's willingness to protect a women's right to choose to have an abortion.

Throughout the hearings, the members of the Committee explored Judge Ginsburg's judicial philosophy and constitutional methodology, as well as her position on constitutional questions relating to women's reproductive freedom, civil rights, freedom of speech, separation of powers and criminal law. The committee also held a closed session from 10:06 to 11:50 am on the last day of the hearing to question Ginsburg privately about her failure to list the waiver of a country club fee as a gift on financial disclosure forms. Although pleased by her record, Senators were disgruntled over her lack of responsiveness and her unwillingness to answer all the committee's questions.[65] Senator Orrin Hatch, in particular, grew exasperated with her evasiveness when questioning her about the death penalty, snapping "It's not a tough question."[66] However, from the outset, Ginsburg had stated that she hoped the Committee would evaluate her qualifications principally on the written record.[67] Despite irritation over Ginsburg's "closed mouthedness," the Committee unanimously confirmed her nomination.

Affirmation

On August 2, 1993, the Senate entertained floor debate over Ginsburg's nomination to the Supreme Court. Not surprisingly, little debate ensued. In fact, all but one of the twenty-six Senators who spoke voiced support for the nominee. Democrats commended the President for selecting a nominee not on the basis of partisanship or ideology, but rather on the basis of standards that define judicial competence. Republicans, who did not support Ginsburg's politics, recognized that it was the President's prerogative to select whom he wanted for the position,

---

[64] The sixth, and last panel, was comprised of Angela M. Bradstreet, president California Women Lawyers; Carlos Ortiz, president of the Hispanic National Bar Association; and John D. Feerick, president of the New York Bar Association.

[65] Senator Biden expressed his sentiments thusly during the confirmation hearing: "[Judge Ginsburg] you do have style that is precise and on occasion seems less expansive when you answer questions, but you have given us some significant substance on issues of privacy and equal protection, freedom of speech, and constitutional methodology. Still, I [would] have to say like other recent nominees, you have given us less than I would like." Quoted on the *McNeil/Lehrer News Hour*, July 22, 1993, (Transcript 4716).

[66] Ibid.

[67] Ginsburg, at the confirmation hearings, explained to the Senate Judiciary Committee that since they had been supplied with hundreds of pages about her and thousands of pages she had penned; her writings as a law school teacher, mainly about procedure; ten years of briefs she filed when she was a courtroom advocate of the equal stature of men and women before the law; numerous speeches and articles on the same theme; 13 years of opinions counting the unpublished together with the published opinions, well over seven hundred of them; all decisions she had made as a member of the U.S. Circuit and several comments on the role of judges and lawyers in our legal system, they should use these written records to evaluate her. *Federal News Service*, July 20, 1993.

and that unless the nominee was incompetent or unethical the Senate was obliged to defer to his wishes. In contrast, Jessie Helms (R-SC), the sole dissenter, maintained that it would be hypocritical for him "to keep silent about Mrs. Ginsburg's beliefs, let alone [to] let her nomination be quietly confirmed by the Senate, like a ship passing in the night."[68] Furthermore, he chastised his Republican colleagues on the Judiciary Committee for letting Ginsburg walk away from the hearings virtually unscathed by critical scrutiny of her position on a variety of legal policy issues. However, Helms' complaints fell on deaf ears and on August 3, 1993, the full Senate confirmed Ginsburg's nomination by a vote of 96-3.

Articulation Level

When comparing the recruitment of Ruth Bader Ginsburg to traditional Supreme Court recruitment processes, hints of movement towards a more moderate articulation level appear. At the outset, President Clinton sought advice from a number of people. Moreover, from the beginning, those potentially interested in who was to be nominated were drawn into the process by news leaks concerning who was under consideration. A wide range of individuals and organizations representing a variety of interests were involved in screening potential candidates. First, President Clinton—like Presidents Carter and Reagan before him—delegated the task of initiating and screening potential candidates to his White House Counsel. However, the President controlled the process by laying out the criteria his advisers ought to use in their selection. Although the Clinton administration was looking for a "pro-choice candidate," its efforts were tempered by its concern over candidates' confirmability. The Clinton administration did not want to expend political capital on yet another contentious confirmation battle. Thus, the President was sensitive to the views of the members of the Senate Judiciary Committee and of organized interests. In contrast to the political criteria applied by the White House Counsel, organized interests and members of the Senate Judiciary Committee, the ABA's Standing Committee on the Judiciary emphasized legal criteria, as did a number of Senators.

When screening candidates, the Senate Judiciary Committee heard from a wide variety of interests. Most witnesses who gave testimony were from the legal establishment and argued for confirmation, downplaying the causes she had advocated and emphasizing her concern for the rule of law. The public and private organizations that opposed Justice Ruth Bader Ginsburg criticized her stance on abortion. Some members of the Senate Judiciary Committee were also disturbed by Justice Ginsburg's liberal orientation. They wanted her assurance that she would not act as a judicial legislator, although she had already proven herself to be centrist on the Court of Appeals for the District of Columbia. The confirmation hearings constituted a learning experience for the Justice,

---

[68]   139 *Congressional Record*, Monday, August 2, 1993, s10076.

as well as a screening stage designed to allay the fears of Senators and the public.

How might Ginsburg's recruitment process have shaped her perceptions of the proper role of a federal judge in a constitutional democracy? It may be, as her record indicates, that even before her recruitment she was committed to balancing accountability and independence, and the relatively open and high profile recruitment process only further reinforced this commitment. It may be, as well, that her recruitment experience made her more sensitive to the judge's dilemma. Early indications are that perhaps the recruitment process has had this tempering effect.

Justice Ginsburg has remained a centrist, balancing judicial independence against political and public accountability in her first term. "True to her words, she [has] not aligned herself with any ideological wing" and "[her] decision-making patterns have placed her in the middle of the Court."[69] However, as the recruitment experience begins to fade in time, the prerogatives of office may replace what was initially learned. Recruitment is indeed important in explaining judicial behavior, but it is only one among a number of variables that shape a Justice's perspective.

---

[69] Christopher E. Smith, "The First-Term Performance of Justice Ruth Bader Ginsburg," *Judicature* 78 (September-October 1994): 80.

Chapter Ten

U.S. Courts of Appeals Selection

The Courts of Appeals were created in 1891, "as a result of increased federal court caseload and the impracticality of having Supreme Court justices sit on circuit."[1] Today, thirteen Courts of Appeals review District Court decisions and enforce, as well as review, the decisions of a variety of federal executive agencies that are empowered with quasi-judicial functions. All but one of these courts, the U.S. Court of Appeals for the Federal Circuit, are contained within multi-state jurisdictions.[2] Except for Federal Circuit judges, all judges of these courts must be residents of the circuit at the time of their appointment. Moreover, they must remain within the circuit even after going to senior status since the Chief Justice of the United States may request that these judges continue to preside over cases filed in the circuit. Between four to twenty-eight members comprise each court. Three-judge panels hear most cases; however, in particularly controversial cases the entire membership of the court may sit *en banc*.[3]

The creation of intermediate Courts of Appeals altered the character of the federal judiciary. It enabled the Supreme Court to focus primarily on "institutional review"—the mediation of interbranch disputes and determination of general principles of legal policy. It has diverted "error correction"—holding trial courts and agencies accountable under the law—into Courts of Appeals, putting Courts of Appeals at the center of federal adjudication. Moreover, since most of their business is mandatory and their decisions are usually final, these courts are the final stop for the vast majority of federal litigants.[4]

---

[1] Stephen L. Wasby, *The Supreme Court in the Federal Judicial System* (Chicago: Nelson/Hall, 1993), p. 41.

[2] In 1982, Congress created the Federal Circuit when it fused the Court of Claims and the Court of Customs and Patent appeals. The Federal Circuit has twelve judgeships and its jurisdiction includes all cases arising under patent laws and Little Tucker Act cases, as well as cases resulting from decisions made by the Merit System Protection Board, the Claims Court, the Court of International Trade, the Court of Veterans' Appeals, and certain other administrative agencies. Daniel Meador, "A Challenge to Judicial Architecture: Modifying the Regional Design of the U.S. Courts of Appeals," *University of Chicago Law Review* 56 (Spring 1989): 603.

[3] Henry J. Abraham, *Judicial Process: An Introductory Analysis of the Courts of the United States, England, and France* 6 ed. (New York: Oxford University Press, 1993), pp. 162-165. In the ninth circuit of 28 judges, 11 can serve *en banc*.

[4] J. Woodford Howard, Jr., *Courts of Appeals in the Federal Judicial System: A Study of the Second, Fifth, and District of Columbia Circuits* (Princeton: Princeton University Press, 1981), p. 7.

The Recruitment of Judges to Courts of Appeals

The recruitment process for Courts of Appeals differs significantly from Supreme Court recruitment since these courts represent regional circuits instead of the entire nation and their decisions apply only to their particular circuit. As a result, actors such as the Attorney General, the Deputy Attorney General, White House advisers and home-state Senators share roles in the initiation and screening of potential candidates, sometimes even supplanting the President.

Initiation

As happens with Supreme Court Justices, the President appoints judges to Courts of Appeals with the advice and consent of the Senate. However, as Sheldon Goldman notes, "behind this simple statement lies a complex reality of customs, pressures, expectations, and constraints that operate on the participants" in the recruitment process.[5] In contrast to Supreme Court recruitment, the President shares this role not only with his advisers in the White House and the Department of Justice, but also with home-state Senators and local politicos within the circuit where the vacancy occurs. Who will play the prominent role in both the initiation and screening phases depends largely upon the individual President, the state claiming the vacancy and whether the Senators from the state in question come from the President's party.

Generally, the Chief Executive, advised by his White House staff and Attorney General, will play a greater role in seeking and promoting nominees if neither of the home-state Senators are of his party. However, if home-state Senators come from the President's party, or if an influential senior Senator such as the Chair of the Judiciary Committee takes an interest in a particular appointment, then the President will usually comply with their recommendations.

Although the convention of "senatorial courtesy" provides home-state Senators with a certain amount of leverage to control lower court nominations, "the balance of power shifts at least slightly in the President's direction when the nominations for the Courts of Appeals rather than District Courts are being considered."[6] Whether Presidents take this initiative is largely dependent upon their "perceptions of the role of the federal government and of the Courts of Appeals' ability to affect accomplishment of administration goals."[7] Presidents

---

[5] Sheldon Goldman, "Judicial Appointments to the United States Courts of Appeals," *Wisconsin Law Review* (Winter 1967): 188.

[6] Donald R. Songer, "The Policy Consequences of Senate Involvement in the Selection of Judges to the United States Courts of Appeals," *Western Political Quarterly* 35 (March 1982): 107. See also Joel B. Grossman, *Lawyers and Judges: The ABA and the Politics of Judicial Selection* (New York: Wiley, 1965).

[7] Rayman L. Solomon, "The Politics of Appointments and the Federal Courts' Role in Regulating America: U.S. Court of Appeals Judgeships from T.R. to F.D.R.," *American Bar Foundation Research Journal* (1984): 285.

concerned with the policy potential of the Circuit Courts tend to take control of the initiation stage of the recruitment process, forcing home-state Senators to defer to their selection.[8]   If only interested in the patronage potential of an appointment, Presidents tend to take little interest in Circuit Court recruitment, usually yielding to the aspirants recommended by the Senators who claim home-state status. However, in the case of an intraparty split or if home-state Senators recommend an unqualified candidate, the executive may intervene.

If a President chooses to take control of the initiation process, Senators have a number of strategies for preventing the nomination of candidates they view as unacceptable. At the formal screening stage (or after the President has formally nominated a Circuit Court candidate) home-state Senators can refuse to return their blue slips or, during informal evaluation of the candidate, they can publicly announce who they wish to fill the position before the President is able to make a formal nomination. However, the Chief Executive is not without recourse. The President can refuse to send the recalcitrant Senator's candidate to the Senate, hoping that those annoyed by the delay in filling the vacancy will pressure the Senator to support the President's choice. The Chief Executive can also make recess appointments, which do not require immediate Senate approval, gambling that by the time the Senate has reconvened the candidate will have proven worthy, making senatorial rejection difficult, at best. In addition, a President can ignore the convention of allocating judgeships to a particular state and nominate a judge from a neighboring state. He can also use negative evaluations from either the FBI or the ABA to persuade Senators to drop their support of their preferred candidate.[9]

Although the President must determine whether the executive branch will take an active role in the initiation of Circuit Court candidates, his advisers in either the Department of Justice or the White House are responsible for searching for and compiling relevant information on candidates. Presidents are more likely to rely upon the Attorney General and other Department of Justice advisers to ease the burden of discovering lower federal court candidates. Today within the Justice Department the Office of Policy Development orchestrates initiation and screening efforts through a judicial selection committee that meets regularly to discuss candidates and assess the progress of investigations. The Justice Department lawyers who run the investigations gather and analyze relevant information as well as interview prospective candidates. Interviews, sometime lasting over an hour, focus on the candidates' professional experience, their experiences as practitioners of law, and their understanding of policy issues facing the courts. The Assistant Attorney General of the Office of Policy Development and his staff also use their vast network of friends and acquaintances as sources for candidates. In addition, they canvass lawyers in the Department of Justice to gain relevant information about prospective nominees, since "these

---

[8] Ibid.

[9] Ibid., 291-292.

lawyers come from all sections of the country and usually have extensive professional and political contacts in their home states."[10]

Of course, a pending vacancy on a Circuit Court bench is well known, prompting aspirants to contact their Senator and the White House Counsel. Often a judge or lawyer may be invited to apply. This initiates a process of filling out questionnaires and gathering endorsements. Following the initiation and screening efforts of the Office of Policy Development, the Attorney General, or his or her designee, consults with the President or President's White House Counsel or the President's Committee on Federal Judicial Selection.

Federal judicial recruitment may change to some degree with each new administration. These changes usually result in a shifting of some responsibilities and, consequently, lead to reallocating the degree of influence certain actors have over appointments. For instance, such a shift occurred when President Jimmy Carter created, under executive order 11972, U.S. Circuit Court Nominating Commissions.[11] President Carter's purpose for establishing the nominating commissions was two-fold: (1) he wanted to de-emphasize political considerations in the recruitment process and focus on selecting circuit judges "according to their professional merit and potential for quality service on the bench"; and (2) he wanted to create a mechanism that would enable him to appoint more women and ethnic minorities on the bench.[12] The Circuit Court Nominating Commissions were to be the primary actors in the initiation phase as well as in the process of screening candidates for Courts of Appeals. Generally, the commissions expanded considerably the initiation phase of recruitment both by allowing more participants to be involved, and by recruiting a broader and more diverse list of possible candidates.

From the outset, President Carter's Circuit Court Nominating Commissions met with controversy. Most importantly, Senators were reluctant to relinquish their control over Courts of Appeals nominations; as a result, they often refused to endorse commission recommendations, delayed confirmation hearings, and threatened to undermine the panels' efforts if the nominees did not comport with their personal preferences. The ABA found the panels to be problematic because, in an effort to meet affirmative action goals, commissions would often set aside the ABA's requirement of 12-15 years of legal experience.

[10] Goldman, "Judicial Appointments to United States Courts of Appeals," p. 196.

[11] Executive order 11972 was later replaced by executive order 12059. The latter differed from the original executive order in that it required that there would be at least one lawyer from each state within the panel's jurisdiction, guaranteeing at least minimal contact with the court's legal community. It also revoked the requirement that five names be submitted to the President, as well as the time requirement and the confidentiality requirement.

[12] When President Carter took office there were only two African-Americans and one woman on the Courts of Appeals. Larry C. Berkson and Susan B. Carbon, *The United States Circuit Judge Nominating Commission: Its Members, Procedures and Candidates* (Chicago: American Judicature Society, 1980), p. 2.

The most controversial aspect of the commissions' mandate, however, was President Carter's effort to make the federal bench more representative. Carter endorsed the maxim that "the governing institutions of democracy should reflect the spectrum of interest of the governed and this should be done by dispersing the power to govern among representatives of diverse groups."[13] Moreover, representativeness on the bench would heighten the judiciary's sensitivity to complex and controversial social issues.[14]

Critics, however, maintained that the mandates of merit selection and affirmative action were inherently irreconcilable. To them, affirmative action required "quota mentalities [that] were inconsistent with the American ethic"[15] and resulted in placement of mediocre judges on the appellate bench. Because of the considerable controversy generated by the Circuit Court Nominating Commissions, they were discontinued by subsequent Republican administrations. Republican Presidents Reagan and Bush preferred to centralize judicial selection apparatus in the executive because it strengthened the President's ability to place on the bench exclusively individuals who supported the administration's specific policy concerns.

Screening and Affirmation

The FBI, the ABA's Standing Committee on the Federal Judiciary, and the Senate Judiciary Committee screen lower federal court candidates, as well as Supreme Court nominees. The FBI's role in screening remains the same at each court level. In contrast, the role of the ABA's Standing Committee and the Senate Judiciary Committee are somewhat modified, and tend to be abbreviated at the Circuit Court and District Court levels. We will save discussion for how the ABA's Committee investigates lower court candidates for Chapter 11, and here turn instead to the Senate Judiciary Committee's evaluation of Circuit Court nominees.

The Senate Judiciary Committee's Circuit Court nomination hearings are generally low-key, rarely escalating to the level of controversy that Supreme Court hearings do (although there are some notable exceptions as our case study will demonstrate). Circuit Court nomination hearings tend to be "kinder and gentler" because undesirable or controversial candidates have been screened out by home-state Senators before their names reached the Committee. Usually only a three-member Subcommittee, designated by the chair of the Committee, investigates lower court nominations. However, the degree to which the Subcommittee scrutinizes Courts of Appeals nominees (in most instances) is greater than the level of attention given to District Court nominees. Nevertheless, when

---

[13] Quoted in Elliot Slotnick, "Lowering the Bench or Raising It Higher," *Yale Law and Policy Review* 1(1983): 275.

[14] Ibid., 270.

[15] Ibid., 275.

compared to the Senate Judiciary hearings at the Supreme Court level, the number of extra-constitutional actors (private and public interest groups, individuals who oppose or endorse the candidate, the media) participating in the hearing and this phase of the screening process more generally is greatly reduced. After conducting its investigation, the Subcommittee evaluates the candidate and passes on its recommendation to the full Committee, which then votes on the candidate. Once the vote has been taken, as with Supreme Court nominees, the Committee sends its vote to the full Senate which then either rejects or confirms the candidate. More often than not, the full Senate will affirm the nominee with little to no discussion.

Articulation Levels

When compared to the *initiation* of Supreme Court candidates, it is clear that more actors tend to be involved effectively in the *initiation* of Courts of Appeals candidates. Whereas officials in the Justice Department and the White House play merely an advisory role in Supreme Court recruitment, in Courts of Appeals recruitment their role is much broader. Moreover, in Courts of Appeals recruitment Presidents are sometimes forced to share the prerogative of naming judicial candidates with home-state Senators of their party. The increase in the number of effective actors in the initiation phase can have an important effect on Courts of Appeals candidates because it exposes them, from the outset, to a number of competing conceptions of a judge's role. For instance, a candidate who comes into contact with both the Department of Justice (which emphasizes legal norms) and the White House (which emphasizes political and representational norms) will be made cognizant immediately of the competing demands inherent within the "judicial dilemma."

In contrast, the number of actors effectively involved in the formal stage of screening is somewhat reduced at the Courts of Appeals level. Although the Federal Bureau of Investigation, the American Bar Association's Committee on the Federal Judiciary, and the Senate Judiciary Committee all evaluate lower court nominees, as well as Supreme Court nominees, the degree to which the ABA and the Senate, in particular, scrutinize Circuit Court nominees (and District Court nominees for that matter) is somewhat reduced. Like with District Court nominees, only a single member of the ABA's Standing Committee investigates Circuit Court candidates.

The abbreviated investigation of the ABA's Committee notwithstanding, it is important to note that if it were not for the American Bar Association's investigation, the number of effective actors in the formal screening of Circuit Court and District Court judges would be even smaller. Since its inception during the Eisenhower presidency, the Bar Association's investigation has gone a long way towards democratizing the recruitment process by allowing a greater number of individuals to participate indirectly in the formal screening of all federal court nominees.

The Senate Judiciary Committee's investigation of Courts of Appeals candidates tends also to be somewhat constrained, with only a three-member Subcommittee conducting a hearing. Interest groups and individuals that either want to endorse or oppose the candidate tend not to turn out in the same numbers as they do for Supreme Court hearings. Indeed, the public is often oblivious to the fact that a Circuit Court nomination hearing is even being held. This tends to be the case because home-state Senators and the President, through a process of negotiation, have usually agreed upon a candidate before the formal nomination, ensuring little conflict and thereby increasing the likelihood that a judge who goes through this screening experience will have a tendency to view the judicial dilemma as irreconcilable and lean either towards political accountability or judicial independence. Simply stated, confirmation hearings that are mere formalities increase the likelihood that the candidate will lean towards political accountability to particular political entities (the President or home-state Senators) or they will be further removed from the pull of accountability, embracing the role the framers originally intended for federal judges.

However, when powerful home-state Senators or senior Senators have competed with the President for the nomination of favored candidates, Courts of Appeals nomination hearings have the potential for becoming as contentious as recent Supreme Court hearings. When the President and the Senate are at odds over a Circuit Court candidate, the Senate Judiciary Committee may deliberately delay confirmation hearings or attempt to embarrass the President by making the confirmation hearings a political spectacle. Clearly, the more contentious the Senate Judiciary hearings, the more likely it is that the candidate will be exposed to a variety of competing expectations, again nudging him or her in the direction of accountability. Contentious hearings will also result in greater involvement by organized interests, again potentially convincing the candidate that a balance between independence and accountability is necessary. Similarly, the more contentious the Senate's final vote, the more likely the judicial candidate will attempt to reconcile the competing demands of his supporters and detractors.

Courts of Appeals recruitment tends to fall somewhere between Supreme Court and District Court affirmation on the articulation continuum. It may be less contentious, and therefore involve, on the whole, fewer effective participants than Supreme Court recruitment processes; but the process may be more contentious and involve more participants than is the case in District Court recruitment events. Although Courts of Appeals recruitment, relatively speaking, seems to fall in between Supreme Court recruitment and District Court recruitment processes, it is important to note that Circuit Court judges are one step removed from the national scene (unlike Supreme Court judgeships) and one step removed from the local scene (unlike district court judgeships), making them in some senses independent to a considerable degree. Circuit Court candidates receive less media attention and less national attention than Supreme Court candidates and less local attention than District Court candidates. Although these appellate judges experience a more diverse recruitment process when compared with their trial counterparts, it can be argued that Courts of Appeals judges remain relatively independent and as a result may have a tendency to adopt a trustee role.

Recruitment of John Noonan Jr. to the Ninth Circuit Court of Appeals

In October 1985, President Ronald Reagan announced the nomination of John Noonan, Jr. to the Ninth Circuit. Noonan was a known conservative legal scholar from the University of California Law School at Berkeley, and an avid anti-abortionist. His appointment appeared to have the potential for considerable controversy.

Initiation and Screening

When campaigning for the presidency, Reagan promised "to appoint federal judges who would shun judicial and social activism."[16] Throughout his two terms in office Reagan stood by his promise, maintaining that he would only nominate judges who would adhere to "judicial restraint" and "who under[stood] the dangers of judicial activism."[17] Moreover, he continued to openly criticize "those who viewed courts as vehicles for political action and social experimentation."[18] Reagan's top aides mirrored the President in their unwillingness to initiate the candidacies of those who did not "harbor the deepest regard for the Constitution and its traditions—one of which [was] judicial restraint."[19] In 1985, when asked about the administration's goals concerning the recruitment of federal judges, Attorney General Edwin Meese, who played a critical role in the initiation and evaluation of potential candidates, explained that although the Reagan administration wanted to "find people of the highest quality," it also wanted candidates who properly understood that the appropriate function of a judge "is to interpret the law, not to make the law."[20]

During Reagan's second term as President, Grover Rees III, Edwin Meese's special assistant in the Justice Department, was charged with recruiting judges who would reshape the federal judiciary in the Reagan image. Rees's role entailed screening nominations for "ideological irregularity." He proved to be a formidable screener—no names reached the White House without his approval. Some speculate, however, that those who came before Rees only had to

---

[16] "BC cycle," *U.P.I.*, Sunday, November 3, 1985.

[17] Ibid.

[18] Speech on October 21, 1985 quoted in "BC cycle," *U.P.I.*, Sunday, November 3, 1985.

[19] "BC cycle," *U.P.I.*, Sunday, November 3, 1985.

[20] Ibid.

utter a single phrase to garner his support: *"Roe v. Wade* [the Supreme Court abortion case] was wrongly decided."[21]

In the early years of President Reagan's presidency, the administration established an elaborate process to initiate and screen candidates for all levels of the federal bench. The process involved the following steps. First, those candidates being considered for a federal judgeship received and were required to complete a ten-page questionnaire. A day-long interview then followed at the Justice Department. After the intensive interview, ten senior officials from the White House and the Department of Justice, meeting on Thursdays in the White House's Roosevelt Room, scrutinized the candidates based upon the information compiled both from the questionnaires and the interviews. Those in attendance at this meeting included: Attorney General Edwin Meese, Grover Rees III, presidential counsel Fred Fielding, and legislative affairs coordinator Max Friedersdoerf.[22] If a candidate was approved both by this special administrative committee and the Attorney General, the name was then (and only then) forwarded to the President.[23]

In October of 1985, John Noonan's nomination had successfully worked itself through this intense and thorough screening process.[24] The fifty-seven year old law school professor, interestingly, did not fit the administration's age profile;[25] however, he had a solid record of pro-life activism, thus explaining the Assistant Attorney General's support of the nomination—the Reagan administration's contention, notwithstanding, that it did not have a litmus test for screening candidates.[26]

Noonan's history of pro-life activism spanned a number of decades. In 1976, *U.S. News & World Report* cited Noonan as saying "Anti-abortion forces are strong and growing stronger. They are going to make abortion a major issue

---

[21] When teaching at the University of Texas Law School, Rees—an avid supporter of "judicial restraint"—wrote that if put into practice it would have dramatic effects: "In constitutional cases we should trust judges less and the law more. I can understand that some people would choose differently: if the Constitution were interpreted the way I believe it should be interpreted, states could have anti-abortion laws [and] prayer would be endemic in the schools." Aric Press and Ann McDaniel, *Newsweek*, October 14, 1985.

[22] It has been reported that this was a "principals only meeting—so important that no deputies may attend in their master's stead." Ibid.

[23] *Time,* November 4, 1985.

[24] Hints of Noonan's impending nomination first became public on October 6, 1985. The *Los Angeles Times* reported that "John Noonan Jr., a law professor at UC Berkeley [had been] mentioned for the Ninth Circuit Court of Appeals in San Francisco."

[25] Rees, while denying there was a litmus test for screening candidates, openly admitted that "there [was] a conscious attempt to avoid appointing people who [would] be on the bench only a few years." Ibid.

[26] Ibid.

in the presidential elections."[27]   On May 18, 1982, Noonan appeared on the *McNeil/Lehrer Report* to discuss the Reagan administration's warning that hospitals which denied food or treatment to handicapped babies would lose their federal funding. Noonan supported the administration's action, contending that despite

> the pro-choice mentality, the mentality that says it's the parents' choice whether a child should live or die...no child is the property of his or her parents; a child is a person. And ever since the Declaration of Independence we've taken the position that all persons are created equal. And these little children are not property of the parents to be disposed of; it isn't the parents' right to decide whether they survive or not. Once they are here, they are well one of us, and we have a really profound obligation to keep them going.[28]

Noonan testified before the Senate, in January of 1984, warning that "the ERA [Equal Rights Amendment] would eliminate all existing restrictions on abortions and require federal and state funding for the procedures." Moreover, "it would provide a constitutional basis for all abortion rights."[29] He advocated, as a result, the inclusion of "the so called abortion neutralizing clause"[30] to the amendment, "reasoning that if the ERA would have no effect on abortions why won't its supporters say so?"[31]   Professor Noonan had also been a member and the president of Americans for Life, an anti-abortion group.   In addition to his overt public and political support of the "pro-life" position, Noonan had authored a book, *The Private Choice: Abortion in America in the Seventies*[32] and a number of articles outlining his legal position on the topic.[33]   In light of Noonan's substantial record on the abortion controversy, the Reagan administration considered him to be one of its "shining stars,"[34] and they were fairly confident about the position he would take on potential abortion litigation.[35]

---

[27] March 1, 1976.

[28] *The McNeil/Lehrer Report*, May 18, 1982, (Transcript 1732).

[29] "PM cycle," *U.P.I.*, Wednesday, January 25, 1984.

[30] Pro-lifers wanted to modify the ERA amendment with a clause that specified that nothing in the proposed amendment granted or secured any right relating to abortion or the funding thereof. Ibid.

[31] Ibid.

[32] (New York: Free Press, 1979).

[33] Articles focusing on the constitutionality of abortion include: "The Supreme Court and Abortion: Upholding Constitutional Principles," *Hasting Center Rep.* 6 (Winter 1980): 32; "The Experience of Pain by the Unborn," in T. Hilgers, et al., eds. *New Perspectives on Human Abortion*, (1981), p. 205; "The Right of Abortion Funding," *Human Life Review* 20 (Spring 1981); "The Akron Case," *Human Life Review* 5 (Summer 1983); "The Root and Branch of Roe v. Wade," *Nebraska Law Review* 63 (1984): 668.

[34] When considering Noonan's nomination, one Justice official proudly stated that "[He] is one of the five smartest guys in the world." *Time*, November 4, 1985.

On Friday October 11, 1985, President Reagan announced the pending nomination of John Noonan. Immediately thereafter Senator Bob Packwood (R-OR), a leading congressional advocate of a woman's right to an abortion, voiced his opposition to the nomination; in doing so he maintained that "the man [was] avid anti-choice and pro-right to life."[36] Although Packwood saw little hope of derailing Noonan's nomination, barring some unknown skeleton in Noonan's closet, he promised to ask Senate Majority Leader Robert Dole (R-KS) to delay the confirmation vote on Noonan. If Dole refused to do so, Packwood planned to instigate a filibuster.[37] Women's rights groups also came out in opposition to the appointment, as they had done with previous Reagan appointees, warning that an appointee such as this would "result in the amending of the Constitution by judicial appointment, further obstructing the rights of women and minorities."[38] Still others voiced concern over his lack of judicial experience.

Ignoring opposition within his own party from a home-state Senator (who had made a claim on a home-state right to the nomination), the President nominated Noonan to the Ninth Circuit Court of Appeals on October 16, 1985. Attempting to expedite the process, a mere two days later President Reagan sent the nomination to the Senate Judiciary Committee. There it sat for another month.

Some observers of President Reagan's recruitment process speculate that "while Reagan's Justice Department [was] responsible for screening candidates, the Senate Judiciary Committee had become the real battleground for the judgeships."[39] Given the political and philosophical divisions between Democrats and Republicans on the Judiciary Committee, Noonan's appearance before a Subcommittee of the full Committee on November 6, 1985 seemed crucial.[40] The

---

[35] When rumors about Noonan's impending nomination became too numerous to be ignored, one reporter contended that: "Some judicial candidates don't have to be asked their views on potential litigation. They volunteer them. John Noonan...calls himself a 'pronounced critic' of the Supreme Court's decision legalizing abortion. Compare that with what Sandra Day O'Connor said about that case in 1981, during her confirmation hearings for the Supreme court: I feel it is improper for me to endorse or criticize that decision, which may well come before the Court in one form or another." *Los Angeles Times*, October 6, 1985.

[36] Tom Towslee, "BC cycle," *U.P.I.*, October 13, 1985.

[37] Senator Packwood not only opposed Noonan's nomination on philosophical grounds, but was also opposed to it because he and Senator Mark Hatfield, also from Oregon, had been pushing for the nomination of U.S. District Court Judge Owen Panner of Portland, Oregon, to the Ninth Circuit Court of Appeals. He felt that it was unfair that all the President's new nominations had been from California, contending that "Oregon deserved an appointee because of the case load the state generat[ed] and the state's population." Ibid.

[38] Statement by Eleanor Smeal, the President of the National Organization for Women, quoted in Judi Hasson, "BC cycle," *U.P.I.*, Sunday, November 3, 1985.

[39] Ibid.

[40] Senate Judiciary Committee Report, S521.52.14 1985.

Subcommittee was comprised of Senators McConnell (R-KY) and Simon (D-IL); Senator Mathias (R-MD) joined the hearing later. Senator Wilson (R-CA), Noonan's sponsor, introduced the nominee to the Subcommittee. His oral testimony focused on Noonan's impressive resume, highlighting his scholarly work and his tenure as a professor at the University of California School of Law. Noting a need for brevity, Senator Wilson capped Noonan's remarkable career by saying:

> John Noonan is a well-educated man who has a deep understanding of and respect for the law. It is clear from his life as a philosopher of the law, and as a teacher and practitioner of the law, that he is superbly qualified for the role of a circuit judge. He understands the role and the importance that it serves in our legal system, and the role that our legal system plays in our constitutional form of government.[41]

A written statement from Senator Orrin Hatch (R-UT) supporting the nominee became part of the record. Hatch's written recommendation joined letters from an esteemed group of legal scholars and law professors who urged that Noonan be confirmed. Letters came from Jesse Choper, Dean, University of California, Berkeley;[42] James Vorenberg, Dean, Harvard Law School;[43] Erwin N. Griswold, former United States Solicitor General;[44] Guido Calebresi, Dean, Yale Law School.[45]

Senator McConnell questioned Noonan first. One aspect of his questioning focused on "how the [candidate] would resolve the conflict between [his] conscience and [his] sense of judgment and the clear meaning of a constitutional or statutory provision?"[46] Noonan responded that "I think there is no doubt that a federal judge deciding the case has the obligation of following the statute, following the Constitution, following precedent."[47] Responding to reservations voiced by a California women's lawyer group over Noonan's pro-life stance, Senator Simon continued along the same vein of questioning, asking "if the law states something whether it is the field of abortion or any other field that you happen to disagree with that law, how do you regard your position as a judge? How do you handle that as a judge?"[48] Noonan responded cautiously by saying:

---

[41] Ibid., 1019.

[42] Ibid., 1065-66.

[43] Ibid., 1067.

[44] Ibid., 1068.

[45] Ibid., 1069.

[46] Ibid., 1025.

[47] Ibid.

[48] Ibid.

> Senator Simon, I believe there is a very large difference between exercising one's rights as a citizen, one's basic political rights which I have been exercising, and what I feel bound to do as a judge. As a judge I would feel absolutely constrained to follow the applicable statute, the applicable constitutional provision, the applicable Supreme Court precedent.[49]

Estelle H. Rogers, the National Director of the Federation of Women Lawyers' Judicial Screening Panel, testified in opposition to Noonan's candidacy. She was the only "outsider" to come before the subcommittee, and the only person to formally oppose Noonan's nomination. She argued that the Federation of Women Lawyers was "deeply concerned about the fitness of [the nominee] to sit on the Ninth Circuit Court."[50] Although part of their concern stemmed from Noonan's well publicized views on abortion, they were more worried about "the intemperate zeal with which he held and expressed [those values]."[51] The "feminist lawyers" she represented doubted that the "passion," "emotional pitch," and "fervor" that pervaded Noonan's works on the subject would really dissipate "with the incantation of the oath of office."[52] Moreover, the Federation of Women Lawyers also questioned the purpose of nominating an individual "who [had] seriously proposed the overturning of *Roe v. Wade.*"[53]

Senator Mathias (R-MD) joined the hearing and, as well as a number of other inquiries, he asked if Noonan would have a difficult time applying the law, if it were in fact contrary to his strongly held beliefs. Professor Noonan's response drew a sharp distinction between a lawyer's role and a judge's role:

> I feel there is a very sharp difference between the role of advocate and the role of judge.... I would have felt I was doing less than I could if I had been less than wholehearted in the causes in which I have been an advocate. But when one takes off the garb of an advocate and puts on that of a judge, it is a very different role. And I would be surprised and ashamed if I became an advocate as a judge. I feel a strong constraint to follow the law, to follow the precedents—and that is something very different from my role as advocate.[54]

Mathias also inquired about the candidate's lack of judicial experience, as well as his "qualified" rating from a divided Standing Committee on the Judici-

---

[49] Ibid.

[50] Ibid., 1050.

[51] Ibid.

[52] Ibid., 1050-1051.

[53] Ibid., 1051.

[54] Ibid., 1060.

ary. Noonan was unsure why he had been given the barely acceptable rating, but he assumed that it was somehow connected to his lack of extensive trial experience. The Senator, taking a small jab at the Reagan administration, consoled Noonan by saying that "in comparison with some of the other nominees who have been before us recently, you have extensive trial experience."[55]

Affirmation

Although Noonan's confirmation hearing lasted only one day, it took the Senate Judiciary Committee another two weeks to clear his nomination (November 21, 1985), and that was not without some difficulty.[56] On the day that the Committee unanimously affirmed his nomination, angry Democrats publicly announced that they would "try to block all nominees for federal judgeships until the panel's Republican majority [gave] them more time to examine the candidates."[57] In addition, ranking Democrat Joseph R. Biden demanded that questions from Democrats be included in the panel's questionnaire to nominees and that at least three weeks notice be given for each confirmation hearing, plus another two weeks be allowed for each vote.[58] According to Biden, Democrats needed more time to scrutinize the backgrounds of controversial nominees.

How then did one of President Reagan's more controversial nominees, John Noonan, get past the embittered minority? A political deal expedited the process. Democrats agreed to affirm Noonan's confirmation, only after they obtained assurances that they would get to vote on the nomination of former CIA General Counsel Stanley Sporkin to the U.S. District Court. Sporkin's confirmation vote had been on hold for seventeen months due to the diligence of conservative Senator Jeremiah Denton (R-AL), one of Sporkin's most strident critics. During the long delay Denton had demanded and was granted four closed hearings "on allegations that Sporkin [had] improperly intervened in an FBI probe of a leak of classified Central Intelligence Agency information."[59] Thus, when the Republican majority of the Senate Judiciary Committee promised that Sporkin's nomination would reach a vote by December 12, the Democrats agreed not to delay the vote further on John Noonan. What is important, however, is that Noonan's appointment was achieved without compromising those qualifications that had recommended him to the Reagan administration at the outset. On December 17, 1985, the full Senate confirmed Judge John

---

[55] Ibid., 1064.

[56] Howard Kurtz, "Democrats Threaten to Stall All Nominees for Judgeships: More Time Asked to Examine Candidates," *The Washington Post*, November 22, 1985.

[57] Ibid.

[58] Ibid.

[59] *The Washington Post*, December 5, 1985, p. A14.

Noonan's nomination; no debate ensued, and he was quietly approved by a unanimous voice vote.

Articulation

John Noonan's recruitment appears to be representative of a low articulation experience. Although the Reagan Administration did not follow the traditional Circuit Court recruitment process, this route to selection did not necessarily move the recruitment process away from a low-level articulation experience. Certainly, a number of participants were involved in the initiation and initial screening. The Attorney General, the Assistant Attorney General, and ranking White House and Department of Justice officials sitting on the President's Committee on Judicial Selection each played a critical role in the process. However, they did not bring a wide range of competing norms to the recruitment process. As a result, the initiation and subsequent screening ensured that candidates like Noonan were not exposed to many competing expectations. Moreover, with President Reagan's party in control of the Senate, the President and his political advisers did not have to be *as* concerned about the conformability of their nominees as in cases of divided government. Thus, the screening process did little to dampen the ideological fervor of Reagan's nominees.

However, the ideological criteria heavily emphasized by the Reagan administration were somewhat offset by the ABA's Standing Committee on Judiciary and by the Senate Judiciary Committee. In giving a contested rating of "qualified" for Judge Noonan, the ABA was sending a strong message to the Reagan administration. The ABA, an extra-constitutional actor in the screening process that emphasizes legal norms, clearly found the President's willingness to place heavy emphasis on ideological compatibility at the cost of legal experience to be problematic.

The Senate Judiciary Committee, although controlled by Republicans, also may have tempered Noonan's activist views. The Senators who conducted the confirmation hearing emphasized different aspects of the "rule of law," and each questioned the nominee about his ability to distinguish between the role of an advocate and the role of a judge in a democratic society. Senators wanted public assurances that candidate Noonan would not act as a judicial legislator once placed on the bench—Democrats because they did not want Noonan and his fellow conservatives to whittle away at *Roe v. Wade*, and Republican's because adherence to a strict constructions philosophy permitted a more conservative reading of the Fourteenth Amendment. Thus, Senators from both parties used the hearing as a vehicle for educating the candidate about their expectations of the appropriate role of a judge in American society.

With respect to interest group participation in the formal screening process, although there were rumblings of disquietude when Reagan first made the nomination, only one individual came before the Subcommittee to oppose Noonan's nomination. So few actors in the formal screening process ensured that the nominee was exposed to few divergent views. The relative haste in which President Reagan appointed Judge Noonan prevented potential participants from entering into the recruitment process (as had been the case in the Ginsburg appointment).

All indications from the recruitment process experienced by Judge John Noonan are that he will continue to hold those views that brought him to the attention of President Reagan's recruiters in the first place. However, as we have suggested, once on the bench a judge comes under a variety of influences that may reinforce the recruitment experience or mitigate (or even override) what is learned through that experience.

Chapter Eleven

Recruitment to Federal District Courts

There are ninety-four U.S. District Courts, each of which is contained within state boundaries, assuring that the District Court judges are "subjected to the continuing political and social influences of their locale and region."[1] Population growth and an increase in the volume of litigation, however, have forced Congress to divide the larger states into more than one district. New York, for instance, has four U.S. District Courts. These same factors have also led to the establishment of multiple judgeships in each district. Today, there are 649 District Court judgeships, with all districts having two or more judges.[2]

Initiation

In the beginning of the Republic, the President took the initiative in searching for and nominating federal trial judges. However, the evolving practice of "senatorial courtesy" added considerably more complexity to the District Court recruitment process. Senators and local party leaders have good reasons for using senatorial courtesy to control the initiation of District Court judges. First, Senators believe they have a greater degree of knowledge than the President does about the qualifications, background, and record of the judges in their state.[3] Second, and more importantly, federal judgeships are desirable,

---

[1] The sole exception to the use of state boundaries for designating court jurisdiction is the district of Wyoming, which includes the Montana and Idaho portions of Yellowstone National Park. Harry P. Stumpf, *American Judicial Politics* (New York: Harcourt, Brace Jovanovich, 1988), p. 107.

[2] A number of assistants help District Court judges carry out their duties. The most important and influential of these is the group of parajudicial U.S. Magistrates. The Federal Magistrate Act of 1979 outlines the requirements for the selection of U.S. Magistrates: "candidates are appointed by District Court judges for eight and four-year terms of office, and they must have been a member of the bar for at least five years prior to selection." A provision in the Magistrate Act also requires District Court judges to establish a merit panel comprised both of lawyers and nonlawyers "to advertise the vacant position, evaluate the applicants, and submit a list of five nominees." The purpose behind instituting the merit selection of magistrates was to make the candidate pool more diverse. Nonetheless, District Court judges frequently select individuals who were close associates or their former law clerks. Henry J. Abraham, *The Judicial Process...*, 6 ed. (New York: Oxford University Press, 1993), p. 161; and Stephen L. Wasby, *The Supreme Court in the Federal Judicial System* (Chicago: Nelson-Hall, 1993), p. 48. See also Steven Puro, Roger L. Goldman, and Alice Padawer-Singer, "The Evolving Role of US Magistrates in the District Courts," *Judicature* 64 (May 1981); Carroll Seron, "Magistrates and the Work of Federal Courts: A New Division of Labor," *Judicature* 69 (April-May 1986); and Christopher E. Smith, "Who Are the U.S. Magistrates?" *Judicature* 71 (October-November 1987).

[3] Chase maintains that neither the President nor individual Senators are in the position to know whether a candidate will turn out to be a good nominee. However, if who has better knowledge

prestigious positions, making them politically important to Senators and the local party elite. These factors ensure that Senators will jealously guard their power to initiate candidates.

Before sending a list of candidates to the President, Senators or state and local politicos often seek the advice of judges sitting on the District Court bench where the vacancy exists.[4] Prospective candidates may also look to the bench, as well as other important political figures in the state, for endorsements. This type of campaigning, despite its prevalence, is usually done behind closed doors. Some aspirants to the bench may also establish visible legal or political profiles in the hopes of attracting the attention of a presidential administration. Thus, they actively participate in party politics, sit as chairs of national and state campaigns, and serve as party spokespersons.

Although Senators play a prevalent role seeking out candidates, Presidents can become the primary actors in the initiation stage if they choose to do so. Harold Chase notes, "where a President wants to ensure a high level of appointments, he has the legal powers which afford him considerable coin with which to bargain with the Senators individually or collectively."[5] Although it is more reasonable for the two parties to confer and come to an agreement over a candidate, if they cannot reach a consensus the President does not abdicate his power.

Traditionally, the Attorney General and other key members of the Department of Justice have played an important role in District Court recruitment. Often Presidents would leave the recruitment process entirely in their Attorney General's hands, offering little or no guidance. In recent years, the President's White House advisers have come to play a significantly more active role in filling vacancies on both District Court and Courts of Appeals benches. Thus, although senatorial courtesy gives Senators primary control over recruitment, Senators now must not only contend with the Department of Justice but they also must be concerned with the political currents emanating from the White House.

Screening and Affirmation

Although the amount of screening done on a candidate varies depending upon who played the primary role in initiating candidacies, it is the President who plays the reactionary role in screening. Because Senators of the President's party take a proprietary view towards District Court recruitment and will make

---

about a candidate is dependent upon resources, then the President wins hands down. Yet, this does not mean that Presidents will always choose more competent individuals. Harold Chase, *Federal Judges: The Appointing Process* (Minneapolis: University of Minnesota Press, 1972), p 11.

[4] John B. Gates and Charles A. Johnson, eds. *The American Courts: A Critical Assessment* (Washington D.C.: CQ Press, 1991), p. 193.

[5] Chase, *Federal Judges*, p. 14.

life difficult if thwarted, the President usually accepts the Senator's candidate unless the individual is grossly unqualified. However, when a President chooses not to acquiesce to the Senator's choice, he may choose one of three possible lines of action: (1) he can refuse to fill the vacancy; (2) he can go ahead and nominate his favored candidate and risk a contested confirmation; or (3) he can make a recess appointment, recognizing that when the name is sent to Congress at the next session the Senators may choose not to confirm the judge who is already seated.

Sometimes, however, Senators submit a list of candidates instead of a single name to the President or the Justice Department. When this occurs, the Justice Department has the discretion to screen the candidate according to the President's criteria. As a result, candidates may be disqualified not only because the Department of Justice views them as lacking the requisite qualifications, but because they fail to share the administration's political vision, concern for demographic balance or ideological concerns.

Where the candidate is a favorite of the President, home-state Senators play a reactionary role, showing their approval or disapproval through the blue-slip process. Most Presidents will avoid naming a candidate for whom Senators of their party express disdain, making sure to resolve any conflicts before the nomination is formally announced.

District Court nominating commissions, an offshoot of President Carter's efforts to institute a merit selection system at the intermediate appeals level, also played a dual role in initiating and screening candidates. President Carter strongly urged Senators to utilize commissions, and to further encourage the practice he issued an executive order establishing standards and guidelines for the recruitment of District Court judges. The order explicitly stated that the President would only nominate individuals who had a "commitment to equal justice under the law."[6] It also granted the Attorney General the authority both to check the credentials of prospective candidates and to monitor the selection process to ensure that the commissions were considering an adequate number of minorities and females.

Between the years 1976 and 1979, Senators responded to Carter's encouragement by establishing thirty commissions.[7] These commissions varied considerably with respect to number of panels and commissioners, method of appointment and tenure of commissioners,[8] the existence of a written charter,

---

[6] Executive Order 1097, section 1-101.

[7] In 1974, Democratic Senators Lawton Chiles and Richard Stone, in concert with the Florida Bar Association, established the first judicial commission to recruit and recommend candidates for U.S. District Court judgeships.

[8] Senators were involved in the appointment of commissioners to twenty-eight of the thirty commissions. In nineteen of the appointments, they were the sole appointers. In the remaining nine, they shared the role with the state bar. A congressional delegation aided by the state bar or law school deans appointed the commissioners for Kansas and Utah.

and the role of the sponsors in designating preferred candidates for nominations.[9] The demographic backgrounds of the commissioners also varied. Males, females, lawyers and lay persons all sat on the commissions in varying proportions. However, European-American males and lawyers tended to dominate the membership.[10] Despite the prevalence of traditional legal elites on the commissions and the continuing influence of home-state Senators, most researchers have concluded that merit selection commissions opened up and diversified the initiation and screening stages of federal trial court judicial recruitment.[11] The commissioners who sit on the few District Court nominating commissions that remain today screen candidates according to standards set out by the Senators who placed them on the commission.[12]

Once a single candidate has been selected (either through coercion or consensus), the Attorney General, if not having done so already, authorizes the Federal Bureau of Investigation to begin its check of the potential nominee. At the same time the FBI is carrying out its requisite check, the American Bar Association is also conducting its own investigation. The local and state bar associations also play an important role in the screening of a District Court candidate, as can interest groups.

As we have seen from Chapter 8, the ABA's Standing Committee on the Federal Judiciary begins its confidential and thorough investigation of the District Court candidate when a name has been received from the Attorney General's office. The member of the Committee from the circuit in which the district vacancy is located assumes the responsibility of conducting the investigation. Upon completion, an informal report is given the Attorney General and when the nomination is officially announced by the President, the results of the ABA's Committee evaluation are reported to the Senate Judiciary Committee in order to facilitate its screening of the nominee.

Interest groups—important actors in the screening of Supreme Court and Circuit Court candidates—at times may become involved in District Court nominations. However, once a nomination has reached the confirmation stage, the pleas of interest groups have tended to fall on deaf ears. The media may also interject itself into the screening process by disseminating information that

---

[9] See Table I in Alan Neff, "Breaking with Tradition: A Study of U.S. District Court Nominating Commissions," *Judicature* 64 (December-January 1981): 264.

[10] Of the 404 commissioners who served on the 30 commissions, 84.9 percent were male and 63.8 percent were lawyers. Despite the low percentage of minorities on the commissions, the percentage that did serve was slightly higher than their estimated presence in the general population. Ibid., 269.

[11] When commissioners were asked about recruitment, only thirty-eight of the respondents reported that they did any recruiting. Neff, "Breaking with Tradition...," p. 269.

[12] Individuals nominated by the commissions, however, were more likely to have legal or judicial experience as state judges, government attorneys or professors of law; additionally, they tended to receive high ratings from the American Bar Association.

may positively or negatively affect the likelihood of a candidate receiving an official nomination or being confirmed.[13] However, ironically most U.S. District Court appointments receive only minimal media coverage.

After intense screening, or not so intense screening as the case may be, if the candidate appears to be free of blemishes the President will then officially nominate him or her. Once the candidate's name has been submitted to the Senate Judiciary Committee, and if "senatorial courtesy" is not invoked, a Subcommittee of usually three Senators appointed by the Chair of the Judiciary Committee conducts a public hearing. Since in most cases the home-state Senators already have given the nominee their endorsement, these hearings are most often a mere formality. However, during contentious confirmation battles, District Court Senate Judiciary hearings may become intensely heated affairs that continue on for a number of months. Upon the conclusion of the hearings, the Judiciary Committee issues its recommendation and then the full Senate votes on the nominee. In most cases, the nominee is immediately and unanimously confirmed. Infrequently, the nominee is confirmed by a bare majority, or is rejected altogether.

Articulation Model

Generally, the least number of effective actors are involved in each of the stages of District Court recruitment, suggesting that recruitment processes at this level will tend to produce judges who either view themselves as delegates or trustees. Most District Court candidates will not experience high articulation recruitment processes that will socialize them to appreciate the need to counterbalance the expectations of impartiality and independence against the demands of political and public accountability. Instead, they will go through low articulation experiences, where the few effective actors involved will either emphasize political accountability at the cost of independence or judicial impartiality at the cost of recognizing the mores and needs of the citizenry. That District Courts are located in the region over which they have jurisdiction, and that neither the President nor Congress scrutinizes the activity of District Court judges to the same extent they scrutinize the activity of Circuit Courts and Supreme Court judges, may further mitigate or enhance the effects of the recruitment experience.[14]

However, it is important to recognize in any given appointment (and this holds true for Supreme Court and Circuit Court appointments as well) the number of participants and their efficacy can vary—the level of the appointment and

---

[13] Neil McFeeley, *Appointment of Judges: The Johnson Presidency* (Austin: University of Texas Press, 1987), pp. 24-25.

[14] One may note that the executive branch may have better knowledge than Congress about decisions of District Court judges because its legal officers, United States Marshals and District Attorneys, both have direct contact with them. However, appointments to both positions result from "senatorial courtesy," thus assuring that these officers have a dual loyalty to both the executive and the Senators in their home state.

the institutional norms and conventions notwithstanding. In some cases, District Court recruitment may involve only a few actors, whereas in a few other cases many participants may play a role. Moreover, not only the number of participants but what interest they may represent may vary from appointment to appointment. The variation in interest may have an important impact on the type of judge finally selected since some participants may emphasize legal norms over democratic norms, whereas others may emphasize the reverse. Variation in number, type, and efficacy can occur across districts and between districts. Thus, each recruitment process must be seen as an idiosyncratic event that falls somewhere on the continuum between a low and moderate articulation system. Once affirmed, other norms come into play and may, in time, balance what was learned from the recruitment experience. Of course, the lifetime tenure of federal judges encourages independence. As a result, nominees once placed on the bench find a diminishing need to be attentive to demands for accountability.

Case Study: The Eastern District of Washington

In 1984, Congress created a third judgeship in the Eastern District of Washington in response to burgeoning caseloads.[15] Once the judgeship had been officially authorized, individuals began to discreetly vie for the position.

Initiation

Interested parties, such as Justice Carolyn Dimmick[16] and Judge Robert J. Bryan,[17] began to notify Republican Senators Slade Gorton and Dan Evans either directly or indirectly.[18] Unlike their Democratic predecessors, Gorton and Evans decided not to use a District Court Nominating Commission.[19] Thus, interested parties were forced to independently vie for the seat.[20] When

---

[15] At that time the District Court for Eastern Washington ranked number one in the nation in caseload per jurist. *Spokesman-Review*, October 3, 1985, p. A1.

[16] Former Washington State Supreme Court Justice who now sits on the federal district bench in Seattle.

[17] Kitsap County Superior Court Judge.

[18] Interview, Alan McDonald, April 23, 1994.

[19] Although a District Court Nominating Commission was not used, the Senators did request that the Washington State Bar Association and the Federal Bar Association convene a joint committee to make recommendations. *United Press International*, July 23, 1984, Monday BC cycle.

[20] When asked if the absence of a judicial selection committee was problematic, Judge McDonald maintained that "judicial selection committees [were] not important, because the Senator will get whoever they want on the list." According to McDonald in 1990, although Senator Gorton used a District Court Nominating Commission, and he appointed the President of the Washington State Bar Association to select the commission's members, he was still able to control the selection process because the President of WSBA had served as Gorton's assistant when he was Attorney

considering candidates for the position, Gorton and Evans "[sought] candidates with philosophies compatible with the conservative views of President Reagan.[21] According to the Senators, the President wanted nominees who were young enough "to ensure a fairly long tenure, meaning that the new judges probably [would] not be much older than 55 years."[22]

Alan McDonald, a lawyer practicing in Yakima, had no personal interest in the new seat. Feeling perfectly content with his private practice, he never gave filling the new judgeship "a moment's thought."[23] Yet, numerous acquaintances who were interested in the position did ask that he put in a good word for them with Senator Gorton, a close personal friend. McDonald, wishing to avoid being placed in the untenable position of choosing between friends, declined to do this favor. However, a particular friend, whom McDonald considered to be extremely well-qualified, asked that he speak to Gorton on his behalf and Judge McDonald consented. Because McDonald felt that person was well-suited for a federal judgeship, he arranged to meet with Gorton between flights at the Spokane Airport. At the meeting, McDonald began to discuss the qualifications of his friend, only to be interrupted by the smiling Senator who said "Alan, ever since this judgeship became available, I have had you in mind."[24] After McDonald acquiesced, allowing Gorton to consider him for the position, his name along with the names of Carolyn Dimmick and Robert J. Bryan[25] was sent to the White House.

Screening

Once the President authorized the nomination, McDonald was interviewed and investigated by John Gavin, one of the Ninth Circuit representatives for the Standing Committee on the Federal Judiciary and "an old and dear friend" of the Yakima lawyer.[26] Despite their friendship, the interview lasted a couple of hours and was quite intensive, because John Gavin "made no assumptions about his friend's qualifications or competence."[27] A Justice Department's interview

---

General. As a result, the panel had a very good idea of what, if not whom, the Senator was looking for. Interview, Alan McDonald, April 23, 1994.

[21] *United Press International*, July 23, 1984, Monday BC cycle.

[22] Ibid.

[23] Interview, Alan McDonald, April 23, 1994.

[24] Ibid.

[25] Judge Bryan was later considered, but not nominated for an opening on the Ninth Circuit Courts of Appeals.

[26] Interview, Alan McDonald, April 23, 1994.

[27] McDonald confirms that the ABA plays a "highly important role in the appointment process because a professional assessment is important." He advocates, however, that the state and local bar "should play an increasing role" in assessing prospective candidates. Their participation

immediately followed the ABA interview. Contrary to the assertions of the popular press, McDonald was not subjected to a litmus test.[28] However, when one of the DOJ investigators inquired about what he thought his judicial philosophy might be, McDonald's response was "I don't know."[29]

This aspect of the screening process took considerably longer than was initially expected. When McDonald's nomination first surfaced, many thought he would be on the bench by April 1, 1985. However, he did not clear the necessary hurdles until June, and then the "nomination was left on the White House steps where it sat."[30] Bill Morlin, staff writer for Spokane's *Spokesman Review*, reported that many presumed the delay was "tied to political differences between the White House and one or both of Washington's Republican Senators."[31] Voicing a similar conclusion, an editor for the *Spokesman Review* condemned the delay, seeing it as "an effort to contaminate the judiciary with politics."[32] When the nomination was first expected, President Reagan and Senator Gorton had "squared off" over the federal budgets and the question of raising taxes.[33] Gorton had led the Senate opposition against the White House's budget proposal. Some asserted that Reagan's attempts to "stock the judicial pond with young conservative ideologues"[34] also played a role in the delay, suggesting that members of the "Far Right" were opposed to the fifty-seven year old McDonald's nomination because of his age and lack of a judicial record.[35]

The delay put McDonald in somewhat of an awkward position. He had been waiting for official word since May and had already left his private-practice, expecting to sit on the bench by mid-summer. When questioned about the delay in early fall, McDonald conceded that although he had "had a wonderful summer vacation," he was a bit "puzzled by the protracted appointment process."[36] On September 12, 1985, President Reagan finally acted on the

---

would "enhance" the process, since the members of state and local bars know the candidates better." Ibid.

[28] Moreover, most newly appointed judges that McDonald met at "judges' school" after his own appointment had not been confronted with a litmus test either. Ibid.

[29] Ibid.

[30] *Spokesman-Review*, September 5, 1985, p. A8.

[31] Ibid.

[32] *Spokesman-Review*, September 6, 1985, p. 4.

[33] Ibid.

[34] Ibid.

[35] Speculation over McDonald's capacity to fill the position, however, did not arise. The private practitioner was considered to be "one of the best trial lawyers in the state." Ibid. Prior to becoming an associate and then partner in the firm of Halverson and Applegate (1954-1984), McDonald had served for a brief two-year stint (1952-1954) as Deputy Prosecuting Attorney for Yakima County.

nomination, sending it to the Senate Judiciary Committee. A little over two weeks later (October 2, 1985) McDonald appeared before a Subcommittee of the Senate Judiciary Committee. Only two members of the Subcommittee, McConnell (R-KY) and Simon (D-IL) were present at the hearing. Senator McConnell questioned McDonald first, asking if he thought that going from being a trial lawyer to a federal judge would be a difficult transition. McDonald responded by saying that the skills required to be a good trial lawyer and to run a successful law practice had adequately prepared him for the position. The remainder of McConnell's questions focused on McDonald's potential for judicial activism. In particular, McConnell wanted to know "if there were everyday circumstances under which a judge should attempt to establish new judicial precedent," and if so what criteria would McDonald use to consider the propriety of revising existing precedent?[37] McDonald answered by saying:

> Well this is an area I would approach gingerly. I think again calling upon my experiences as a practicing lawyer all these years, that predictability is so important to those who labor in the vineyards of the law. And I think those occasions [for establishing new judicial precedent] are going to arise only when the precedent is nonexistent or ambivalent.[38]

After McConnell's substantive but nevertheless brief questioning, Senator Simon questioned McDonald about his membership in what appeared to be a male-only club. The American Bar Association had been concerned that McDonald's involvement in this club may have violated its code of ethics, regarding membership in any club that discriminates on the basis of race, creed, or sex. According to McDonald, the bylaws of the club in question, the 26A Dining Club, did not prohibit women from joining. He conceded, however, that women were not encouraged to join, but he qualified this by stating that he did not believe that "any woman in her right mind would be interested in joining it."[39] When asked if he thought he would continue his membership in the club in light of the controversy, McDonald responded affirmatively. Upon hearing this response, Simon warned him to think his response over carefully and to tell the Subcommittee of his final decision before his approval came to a vote.[40]

This proved not to be necessary. Immediately following the hearing, Senator Gorton and McDonald went to Senator Simon and explained that the club was "just an informal group of people who got together," and McDonald had only listed the club "in an excess of caution."[41]

---

[36] *Spokesman-Review*, September 9, 1985, p. A8.

[37] Senate Confirmation Hearing, October 2, 1985, S521-52.11, pp. 383-385.

[38] Ibid.

[39] Ibid.

[40] Ibid.

[41] *Spokesman-Review*, October 4, 1985, p. 17.

Affirmation

The resolution of the controversy guaranteed McDonald's confirmation. On October 7, 1985, the Senate Judiciary Committee reported favorably to the full Senate on his appointment. On October 18, 1985, the full Senate unanimously confirmed his nomination by a voice vote.

Articulation

It was evident that McDonald's recruitment was a typical low articulation experience. Gorton and Evans decided against establishing a District Court Nominating Commission, making the process less pluralistic. Second, Senator Gorton at the outset knew he wanted McDonald for the position, even before the formal recruitment process had begun. As a result, even if a large number of people had applied for the position, their chances of being seriously considered by the Senator were greatly minimized. And last, Judge McDonald never considered the position until it was offered to him. Thus, during the initiation phase, he did not come into contact with a broad array of people who may have represented a variety of perspectives regarding a judge's role in a democratic society. Neither members of the legal community nor advocates of particular interests were able to engage him in such a dialogue.

The lack of a nominating commission participating in screening protected McDonald from the varied inquiries coming from its diverse membership. Gorton, a person interested in political accountability, was the only person with whom he had contact in the initial stages of screening. McDonald's ABA interview and hearing before the Senate Judiciary Committee's Subcommittee were fairly intensive. However, the intensity of the ABA interview is somewhat offset by the fact that he was interviewed by a friend. Only Senator Gorton took a personal interest, and he was the only non-Subcommittee member present at McDonald's Senate Judiciary hearing.

Moreover, to say that McDonald's subcommittee hearing was substantive and rigorous is really not saying much. The substance and the rigor of his hearing in no way compares to the substance and rigor faced by nominees to the Supreme Court or the Circuit Courts. The lack of testimony from outsiders either in support or opposition to the candidate is a clear indicator of this. McDonald had the full advantage of senatorial courtesy, which assured Senate Judiciary Committee approval and, thereby, allowed the full Senate to merely rubber-stamp his nomination.

McDonald's recruitment tended to be characteristic of a low articulation style that is commonly associated with traditional federal District Court appointments, suggesting that as a judge he would lean either towards a more accountable view of his role or a more independent view. As a federal judge, McDonald recognizes the vulnerability of a judge concerning public pressure—if the public elected federal judges and they did not serve for life, they might reach very different outcomes. As a result, McDonald supports insulating federal District Court judges from the undue influence of the citizenry. He believes that "somewhere in the judicial system there has to be one group of judges that are isolated from democratic rule," maintaining that the framers evidenced great wisdom when they made certain exceptions to democratic rule.[42] Moreover, McDonald is not so much concerned with how the public receives his opinions, expressing that "in his own experience in the Vineyards of Eastern Washington, it [does not] matter how it will sound to the public.[43] Thus, Judge McDonald seems to view his role as a federal District Court judge as being independent from the demands of the citizenry.[44]

---

[42] Interview, Alan McDonald, April 23, 1994.

[43] Ibid.

[44] Judge McDonald went on senior status in January, 1997.

Chapter Twelve

Epilogue

Earlier we had cautioned that in addition to what is learned from the recruitment experience a number of other important influences mold the behavior of judges on the bench. Only a fortunate few of the many who aspire to state and federal benches, whether elected or appointed, survive the winnowing recruitment process. Throughout the selection process these fortunate survivors absorb particular perspectives regarding what is expected of them as judges. At the same time, they also retain personal values and views of the legal and political world that either coincide with or are permitted by the demands or desires of active participants encountered throughout the recruitment process. It has been argued throughout this monograph, and demonstrated in a series of close analyses of a number of specific cases, that the numbers and diversity of active participants involved throughout the recruitment sequence determine the level of *articulation* ascribed to any recruitment experience. The level of articulation, in turn, influences the views of the newly selected judge with respect to the judge's dilemma—i.e., political accountability, and judicial independence.

Recruitment may end once appointed or elected judges don the robes of office, but the process of molding the individual jurist to the judicial position continues. Once on the bench, certain restraints are brought to bear and certain opportunities for self-initiated action are presented. The office itself requires new judges to observe particular **norms** and **rules**. The **norms** are the "oughts'" born of others' expectations, that constrain the judges' behavior. These norms mean, for example, that judges ought to be civil with one another and with attorneys and jurors. They ought not to dissent frequently, nor should they be seen too often in the company of attorneys who practice before them, nor should they avoid their share of court-related duties.

Although no formal punishments are necessarily associated with violations of judicial norms, the symbolic and informal rewards for following their dictates are indeed numerous. The "team player" or social and task leader may be elected as Chief Judge by colleagues, or be awarded "Judge of the Year" by the bar association. Perhaps the senior judge awards the coveted opinion writing assignment to the cooperative judge. In contrast, ignoring the norms could lead to informal forms of disapproval and professional isolation. The opportunity to draft an opinion may be withheld from a judicial maverick, or the Chief Judge may appoint him or her to night court or to another less desirable department of a large trial court.

The Preamble to the Code of Judicial Conduct provides a framework for the norms of office:

Our legal system is based on the principle that an independent, fair and competent judiciary will interpret and apply the laws that govern us. The role of the judiciary is central to the American concept of justice and rule of law. Intrinsic to all sections of this Code are the precepts that judges, individually and collectively, must respect and honor the judicial office as a public trust and strive to enhance and maintain confidence in our legal system. The judge is an arbiter of facts and law for the resolution of disputes and a highly visible symbol of government under the rule of law.[1]

The **rules** associated with judicial office are another type of stricture, but these stipulations involve sanctions. The threat (or occasional actual use) of punishments usually assures observance of the rules of office. The sanctions may vary from the ultimate penalty of impeachment or forced retirement, to the gentler penalty of removal from certain cases, to private admonishment. For example, one common rule holds that judges must recuse themselves from cases argued by former law partners or cases involving companies in which judges hold stock. The Washington State Constitution establishing the Commission on Judicial Conduct deals with rule violation thus:

There shall be a commission on judicial conduct, existing as an independent agency of the judicial branch....Whenever the commission concludes, based on an initial proceeding, that there is probable cause to believe that a judge...has violated a rule of judicial conduct or that a judge...suffers from a disability...the commission shall conduct a public hearing or hearings and shall make public all those records....

Upon the completion of the hearing or hearings, the commission in open session shall either dismiss the case, or shall admonish, reprimand, or censure the judge...or shall censure the judge...and recommend to the Supreme Court the retirement of the judge....[2]

The recruitment experience begins the familiarization of judges with the norms of office. A candidate who appears to reject or openly defies the norms may lose the elections or be dropped from consideration for an appointment. Clearly, the screening process is designed to reveal past and potential norm violations. As screeners attempt to measure a candidate's "integrity" or "temperament," they are looking for clues about her or his likely acceptance of the norms of office. The formal affirmation of a judge authorizes the imposition of the rules of office. At this point, ignoring the rules may lead to formal reprimands, with serious violations even leading to dismissals.

Additional requirements of office impinge upon what a new judge has already learned and retained from the recruitment experience. A variety of

---

[1] "Preamble," *Code of Judicial Conduct*, State of Washington (1995).

[2] *Washington State Constitution*, Article IV, sec. 31.

courtroom and courthouse actors such as other judges, attorneys, jurors, litigants, staff, etc. place demands upon a judge. Relations with each of these participants in the judicial process generate their own norms and rules. Ideally, the recruitment experience should inform a judge of the variety of requirements of office and those personal views that survive the recruitment experience should reinforce those requirements.

Also important to shaping a judge's perspectives are the kinds of issues that are brought to the court for resolution. For example, judges sitting on an urban trial bench, likely, must confront numerous criminal, landlord-tenant and labor cases. A rural bench must resolve land use, water, and farming issues. Each court to some considerable degree represents the particular economic and social make-up of its community, which again, should have been evident during recruitment. Likely, those candidates who appeared not to be representative of their constituencies were screened out. Of course, legislative enactments prompt the kinds of cases brought to the courts as well, and higher courts provide precedents to be followed. Nonetheless, each jurisdiction puts its own twist on laws and precedents in the trials, settlements, and practices unique to that bench.

The broader point we are making here is that, besides important recruitment experiences, other influences are brought to bear on a judge, constraining or reinforcing her or his preferences and behavior. The context within which the judge must function places a variety of sometimes-conflicting demands on the jurist. Even a single trial judge, lord of his or her own fiefdom, must react to issues and persons under a variety of situations requiring particular responses.

Of course, the longer a judge is removed from the recruitment experience, the greater the opportunity for modification of what was originally learned. Indeed, the longer the term of office, the greater the tendency to forget the lessons of recruitment. The lifetime appointments of federal judges limited only by the "good behavior" rule provide considerable independence, once affirmation has occurred. In contrast the trial judge who must face the voters or gain reappointment every four or six years should not forget the lessons learned from the previous recruitment experience. Even for those judges fortunate enough to enjoy long tenures, the lessons learned from recruitment and the views that survive the experience provide the basis for what follows in the judge's career. In some cases the post-recruitment influences merely re-enforce what was gained from the selection process. In other cases, however, the new influences still must work with what recruitment has instilled, often delaying acceptance of the conflicting norm of office. It is not an overstatement to argue, as we have, that to understand much about judging we must know what transpires before the judge dons the robes of office.

Remaining, however, is the question of the correct measurement of the results of recruitment. What can we expect of the "trustee," the "delegate" or the "steward"? How might the judge who is a product of a high articulation recruitment experience decide cases? What difference does the level of judicial selection articulation make? The model predicts that the judge who survives a high articulation recruitment assumes either a "steward" or "politico" role. Such a judge would tend to balance the requirements of independence with the demands of accountability. A jurist who comes to the bench by means of a low articulation experience would be drawn to a "delegate" or "trustee" role. The delegate, accountable to one or two recruitment actors, begins his or her career burdened with a sense of obligation to that restricted set of actors. The trustee, who achieved a judgeship with a minimum of recruitment activity, remains largely independent and relatively free from obligations.

A product of high articulation is initially drawn toward a center position between **activism** and **restraint**. The low articulation product is drawn either to an activist position as a trustee in which he or she is relatively free to pursue preferences unimpeded by selection obligations or as a delegate drawn to a position in which her or his preferences are checked by those who put him or her on the bench. Research on judicial activism and restraint has a long tradition in public law, which need not be repeated here.[3] However, for us the difficulty arises when attempting to separate that activist or restraintist behavior attributed to recruitment from that which is the result of the demands of the judicial position.

Focusing on change provides an opportunity to separate recruitment role behavior from position behavior. If a newly appointed or elected judge changes his or her activism-restraint behavior gradually and consistently as the jurist settles into the court and moves away from the time of initial selection, we might suspect that changing behavior is a product of position norms and rules. If, in contrast, a judge remains consistent over time we might predict that the recruitment role remains strong or is reinforced by position norms and rules. As judicial behavior changes immediately prior to an election or reappointment, the anticipation of the demands of recruitment may be responsible.

Not only does the recruitment experience bear on those going through the process; it also affects those who are actors in that process. To understand the full scope of selection processes, we need to know how such important actors as voters, bar associations, Governors, Presidents, Senators, or County Commissioners view it. For example, public confidence in courts may vary systematically with articulation levels and this confidence or trust may persist despite the changes that the position may impose on the judge. Does the public have greater confidence in judges who are products of a high articulation recruitment than they do in a judge appointed by a Governor or President after little consultation and little involvement of others? This is a question which is both timely, given American's flagging trust in government, and of inherent interest to students of public law. Perhaps over the long run understanding how

---

[3] See Stephen C. Halpern and Charles M. Lamb, eds. *Supreme Court Activism and Restraint* (Lexington: Lexington Books, 1982).

recruitment affects those involved in recruiting judges is as important as understanding how it affects those recruited. There is indeed much yet to be learned about judicial recruitment.

Appendix A

Judicial Elections, Articulation, and Role Orientations: An Empirical Test[1]

In the 1994 Washington primary elections, a total of 121 candidates contested for 41 available positions for the Municipal, District, Superior, Appeals and Supreme courts throughout the state. In the November balloting, two Supreme Court seats, and two Superior, one Municipal and 36 District court spots were on the ballot. The data for the following report came from a mail survey of all candidates for all state contested judicial positions in both the primary and general elections, and from an initial random sample of 1,000 registered voters in the two elections in Spokane County, the most populous county in Eastern Washington.

The primary ballot in Spokane featured three Supreme Court, a Superior Court and four District Court races. A total of 85,158 voters participated in the primary (40% of registered voters) and 147,219 in the general election (68% of registered voters). The average roll-off for the Supreme Court races was 22% in the primary and 21% in the general election in Spokane County. Roll-off was 12% for the hotly contested Superior Court, and 12% for the closest District Court race. The turn-out for Spokane may have been high for a mid-term election because of the hotly contested race for Congress between then Speaker of the House, Tom Foley, and the ultimate winner George Nethercutt.[2]

Of the 121 primary candidates, 70 (58%) responded to the survey. Of the 90 general election candidates, 55 (61%) responded.[3] Of the sampled voters 30% responded to the primary mailings and 32% of those surveyed in the general election responded. Again, the response rate is marginal, but the respondents appear to represent the characteristics of the attentive voters in Spokane County.[4]

---

[1] Based on Nicholas P. Lovrich, Elizabeth A. Mazzara and Charles H. Sheldon, "Judicial Elections, Campaigning, Voting, Knowledge and Canon 7." Paper delivered at the 1995 Annual Conference of the Western Political Science Association, Portland, Oregon, March, 1995.

[2] Foley was able to generate only 35% of the total vote in the primary whereas Nethercutt defeated three other Republican challengers with 32% of all the votes, moving on against Foley in the general election where he won by a margin of about 3,000 votes.

[3] Candidates from all levels of the judiciary ranging from the Supreme to Municipal Courts responded. There were comparable numbers of winners and losers, and all county jurisdictions involved were represented.

[4] For example, the ages varied from 20 to 90; 20% had a high school or less education, 36% had some college, and 44% were college graduates. Their party preferences and political ideology was nearly evenly divided between Republicans, independents and Democrats and between

What the Articulation-focused Model Predicts

The concern here is to test, with the judicial candidates and the county voters, four of the central contentions that the articulation-focused recruitment model generates. The contentions are:

1.   The candidates that are products of a higher articulation experience (high contestedness, close competitiveness and heavy voter participation) will tend to have a demonstrably more balanced view concerning accountability and independence than will candidates associated with a low articulation experience. They will tend to favor **steward** or **politico** roles.

2.   The products of a lower articulation experience will tend to have more extreme perspectives regarding accountability or independence and, consequently, they will be drawn more often to **trustee** or **delegate** roles than candidates associated with a high articulation contest.

3.   The more knowledgeable voters will tend to prefer a balanced recruitment role—either the **steward** or the **politico** roles—for judges, while the less informed will tend to prefer a less balanced **delegate** or **trustee** role for judges.

4.   The more knowledgeable voters will have been involved more frequently in both the primary and general elections, will vote more often for judges, and will hold courts in higher regard, than less knowledgeable voters.

Because of the numerous and often competing interests involved in a higher articulation election, it is expected that its pluralistic nature will compel some judges to compromise the interests they have absorbed from the recruitment sequence, balancing the demands placed upon them and adopt a steward role. Alternatively, some judges may play one interest against another or lean toward one interest at one time and toward another later—in the manner of a classic politico role.

In contrast, the products of a low or lower articulation recruitment system will be largely free to search for answers from their own storehouse of preferences, beliefs or views of the law, relatively unencumbered by outside interests.   The trustee role fits them well.   On the other hand, if a low articulation system has seen but one or two actors initiating, screening and affirming judges it is likely that those judges will adopt a delegate role, representing the interests of those few actors.

Again, it should be pointed out that these recruitment roles are but one set among many competing (if not conflicting roles).   For example, a judge may have survived the recruitment process with delegate tendencies, but once on the bench other judges' perspectives, *stare decisis*, case record, and lawyer

---

conservatives, moderates and liberals.   However, in our judgment the respondents represent the sentiments and perceptions of the interested voter who would most often be drawn to the voting booths to cast ballots for judges.   Indeed, 955 of the respondents said they had voted in the general election and 89% indicated they had voted for judges, a lower roll-off vote than occurred in the election.

arguments will have to be considered. Nonetheless, recruitment roles are strongest at the beginning of a judicial career, and that alone adds to their significance.

The informed voter tends to be an active voter, and we postulate that the informed voted likely has a sympathetic view concerning the judge's dilemma. The rule of law and the judge's role in that rule, if not completely understood or accepted, should still contribute to a more supportive perspective regarding courts than if that understanding is absent. Because the September primary always experiences a low voter turnout and attracts political and party activists, it seems likely that primary voters will be more knowledgeable concerning courts and candidates than voters in the general elections. Also, the roll-off regarding judicial candidates is likely to be higher in the general balloting.

Data Analysis

The major contention, of course, is that judicial selection systems have a demonstrable connection to the role orientations of the judicial candidates.[5] The role orientations, in turn, reflect particular views concerning judicial accountability and independence. Table 1 reports the results of testing the first three hypotheses. The assertions made can be tested by constructing a rough approximation of an "articulation scale" and seeing how it connects with judicial candidates' role orientations.[6] The articulation scale is composed of the

---

[5] The role orientation item read: "On a scale of one (strongly agree) to five (strongly disagree) rate your level of agreement with each of the following functions of judicial elections:"
[**Trustee**] "Elections should support those judges who are independent, remain unaffected by the people's demands and rule strictly according to the law." (69% of the respondents gave a positive rating to this function).
[**Steward**] "Elections should inform judges of the general feelings of the people so that the judges and their rulings don't become too isolated from the community." (65% gave this statement a positive rating).
[**Delegate**] "Elections should tell the judges what the people want and judges should follow the people's desires as much as the law permits." (28% gave it a positive rating).
A **Politico** role would be adopted by those judges who weigh all three roles positively, but of equal preference. (13% fell into this category).

[6] The articulation scale was compiled from the following list of possible campaigning activities. The percentage refers to the number of candidates that participated in that activity:

Question: "Please check the space before each of the following campaigning activities in which you (or your committee) participated in the general election."

Activity	Percent Participating
Newspaper advertisements	93%
Lawn signs and bill boards	88%
Candidate "nights" or fairs	80%
Door-to-door campaigning	73%
Speeches—Rotary, Lions, retirements	73%

total number of activities judicial candidates used in their campaigns, and then the more active half compared with the less active.[7] For example, some candidates used lawn signs and newspaper ads only, while others used newspaper ads, lawn signs, door-to-door campaigning, radio, TV, etc. in their campaigns. Those judges running the sparse or low articulation campaigns were compared with the more active judges in high articulation experiences.

Table 1 also suggests that voter knowledge (as perceived by the candidates) is positively related to the recruitment role orientations. The contention was that the more knowledgeable voters would be more receptive to a balanced steward role.

Table 1

CANDIDATE ARTICULATION, KNOWLEDGE, AND ROLE PREFERENCES

JUDGES (General Election)

Preferred Roles	Judicial Candidates Electoral Articulation		Candidate Assessment of Voter Knowledge	
	Low	*High*	*None*	*Some*
	(n=23)	(n=28)	(n=18)	(n=36)
Trustee	83%	67%	78%	64%
Steward	65%	71%	44%	75%
Delegate	39%	21%	11%	36%
*Politico	21%	7%	6%	17%

*= Only a total of 7 respondents were politicos.

Mailings to voters	78%
Interviews with interested groups	68%
Shaking hands at malls, games, fairs	65%
Soliciting endorsements	63%
Appearances before editorial boards	53%
Fund raising, breakfasts etc.	43%
Radio advertisements	35%
Neighborhood meetings	35%
Interviews with bar committees	28%
News conferences	20%
Telephone canvassing	20%
TV	18%
Law firm visits	10%

[7] Twenty-three of the respondents participated in 9 or less of the activities ("less active") while 27 were active in ten or more ("more active").

Table 1 records highly suggestive tendencies. As hypothesized, the more active candidates—or those experiencing a higher articulation campaign—tend to give more credence to the steward role and less to the trustee and delegate than their counterparts who went through a low articulation campaign. Very few respondents were designated politicos. Equally suggestive, the candidates who thought the voters were "slightly" to "well informed" also tended to accept the balanced steward role while those candidates who felt the voters were "poorly informed" tended to be drawn to the trustee role.

Perceptions of voters' informedness and whether the candidates experienced a higher articulated campaign also are associated, but not as expected. Two out of three of those respondents who were conducting an active campaign felt that the voters were informed to some degree. Seven of the ten less active candidates assumed that the voters were arrayed from slightly to well informed.

As a check on the connection between campaign articulation, voter knowledge, and role preferences, an articulation scale is constructed from responses from the voters' survey. The hypothesis is that the more voting sources voters use, the more active they are in voting and the more issues in the campaigns they could identify the higher their articulation experience.[8] Again, the most active half was compared with the less active half. A "knowledge scale" was constructed from voter responses by combining: 1) the number of correct candidate names they could identify; 2) self-rating of level of familiarity with courts; 3) self-rating of informedness; and, 4) a true and false quiz on law and the courts. A comparison between the more knowledgeable half with the less knowledgeable half of the respondents provides clues about the connection between voter knowledge and judicial preference. Table 2 reports the results of the voter comparisons.

---

[8] Questions which were used to construct the voter "articulation scale" were: 1) "Please indicate the one or several sources of information you actually used by circling the letter(s) to the left of the source(s) listed above." (the list contained 15 possible sources, ranging from the voters' pamphlet to discussions with family and friends); 2) whether they voted in the general election; 3) whether they voted in the primary; 4) whether they voted for judges; and, 5) whether they could identify any issues discussed in the campaigns.

Table 2

VOTER ARTICULATION, KNOWLEDGE AND ROLE PREFERENCES

VOTERS (General Election)

Preferred Roles	Articulation			Knowledgeable	
	Low	High		Less	More
	(n=91)	(n=117)		(n=93)	(n=118)
Trustee	42%	47%		43%	47%
Steward	59%	65%		66%	60%
Delegate	56%	54%		59%	52%
Politico	31%	25%		41%	16%

The hypothesized tendencies hold as well for the voters in regard to the articulation level they experienced. Although those less active rated the balanced steward role highest it does not exceed the rating of the more active (59% to 65%) and is only slightly higher than the more passive voter's view of the delegate role. However, the distinction is not as pronounced between the less and more knowledgeable voters. Both favor the steward role with nearly the same emphasis when compared with the other role alternatives. The anticipated balance concerning politico views is absent.[9] The relationship between articulation and recruitment role orientations is enhanced by the data from the voters' survey. The importance of knowledge appears to be that as voters became more knowledgeable they move toward either a steward of trustee role and away from the delegate role preference. Also, they are far less likely to adopt the hybrid politico role which is a frequent choice of less informed voters.

The relationship between articulation and knowledge is evident. The more knowledgeable voters vote more often, vote more frequently for judges, and regard judicial elections as being as important or more important than elections to other public offices. Also they have greater confidence in public agencies, including courts.

---

[9] The model hypothesizes that politicos would be compelled to balance political accountability with political independence in a high articulation situation. Voters would probably not be aware of the importance of interested group efforts, especially at the initiation and screening stages. Perhaps the judicial candidates would be reluctant to admit the political aspects of their campaign.

Table 3

VOTER KNOWLEDGE, ACTIVISM AND GOVERNMENT CONFIDENCE

Knowledgeable

	Less	More
	(n=100)	(n=125)
Voted in Election	93%	98%
Voted for Judges	89%	99%
Voted in Primary	68%	78%
Judicial Elections		
are important	89%	89%

Confidence in Local Public Agencies*

Knowledge

	Less	More
Police	54%	52%
Courts	30%	42%
Schools	44%	45%
News Media	14%	19%
Judges	31%	48%
Lawyers	16%	19%
Hospitals	85%	80%
Gov't Leaders	7%	14%
Legislators	28%	33%
Colleges-Universities	62%	68%

* Question: "Public agencies seek to gain the confidence of the public through their actions and services. Please indicate the confidence you have in each of the following:"

Common sense dictates that voters in the primary election are more attentive and knowledgeable than voters in the general elections. As is often the case, common sense is a poor guide. Actually, the participants in the primary election were not as knowledgeable as their general election colleagues. However, they were only slightly more active.[10] The explanation lies in the

[10] The primary voters used slightly more of the available sources than those voting in the general election. Most of the difference is explained by a 32% vs. 24% reliance on "family and friends" as a source in the primary.

nature of the District Court races. The crucial vote was in the general election with the primary results only narrowing the candidates down to two for each spot. Many of the candidates did little campaigning for the primary, saving their money and energy for the November ballot.[11]

Conclusions

Assuming, as we do, that the ideal purpose of judicial elections is to reach a balance between holding the judges accountable and granting them independence, the research suggests that this goal can be pursued best by providing as much information as possible to the interested voters. To both the judicial candidates and the voters in both the primary and the general elections, a balanced steward role is preferable to the extremes of accountability and independence—the delegate or trustee. Data are absent from the special interests involved in initiating and screening that would contribute to a politico recruitment outlook.

Although we initially attempted, through a random sample of registered voters in Spokane County, to tap both interested voter and more casual voter, our returns clearly indicate that it was the more attentive voters who responded.[12]

Our initial inquiries were whether products of a high articulation system would tend to favor a more balanced view of their role and whether candidates experiencing a low articulation election would tend to be drawn to the extremes of either accountability or independence. This appears to be the case. When related inquiries are made of the voters, support for our contentions is encouraging, at times, but inconclusive in some respects. Voters in both high and low articulation efforts tend to favor the balanced role, as do all voters regardless of their knowledge levels. The data also show that the more active candidates felt more pressures from the constraints of Canon 7. As hypothesized, the more knowledgeable voters have more confidence in state and local government and community agencies.[13]

In an effort to find factors that were strongly associated with articulation variance, several trends were investigated. First, the level of voter activity was

---

[11] Some candidates said they agreed with their opponents not to do much in the primary. Of the 38 District races, only 12 had more than two contestants, requiring some efforts in the primary.

[12] See, Lovrich and Sheldon, "Voters in Judicial Elections: An Attentive Public or an Uniformed Electorate?" *Justice System Journal* 9 (1984): 23.

[13] For the role of trust in government in retention elections see Larry T. Aspin and William K. Hall, "Political Trust and Judicial Retention Election," *Law & Policy* 9 (October, 1987): 451. Our study showed no significant relationship between the degree of voter activity and level of confidence in government.

strongly associated with level of knowledge.[14] Our common sense notion is confirmed. The more knowledgeable the voters, the more active and interested they are. Another interesting trend was that ideological preference was an important factor in the level of voter knowledge and activity. The more liberal the voters the more likely they would be knowledgeable and become a contributor to the high articulation experience.[15]

What is suggested by the analysis from at least these limited Washington State and Spokane County surveys is that to maintain or enhance a balance between public accountability and judicial independence, the voters must become informed and more strongly encouraged to participate. In turn, the candidates must perform an educating function as they campaign and be permitted more flexibility regarding what they can share with the voters.

---

[14] The association between levels of voter activity and knowledge recorded a Chi Square of 16.35 with a $P<.00$.

	Knowledge	
	Less	**More**
Activity		
Low	61%	39%
Hight	34%	66%

[15] The association between level of activity and knowledge and ideology is close. $(P < .01)$

	Conservative	Liberal
Knowledge		
Less	84%	16%
More	49%	51%
Activity		
Less	81%	19%
More	55%	46%

the
PEOPLE
shall
judge

Restoring Citizen Control to Judicial Selection

A Report of the Walsh Commission   March 1996

John Locke, the 17th century Brithish philosopher whose influence is so pervasive in our own political history, stated the then-revolutionary idea that the people should be in control of the mechanisms of government. That principle is the keystone of our report and the effort to restore lost citizen control is at the heart of our recommendations.

We have achieved popular control of the executive and legislative branches of government. But there are special difficulties in imposing effective popular control of the judiciary. In part this is because of the technical character of the judge's work. In part it is because we are trying to, at the same time, protect the independence which is essential for the impartial dispensation of justice.

In recommending the best system for selecting Washington judges, the Commission noted that there are fundamental differences between the role of the judge in a democratic community and that of other elected officials.

•We elect legislators and governors to further our individual policy preferences, to make decisions that will further our personal interests and give voice to our vision of appropriate governmental action.   Legislators and governors should be representative—strong champions of the preferences of their constituents. A law-*making* process marked by lively debate among conflicting policies leads to better and more accountable public policy.

•By sharp contrast, the low-*interpreting and applying* tasks entrusted to judges must be impartial. Judges serve the people through the impartial interpretation of laws made by a democratically elected legislature. It is not the role of the judge in a democratic community to make fundamental policy decisions, to express preferences for one policy over another, or to represent one group over another. To the contrary, impartiality means judges will not favor one view, one group or one policy over another. Indeed, when questions of constitutional authority are raised, judges need to be principled enough to defy current popular opinion in favor of the long run public values expressed in the constitution. So far as it is possible, judges should employ their best independent judgment, their experience and their legal skills in a principled, disciplined and impartial interpretation of the law.

This fundamental contrast in the role of judges as compared to "representative" officials raises important questions about our current system of selecting judges. A method of selection that works well for one kind of official may not be suitable for other kinds of officials. In Washington, judges reach the bench either by appointment or by contested election. As is detailed in the report that follows, both processes have serious problems in today's world for the selection of the neutral, skilled professionals the people demand in their judiciary.

Each state's judicial selection system reflects its judgment of the appropriate balance among competing goals: qualified judges; voter information and judicial accountability;

and judicial independence. The people demand that the judicial selection process be open to all qualified candidates in the state; that all judges be selected on the basis of their honesty, knowledge and judgment; and that the process encourages qualified candidates to seek judicial office. For the selection process to be meaningful, voters must have more information about the candidates, their qualifications as well as their performance once on the bench. Yet neither the selection process nor the performance review process should undermine the ability of a judge to be impartial. The Commission has searched for practical methods of reaching these goals.

Applying the principle of citizen control to an accountable but not truly representative branch of government requires discerning analysis. Things are not always what they seem, and the issues are not resolved by reference to comfortable political slogans. Failure to look clearly at what is actually happening has resulted in a system in which the people are largely excluded from meaningful participation in decisions about judicial selection and tenure. The Commission's recommendations are intended to restore some of that citizen control, to return to John Locke's vision of a community where the people shall judge.

Ruth Walsh
Chair, The Walsh Commission
March 1996

Summary of Recommendations

Length of Practice

All candidates for judicial office shall have been active members of the state bar and/or shall have served as a judicial officer for at least the stated time periods:

- *Supreme Court and Court of Appeals—10 years*
- *Superior Court—7 years*
- *District Court—5 years*

Currently, a person need only to have passed the bar and be a registered voter to qualify for most judicial positions in Washington; yet the qualities of a good judge—balance, sensi-

tivity, judgment—develop only
through experience.

Voters consistently testified
to the Commission that judges
should be experienced lawyers,
and should meet minimum requirements for years of legal
practice.

The recommended experience requirements are within
the range of those in other
states that have addressed this
problem.

Residency

*All candidates for judicial office
shall have resided in the judicial
district or county for the stated
time periods immediately preceding candidacy:*

- *Supreme Court—7 years in
  state*
- *Court of Appeals—5 years in
  judicial district*
- *Superior Court—5 years in
  judicial district*
- *District Court—2 years in
  county*

Judges should know the
communities they serve, and
community members should
have an opportunity to know
their judges. A residency requirement establishes this connection.

Currently, judicial candidates have no significant residency requirement except to be
registered voters.

The recommended residency
requirements are within the
range of those in other states
that have addressed this problem.

Judicial Selection

*Judges shall be selected either
by appointment from recommendations made by nominating commissions or by contested
election.*

The opportunity to participate in selecting judges makes
judicial decisions more acceptable to the people, and elections
encourage judges to listen to the
people.

The consistent frustration of
voters in judicial elections
shows that there is something
broken in Washington's judicial
selection system.

This recommendation responds directly to the need for a
more open and informed appointment process—the method
by which more than 60 percent
of our judges are chosen.

Nominating commissions involve voters in the recruitment
and assessment of qualified
candidates for judicial positions.

Voters express the greatest
frustration when asked to select
new judges; a review of the
newly appointed judge's first 12
months will help voters make a
decision in the contested election.

The contested election ensures access for qualified candidates who, for whatever reason, do not secure a recommendation from the commission.

The combination of a nominating commission process, a judicial performance review system and a contested election provides a reasonable assurance that high quality judges are initially selected.

Retention elections, combined with a published review of the judge's performance, provide voters an opportunity to register approval for all judicial candidates based upon objective information.

Judges confident that their performance lives up to objective criteria need worry less about making unpopular decisions.

The proposed system will assure Washington voters of a system that produces high quality judges whose independence is enhanced and protected, and who remain accountable for performance.

Nominating Commissions

Volunteer citizen nominating commissions shall be created to review and compile a list of recommended candidates from which the appointing authority shall fill all judicial openings.

The nominating commission is a tested solution for promoting citizen participation in the appointment process. Members have the time and the information needed to make comprehensive and largely nonpartisan reviews of each applicant's qualifications for judicial office. The 30 states with such a system offer manuals, checklists and forms as models, and can also provide guidance.

Voters testified that nominating commissions must remain free of political influence. Consequently, their compositions reflect a balance between branches of government, have non-lawyers outnumbering lawyers, feature staggered terms for members, and are broadly based, diverse and representative of the people.

Nominating commissions will create the opportunity for 800 people to participate in the selection process for all judicial openings, with separate commissions serving each court level, and local people serving on local commissions. Currently more than 60 percent of judges in this state are appointed without any significant voter involvement.

A nominating commission will meet only when there is an opening to fill; other states indicate that administrative costs to support nominating commissions are not significant, and that people participate with great commitment.

Judicial Performance Information

A process for collecting and publishing information about judicial performance shall be created under the authority of the Supreme Court.

Voters testified that they wanted more information about the performance of judges. The Commission recommends creating an objective, uniform, comprehensive method for providing voter information about judicial performance.

End-of-term reports will be used to provide information in the judicial voter pamphlet; judges may respond to the review prior to its release. Confidential mid-term reviews will provide the judges feedback for the purpose of self-improvement.

Many models and resources are available for establishing a program to report judicial performance. Most of the states use a commission-type body to oversee the process. The Commission recommends that members of such a group be appointed for limited, staggered terms and be well-trained, diverse, impartial and representative of lay people, judiciary and bar.

Performance review categories should include: legal knowledge, integrity, communication skills, decisiveness, impartiality, interpersonal skills and administrative ability.

Judicial Candidate Information

A process for collecting and publishing information about candidates for judicial office shall be created under the authority of the Supreme Court.

Published criteria and a standard disclosure statement will provide voters with relevant, verified information about all judicial candidates. The standardized format will facilitate candidate comparison.

The Commission encourages the Supreme Court to authorize a disclosure system in which candidates who fail to provide information are identified in the judicial voter pamphlet.

Judicial Voter Information

The Supreme Court shall authorize the publication of a judicial voter pamphlet and encourage other methods for distributing judicial candidate information.

In any given election, as many as 50 percent of those voting choose not to vote for judicial candidates. The Commission believes that widely disseminated information about candidates will have a positive effect on voter participation in judicial elections.

News media representatives reported that Canon 7 of the state *Code of Judicial Conduct* prevented candidates from taking positions on important issues. It is the Commission's view, however, that the Canons do allow candidates to state views on many important issues.

Because current state and county voter pamphlets are distributed after the primary and are under too many restrictions to offer voters comparable information about judicial candidates, a special judicial voter pamphlet should be established without those restrictions and delivered in a timely manner.

Judicial information could also be disseminated on the Internet, with fax-on-demand, with "800" numbers, through symposiums, etc. conducted by local civic groups, and through the media.

The voter information process established by an Ohio Supreme Court rule requires each judicial candidate to file a disclosure statement. The Commission recommends a similar process for Washington.

Public Education

More information shall be made available to students, the public and news media about the na- *ture of the judicial system and the character of the judicial office.*

It was clear from people's testimony that public knowledge about the judiciary was far less than that about the legislative and executive branches of government.

Early education is key. In-school programs would acquaint students with judges and the judicial system. Student knowledge and interest may also increase their parents' participation in judicial elections.

Campaign Finance

Canon 7 of the Code of Judicial Conduct shall be revised to impose limits on campaign contributions by persons or organizations and impose aggregate limits on expenditures by a judicial candidate's campaign committee.

The current state laws and court rules that regulate campaign fundraising and finance reporting for judicial candidates do not impose any limits on contributions and expenditures. Yet testimony from special interest groups indicated that money can and does effect the outcome of judicial elections.

The Commission struggled with the needs for: maintaining both the fact and the appearance of judicial impartiality, encouraging campaign conduct compatible with the nature of the judicial office, and providing adequate time for campaigns without interfering with the business of deciding cases.

Because limits raise constitutional issues, the Commission patterned its recommendation on the Ohio court rule which selects those kinds of spending restraints and contribution limits that promise some benefit and are relatively certain to meet constitutional requirements.

Other types of limits should be explored in the process of redrafting Canon 7 of the Code of Judicial Conduct, for example, time limits for judicial campaigns, time limits for fundraising, and limitations on retention campaign spending.

Conclusion

The Commission believes that the current political climate in Washington is ready to seriously consider the recommendations in this report.   However, leading scholars of judicial reform (e.g., Philip Dubois, Ed., *The Analysis of Judicial Reform*, 1982, and Abraham, *The Judicial Process*, 6th ed, 1993) make it clear that such proposals face difficult obstacles.   Chief among them is political resistance to change. We do not underestimate the strength of the opposition. But Washington has a tradition of farsighted political leaders who have permitted voters to consider proposals such as these. With the support of those leaders, progress is possible.

To further that progress, the Commission recommends that the following immediate actions:
• Legislative committees should hold hearings to review the recommendations;
• The Supreme Court should take action to adopt rules to implement a Judicial Voter Pamphlet, performance information process and judicial campaign reform;
• Political leaders should give voters an opportunity to consider these recommendations by approving the prerequisite constitutional amendments;
• Commission members should volunteer to speak before civic and professional groups to explain the recommendations; and
• Civic and professional organizations should begin to build coalitions to support the recommendations.
Adoption of the Commission's recommendations is a first step toward restoring voter control to judicial selection.   Given our state's com-

mitment to the ideals of citizen control, it is ironic that our judicial selection system excludes meaningful voter input and frustrates informed voting. With the support of farsighted political leaders, we can put in place a system in which, once again, the people shall judge.

Appendix C

Texas   1994
Harris County General Election Ballot

**OFFICIAL BALLOT LABEL — GENERAL ELECTION
HARRIS COUNTY, TEXAS — NOVEMBER 8, 1994**

INSTRUCTIONS FOR VOTING A PUNCH CARD BALLOT

HOW TO MARK YOUR BALLOT WHEN VOTING ON CANDIDATES FOR OFFICES

1. Vote for the candidate of your choice in each race by making a punch hole in the space provided adjacent to the name of that candidate.

2. You may cast a straight party vote (that is, cast a vote for all the nominees of one party) by making a punch hole in the space provided adjacent to the name of that party. If you cast a straight party vote for all the nominees of one party and also cast a vote for an opponent of one of that party's nominees, your vote for the opponent will be counted as well as your vote for all the other nominees of the party for which the straight party vote was cast.

REPLACING A SPOILED BALLOT

If you make a wrong punch, tear, or deface your ballot, return it to the election official and obtain another. YOU MAY NOT RECEIVE MORE THAN THREE BALLOTS IN SUCCESSION.

DEPOSITING THE BALLOT

Check your ballot after voting to make sure that the holes are actually punched through. Deposit your ballot in the ballot box. Do not fold your ballot.

ABBREVIATIONS (PARTY)

Democratic — Dem.   Republican — Rep.   Libertarian — Lib.   Independent — Ind.

PAGINA DE BOLETA OFICIAL — ELECCION GENERAL
CONDADO DE HARRIS, TEXAS — 8 DE NOVIEMBRE DE 1994

INSTRUCCIONES PARA VOTAR CON UNA BOLETA ELECTRONICA

COMO MARCAR SU BOLETA CUANDO ESTA VOTANDO SOBRE CANDIDATOS PARA PUESTOS OFICIALES

1. Vote por el candidato de su preferencia en cada carrera haciendo un agujero en el espacio provisto adyacente al nombre de ese candidato.

2. Usted podrá votar por todos los candidatos de un solo partido político (es decir, votar por todos los candidatos nombrados del mismo partido político) haciendo un agujero en el espacio provisto adyacente al nombre de dicho partido político. Si usted vota por un solo partido político ("straight ticket") y también vota por el contrincante de uno de los candidatos de dicho partido político, se computará su voto por el contrincante tanto como su voto por todos los demas candidatos del partido político de su preferencia.

REEMPLAZANDO UNA BOLETA DAÑADA

Si usted se equivoca, o si rompe o destruye su boleta, devuelvala al oficial electoral y obtenge otra USTED NO PODRA RECIBIR MAS DE TRES BOLETAS SUCESIVAS

PARA DEPOSITAR LA BOLETA

Después de votar, sirvase verificar que las perforaciones transpasen completamente su boleta Deposite su boleta en la caya para boletas No doble su boleta

ABREVACIONES (PARTIDO)

Democratico — Dem   Republicano — Rep   Libertariano — Lib   Independiente — Ind

BALLOT STYLE

238   *Choosing Justice*

GENERAL ELECTION - *ELECCION GENERAL*
HARRIS COUNTY, TEXAS - *CONDADO DE HARRIS, TEXAS*
Page 1   NOVEMBER 8, 1994 - *8 DE NOVIEMBRE DE 1994*

Office	Candidate	Party	#
Straight Party Vote / *Votar Por Todos Los Candidatos De Un Solo Partido Político*	Democratic *(Democrático)*	Dem.	1
	Republican *(Republicano)*	Rep.	2
	Libertarian *(Libertariano)*	Lib.	3
United States Senator / *Senador de los Estados Unidos*	Richard Fisher	Dem.	4
	Kay Bailey Hutchison	Rep.	5
	Pierre Blondeau	Lib.	6
United States Representative / *Representante de los Estados Unidos*	**VARIABLE RACE (SEE OTHER SIDE)**		
Governor / *Gobernador*	Ann W. Richards	Dem.	11
	George W. Bush	Rep.	12
	Keary Ehlers	Lib.	13
Lieutenant Governor / *Gobernador Teniente*	Bob Bullock	Dem.	14
	H.J. (Tex) Lezar	Rep.	15
Attorney General / *Procurador General*	Dan Morales	Dem.	16
	Don Wittig	Rep.	17
	Vicki Flores	Lib.	18
Comptroller of Public Accounts / *Contralor de Cuentas Públicas*	John Sharp	Dem.	19
	Teresa Doggett	Rep.	20
State Treasurer / *Tesorero Estatal*	Martha Whitehead	Dem.	22
	David Hartman	Rep.	23
Commissioner of the General Land Office / *Comisionado de la Oficina General de Terrenos*	Garry Mauro	Dem.	24
	Marta Greytok	Rep.	25
	David C. Chow	Lib.	26

Page 1

Commissioner of Agriculture *Comisionado de Agricultura*	Marvin Gregory	Dem.	27 ◗
	Rick Perry	Rep.	28 ◗
	Clyde L. Garland	Lib.	29 ◗
Railroad Commissioner *Comisionado de Ferrocarriles*	James E. (Jim) Nugent	Dem.	30 ◗
	Charles R. Matthews	Rep.	31 ◗
	Rick Draheim	Lib.	32 ◗
Railroad Commissioner, Unexpired Term *Comisionado de Ferrocarriles, Duración Restante del Cargo*	Mary Scott Nabers	Dem.	33 ◗
	Carole Keeton Rylander	Rep.	34 ◗
	Buster Crabb	Lib.	35 ◗
Justice, Supreme Court, Place 1 *Juez, Corte Suprema, Lugar Núm. 1*	Raul A. Gonzalez	Dem.	36 ◗
	John B. Hawley	Lib.	37 ◗
Justice, Supreme Court, Place 2 *Juez, Corte Suprema, Lugar Núm. 2*	Alice Oliver Parrott	Dem.	39 ◗
	Nathan L. Hecht	Rep.	40 ◗
Justice, Supreme Court, Place 3 *Juez, Corte Suprema, Lugar Núm. 3*	Jimmy Carroll	Dem.	42 ◗
	Priscilla Owen	Rep.	43 ◗
Presiding Judge, Court of Criminal Appeals *Juez Presidente, Corte de Apelaciones Criminales*	Mike McCormick	Dem.	45 ◗
Judge, Court of Criminal Appeals, Place 1 *Juez, Corte de Apelaciones Criminales, Lugar Núm. 1*	Charles F. Campbell	Dem.	48 ◗
	Steve Mansfield	Rep.	49 ◗

Office	Candidate	Party	No.
Judge, Court of Criminal Appeals, Place 2 *Juez, Corte de Apelaciones Criminales, Lugar Núm. 2*	Betty Marshall	Dem.	53 ◗
	Sharon Keller	Rep.	54 ◗
Member, State Board of Education *Miembro de la Junta Estatal de Educación Pública*	**VARIABLE RACE (SEE OTHER SIDE)**		
State Senator *Senador Estatal*	**VARIABLE RACE (SEE OTHER SIDE)**		
State Representative *Representante Estatal*	**VARIABLE RACE (SEE OTHER SIDE)**		
Justice, 1st Court of Appeals District, Place 1 *Juez, Corte de Apelaciones, Distrito Núm. 1, Lugar Núm. 1*	Helen Cassidy	Dem.	64 ◗
	Tim Taft	Rep.	65 ◗
Justice, 1st Court of Appeals District, Place 2 *Juez, Corte de Apelaciones, Distrito Núm. 1, Lugar Núm. 2*	M. B. "Murry" Cohen	Dem.	67 ◗
Justice, 1st Court of Appeals District, Place 3 *Juez, Corte de Apelaciones, Distrito Núm. 1, Lugar Núm. 3*	Michol Mary O'Connor	Dem.	70 ◗
	Mamie Proctor	Rep.	71 ◗
Justice, 1st Court of Appeals District, Place 4 *Juez, Corte de Apelaciones, Distrito Núm. 1, Lugar Núm. 4*	Adele Hedges	Rep.	73 ◗
Justice, 1st Court of Appeals District, Place 5 *Juez, Corte de Apelaciones, Distrito Núm. 1, Lugar Núm. 5*	Eric Andell	Dem.	76 ◗

Page 3

Appendix C 241

Office	Candidate	Party	No.
Justice, 14th Court of Appeals District, Place 1 / *Juez, Corte de Apelaciones, Distrito Núm. 14, Lugar Núm. 1*	Bob Moore	Dem.	79 ▶
	Harvey Hudson	Rep.	80 ▶
Justice, 14th Court of Appeals District, Place 2 / *Juez, Corte de Apelaciones, Distrito Núm. 14, Lugar Núm. 2*	Ross Sears	Dem.	82 ▶
	Wanda McKee Fowler	Rep.	83 ▶
Justice, 14th Court of Appeals District, Place 3 / *Juez, Corte de Apelaciones, Distrito Núm. 14, Lugar Núm. 3*	George Ellis	Dem.	85 ▶
	Richard Edelman	Rep.	86 ▶
Justice, 14th Court of Appeals District, Place 4 / *Juez, Corte de Apelaciones, Distrito Núm. 14, Lugar Núm. 4*	Joe L. Draughn	Dem.	88 ▶
	Maurice Amidei	Rep.	89 ▶
Justice, 14th Court of Appeals District, Place 5 / *Juez, Corte de Apelaciones, Distrito Núm. 14, Lugar Núm. 5*	Ed Cogburn	Dem.	91 ▶
	John S. Anderson	Rep.	92 ▶
Justice, 14th Court of Appeals District, Place 6 Unexpired Term / *Juez, Corte de Apelaciones, Distrito Núm. 14, Lugar Núm. 6 Duracion Restante del Cargo*	Patrice Barron	Dem.	94 ▶
	Leslie Ann Brock	Rep.	95 ▶
District Judge, 55th Judicial District / *Juez del Distrito, Distrito Judicial Núm. 55*	Kathleen S. Stone	Dem.	98 ▶
District Judge, 113th Judicial District / *Juez del Distrito, Distrito Judicial Núm. 113*	Patricia Lasher	Dem.	101 ▶
	Patricia Hancock	Rep.	102 ▶

242 *Choosing Justice*

District Judge, 157th Judicial District *Juez del Distrito, Distrito Judicial Núm. 157*	Michael (Mike) Schneider	Rep.	105 ▶
District Judge, 180th Judicial District *Juez del Distrito, Distrito Judicial Núm. 180*	Susan Spruce	Dem.	108 ▶
	Debbie Mantooth	Rep.	109 ▶
District Judge, 182nd Judicial District *Juez del Distrito, Distrito Judicial Núm. 182*	Laura Ingle	Dem.	111 ▶
	Jeannine Barr	Rep.	112 ▶
District Judge, 183rd Judicial District *Juez del Distrito, Distrito Judicial Núm. 183*	Jay W. Burnett	Dem.	114 ▶
District Judge, 184th Judicial District *Juez del Distrito, Distrito Judicial Núm. 184*	Bob Burdette	Dem.	117 ▶
	Jan Krocker	Rep.	118 ▶
District Judge, 185th Judicial District *Juez del Distrito, Distrito Judicial Núm. 185*	Carl Walker, Jr.	Dem.	120 ▶
	H. Lon Harper	Rep.	121 ▶
District Judge, 189th Judicial District *Juez del Distrito, Distrito Judicial Núm. 189*	Carolyn Marks Johnson	Dem.	123 ▶
	David Jennings Willis	Rep.	124 ▶
District Judge, 190th Judicial District *Juez del Distrito, Distrito Judicial Núm. 190*	Eileen F. O'Neill	Dem.	126 ▶
	John Devine	Rep.	127 ▶

District Judge, 208th Judicial District *Juez del Distrito, Distrito Judicial Núm. 208*	Randy Martin	Dem.	131
	Denise Collins	Rep.	132
District Judge, 209th Judicial District *Juez del Distrito, Distrito Judicial Núm. 209*	Lloyd W. Oliver	Dem.	134
	Michael McSpadden	Rep.	135
District Judge, 228th Judicial District *Juez del Distrito, Distrito Judicial Núm. 228*	Ted Poe	Rep.	137
District Judge, 230th Judicial District *Juez del Distrito, Distrito Judicial Núm. 230*	Joe Kegans	Dem.	140
District Judge, 232nd Judicial District *Juez del Distrito, Distrito Judicial Núm. 232*	Carlos "C.C." Correa	Dem.	143
	Mary Lou Keel	Rep.	144
District Judge, 234th Judicial District *Juez del Distrito, Distrito Judicial Núm. 234*	Donna Roth	Dem.	146
	Scott Brister	Rep.	147
District Judge, 245th Judicial District *Juez del Distrito, Distrito Judicial Núm. 245*	Beth McGregor	Dem.	149
	Annette Galik	Rep.	150
District Judge, 246th Judicial District *Juez del Distrito, Distrito Judicial Núm. 246*	John W. Peavy, Jr.	Dem.	152
	Don Ritter	Rep.	153

Page 6

District Judge, 247th Judicial District *Juez del Distrito, Distrito Judicial Núm. 247*	Dean Huckabee	Dem.	157 ◆
	Bonnie Crane Hellums	Rep.	158 ◆
District Judge, 248th Judicial District *Juez del Distrito, Distrito Judicial Núm. 248*	Woody R. Densen	Dem.	160 ◆
	W. R. Voigt	Rep.	161 ◆
District Judge, 257th Judicial District *Juez del Distrito, Distrito Judicial Núm. 257*	Linda Motheral	Dem.	163 ◆
District Judge, 262nd Judicial District *Juez del Distrito, Distrito Judicial Núm. 262*	Doug Shaver	Dem.	166 ◆
District Judge, 263rd Judicial District *Juez del Distrito, Distrito Judicial Núm. 263*	Ruben Guerrero	Dem.	169 ◆
	Jim Wallace	Rep.	170 ◆
District Judge, 269th Judicial District *Juez del Distrito, Distrito Judicial Núm. 269*	Charles E. "Ernie" Hill	Dem.	172 ◆
	David West	Rep.	173 ◆
District Judge, 270th Judicial District *Juez del Distrito, Distrito Judicial Núm. 270*	Susan Soussan	Dem.	175 ◆
	Richard Hall	Rep.	176 ◆
District Judge, 280th Judicial District *Juez del Distrito, Distrito Judicial Núm. 280*	John Kirtley	Dem.	178 ◆
	Tony Lindsay	Rep.	179 ◆

Office	Candidate	Party	No.
District Judge, 281st Judicial District *Juez del Distrito, Distrito Judicial Núm. 281*	Willard M. Tinsley	Dem.	183 ▶
	William F. "Bill" Bell	Rep.	184 ▶
District Judge, 295th Judicial District *Juez del Distrito, Distrito Judicial Núm. 295*	Bonnie Fitch	Dem.	186 ▶
	Tracy Elizabeth Christopher	Rep.	187 ▶
Family District Judge, 308th Judicial District *Juez Familiar del Distrito, Distrito Judicial Núm. 308*	A. Robert Hinojosa	Dem.	189 ▶
	Georgia Dempster	Rep.	190 ▶
Family District Judge, 309th Judicial District *Juez Familiar del Distrito, Distrito Judicial Núm. 309*	Sherri Cothrun	Dem.	192 ▶
	John D. Montgomery	Rep.	193 ▶
Family District Judge, 310th Judicial District *Juez Familiar del Distrito, Distrito Judicial Núm. 310*	Deborah Wright	Dem.	195 ▶
	Lisa Millard	Rep.	196 ▶
Family District Judge, 311th Judicial District *Juez Familiar del Distrito, Distrito Judicial Núm. 311*	Dinah Bailey	Dem.	198 ▶
	Bill Henderson	Rep.	199 ▶
Family District Judge, 312th Judicial District *Juez Familiar del Distrito, Distrito Judicial Núm. 312*	Sandra R. Peebles	Dem.	201 ▶
	James D. Squier	Rep.	202 ▶
Family District Judge, 313th Judicial District *Juez Familiar del Distrito, Distrito Judicial Núm. 313*	Ramona John	Dem.	204 ▶
	Pat Shelton	Rep.	205 ▶

Family District Judge, 314th Judicial District *Juez Familiar del Distrito, Distrito Judicial Núm. 314*	David O. Fraga	Dem.	209 ◗
	Mary Craft	Rep.	210 ◗
Family District Judge, 315th Judicial District *Juez Familiar del Distrito, Distrito Judicial Núm. 315*	Berta A. Mejia	Dem.	212 ◗
	Kent Ellis	Rep.	213 ◗
County Judge *Juez del Condado*	Vince Ryan	Dem.	215 ◗
	Robert Eckels	Rep.	216 ◗
	W. Sanford Smith III	Lib.	217 ◗
Judge, County Court at Law No. 1 *Juez, Corte de Ley del Condado Núm. 1*	Ed Landry	Dem.	218 ◗
	Gene Chambers	Rep.	219 ◗
Judge, County Court at Law No. 2 *Juez, Corte de Ley del Condado Núm. 2*	Tom Sullivan	Rep.	221 ◗
Judge, County Court at Law No. 3 *Juez, Corte de Ley del Condado Núm. 3*	Carolyn Day Hobson	Dem.	224 ◗
	Lynn Bradshaw-Hull	Rep.	225 ◗
Judge, County Court at Law No. 4 *Juez, Corte de Ley del Condado Núm. 4*	Charles Coussons	Dem.	227 ◗
	Cynthia Crowe	Rep.	228 ◗
Judge, County Criminal Court No. 1 *Juez, Corte Criminal del Condado Núm. 1*	Bill Ragan	Dem.	230 ◗
	Reagan Cartwright Helm	Rep.	231 ◗

Judge, County Criminal Court No. 2 *Juez, Corte Criminal del Condado Núm. 2*	Denise Crawford	Dem.	235 ▶
	Michael Peters	Rep.	236 ▶
Judge, County Criminal Court No. 3 *Juez, Corte Criminal del Condado Núm. 3*	John Petruzzi	Dem.	238 ▶
	Don Jackson	Rep.	239 ▶
Judge, County Criminal Court No. 4 *Juez, Corte Criminal del Condado Núm. 4*	James E. "Jim" Anderson	Rep.	241 ▶
Judge, County Criminal Court No. 5 *Juez, Corte Criminal del Condado Núm. 5*	Hannah Chow	Dem.	244 ▶
Judge, County Criminal Court No. 6 *Juez, Corte Criminal del Condado Núm. 6*	J. R. (Bob) Musslewhite	Rep.	247 ▶
Judge, County Criminal Court No. 7 *Juez, Corte Criminal del Condado Núm. 7*	Shelly P. Hancock	Dem.	250 ▶
Judge, County Criminal Court No. 8 *Juez, Corte Criminal del Condado Núm. 8*	Neel Richardson	Dem.	253 ▶
Judge, County Criminal Court No. 9 *Juez, Corte Criminal del Condado Núm. 9*	Alfred G. "Al" Leal	Dem.	256 ▶
	Analia Wilkerson	Rep.	257 ▶

Judge, County Criminal Court No. 10 *Juez, Corte Criminal del Condado Núm. 10*	Sherman A. Ross	Rep.	261 ◗
Judge, County Criminal Court No. 11 *Juez, Corte Criminal del Condado Núm. 11*	David Mendoza, Jr.	Dem.	264 ◗
	Diane Bull	Rep.	265 ◗
Judge, County Criminal Court No. 12 *Juez, Corte Criminal del Condado Núm. 12*	Joe T. Terracina	Dem.	267 ◗
	Robin Brown	Rep.	268 ◗
Judge, County Criminal Court No. 13 *Juez, Corte Criminal del Condado Núm. 13*	Mark Atkinson	Rep.	270 ◗
Judge, County Criminal Court No. 14 *Juez, Corte Criminal del Condado Núm. 14*	Norma Jean Mancha	Dem.	273 ◗
	Jim Barkley	Rep.	274 ◗
Judge, County Probate Court No. 1 *Juez, Corte Testamentaria del Condado Núm. 1*	John Hutchison	Dem.	276 ◗
	Russell Austin	Rep.	277 ◗
Judge, County Probate Court No. 2 *Juez, Corte Testamentaria del Condado Núm. 2*	Martha Failing	Dem.	279 ◗
	Mike Wood	Rep.	280 ◗
Judge, County Probate Court No. 3 *Juez, Corte Testamentaria del Condado Núm. 3*	Jim Scanlan	Dem.	282 ◗

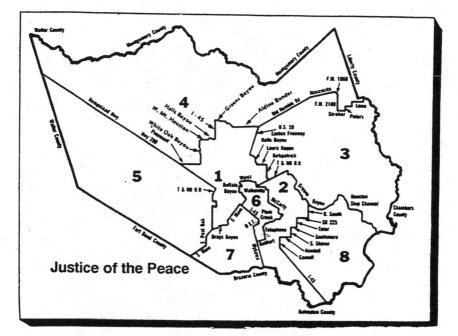

Justice of the Peace

Justice of the Peace, Precinct No. 1, Place 2 David M. Patronella	*Juez de Paz, Precinto Núm. 1, Lugar Núm. 2* Dem. 307
Justice of the Peace, Precinct No. 2, Place 2 George E. Risner Danny Perkins	*Juez de Paz, Precinto Núm. 2, Lugar Núm. 2* Dem. 307 Rep. 308
Justice of the Peace, Precinct No. 3, Place 2 Tony Polumbo	*Juez de Paz, Precinto Núm. 3, Lugar Núm. 2* Dem. 307
Justice of the Peace, Precinct No. 4, Place 2 Tom Lawrence	*Juez de Paz, Precinto Núm. 4, Lugar Núm. 2* Rep. 307
Justice of the Peace, Precinct No. 5, Place 2 Dessiray Bell Bill Yeoman Lloyd R. Walker	*Juez de Paz, Precinto Núm. 5, Lugar Núm. 2* Dem. 307 Rep. 308 Lib. 309
Justice of the Peace, Precinct No. 6, Place 2 Armando V. Rodriguez	*Juez de Paz, Precinto Núm. 6, Lugar Núm. 2* Dem. 307
Justice of the Peace, Precinct No. 7, Place 2 Al Green	*Juez de Paz, Precinto Núm. 7, Lugar Núm. 2* Dem. 307
Justice of the Peace, Precinct No. 8, Place 2 Steve Phelps	*Juez de Paz, Precinto Núm. 8, Lugar Núm. 2* Dem. 307

Appendix D

South Carolina   1996
Joint Legislative Committee Report

Introduction

The Joint Legislative Committee for Judicial Screening is charged by law to consider the qualifications of candidates for the judiciary. The Joint Committee has carefully investigated the candidates currently set for screening and found thirty-eight candidates qualified for judicial office and one candidate not qualified for judicial office. The Joint Committee did not reach a finding as to one candidate's qualifications as four members of the Joint Committee voted to find the candidate qualified and four members voted to find the candidate not qualified. This report details the reasons for the Joint Committee's findings and each candidate's qualifications as they relate to the Joint Committee's nine evaluative criteria.

The Joint Committee's last report, issued in March of 1995, indicated that the Joint Committee had found all candidates treated in that report to be "legally qualified." The Joint Committee defined the term "legally qualified" to mean that the candidates met the requirements for judicial office set forth in the South Carolina Constitution. The Joint Committee determined that each candidate treated in this report meets the constitutional and statutory requirements for the judicial office. The Joint Committee did, however, also make an overall finding as to whether each candidate was qualified or not qualified for service on the bench. The Joint Committee returned to its long-standing practice of making an overall finding as to candidate qualifications (and not simply a finding of legal qualification) because numerous members of the General Assembly requested the Joint Committee do so, and the Joint Committee believes that its report will be more helpful to members of the General Assembly if it includes an overall finding as to each candidate's qualifications.

The Joint Committee conducts a thorough investigation of each candidate's professional, personal, and financial affairs, and holds public hearings during which it questions each candidate on a wide variety of issues. The Joint Committee's investigation focuses on nine evaluative criteria. These evaluative criteria are: integrity and impartiality; legal knowledge and ability; professional experience; judicial temperament; diligence and industry; mental and physical capability; financial responsibilities; public service; and ethics. The Joint Committee's investigation includes the following:

(1)   survey of the bench and bar;
(2)   SLED and FBI investigation
(3)   credit investigation;
(4)   grievance investigation;
(5)   study of application materials;
(6)   verification of ethics compliance
(7)   search of newspaper articles;
(8)   conflict of interest investigation'
(9)   court schedule study;
(10)   study of appellate record;
(11)   court observation; and
(12)   investigation of complaints

While the law provides that the Joint Committee is to make findings as to qualifications, the Joint Committee views its role as also including an obligation to consider candidates in the context of the judiciary on which, if elected, they will serve and, to some degree, govern. To that end, the Joint Committee inquires as to the quality of justice delivered in the courtrooms of South Carolina and seeks to impart, through its questioning, the view of the public it represents as to matters of legal knowledge and ability, judicial temperament, and the absoluteness of the Judicial Canons as to recusal for conflict of interest prohibition of *ex parte* communication, and the disallowance of the acceptance of gifts.

The Joint Committee expects each candidate to possess a basic level of legal knowledge and ability, to have experience that would be applicable to the office sought, and to exhibit a strong adherence to codes of ethical behavior. These expectations are all important and excellence in one category does not make up for deficiencies in another.

This report is the culmination of weeks of investigatory work and public hearings. The Joint Committee takes its responsibilities very seriously as it believes that the quality of justice delivered in South Carolina's courtrooms is directly affected by the thoroughness of its screening process. Please carefully consider the contents of this report as we believe it will help you make a more informed decision. If you would like to review portions of the screening transcript or other public information abut a candidate before it is printed in the Journal, please contact Michael Couick or Nancy Goodman at 212-6610.

This report conveys the Joint Committee's findings as to the qualifications of all candidates currently offering for election to the circuit and family court. In addition, the Joint Committee has found the Honorable John Black, The Honorable Luke N. Brown, Jr., the Honorable Clyde K. Laney, Jr., the Honorable Robert R. Mallard, the Honorable William J. McLeod, and the Honorable Willie T. Smith, Jr., qualified for continued service as retired judges and has communicated its findings to the Supreme Court by way of a letter to the Chief Justice.

Appendix E

New Jersey 1995

Guidelines for Reviewing Qualifications of Candidates
For Original Judicial Office In The State Of New Jersey

PREFACE

"The quality of a court system is determined chiefly by the quality of its judges. Judges should be selected on the basis of ability, character, training and experience, by a process that assures that selection is made on a merit basis... All persons selected as judges should be of good moral character, emotionally stable and mature, in good physical health, patient, courteous and capable of deliberation and decisiveness when required to act on their own reasoned judgment. They should have a broad general and legal education," and under the Constitution of the State of New Jersey have been admitted to the Bar "for at least ten years."*

The eight criteria which follow set out the guidelines adopted by the Board of Trustees of the New Jersey State Bar Association in an effort to standardize the criteria by which candidates for state judicial office are to be judged. These guidelines borrow heavily from the American Bar Association guidelines referred to in the footnote below.

The guidelines which follow attempt to identify those characteristics by which candidates for state judicial office are to be judged by the New Jersey State Bar Association Committee on Judicial and Prosecutor Appointments. These guidelines (with some modifications) are predicated upon the "Guidelines for Reviewing Qualifications of Candidates for State Judicial Office" approved by the American Bar Association House of Delegates in August of 1983.

1. INTEGRITY

A candidate should be of undisputed integrity.

The integrity of the judge is, in the final analysis, the keystone of the judicial system; for it is integrity which enables a judge to disregard personalities and partisan political influences and enables him or her to base decisions solely on the facts and the law applicable to those facts. It is,

---

* The above statement was taken from a document entitled "Guidelines for Reviewing Qualifications of Candidates for State Judicial Office" prepared by the Judicial Administration Division of the American Bar Association.

therefore, imperative that a judicial candidate's integrity and character with regard to honesty and truthfulness be above reproach. An individual with the integrity necessary to qualify must be one who is able, among other things, to speak the truth without exaggeration, admit responsibility for mistakes and put aside self-aggrandizement.   Other elements demonstrating integrity are intellectual honesty, fairness, impartiality, ability to disregard prejudices, obedience to the law and moral courage.

A candidate's past personal and professional conduct should demonstrate consistent adherence to high ethical standards.   The State and County Committees should make inquiry of judges before whom the candidate has appeared and among other members of the Bar as to whether or not a candidate's representations can be relied upon.   A candidate's disciplinary record, if any, should be considered.   The reputation of the candidate for truthfulness and fair dealing in extra-legal contexts should also be considered. Inquiry into a candidate's prejudices that tend to disable or demean others is relevant.   However, since no human being is completely free of bias, the important consideration is that of whether or not the candidate can recognize his or her own biases and set them aside.

2.   LEGAL KNOWLEDGE AND ABILITY

A candidate should possess a high degree of knowledge of established legal principles and procedures and have a high degree of ability to interpret and apply them to specific factual situations.

Legal knowledge may be defined as familiarity with established legal principles and evidentiary and procedural rules. Legal ability is the intellectual capacity to interpret and apply established legal principles to specific factual situations and to communicate, both orally and in writing, the reasoning leading to the legal conclusion. Legal ability connotes also certain kinds of behavior by the judge such as the ability to reach concise decisions rapidly once he or she is apprised of sufficient facts, the ability to respond to issues in a reasonably unequivocal manner and quickly to grasp the essence of questions presented.

Legal knowledge and ability are not static qualities, but are acquired and enhanced by experience and by the continual learning process involved in keeping abreast of changing concepts through education and study. While a candidate should possess a high level of legal knowledge, and while a ready knowledge of rules of evidence is of importance to judges who will try contested cases, a candidate should not normally be expected to possess expertise in any particular substantive field. More important is the demonstration of an attitude reflective of willingness to learn the new skills and knowledge which will from time to time become essential to a judge's performance and of a willingness to improve judicial procedure and administration.

A review of a candidate's academic record, participation in continuing legal education forums, legal briefs and other writings and reputation among judges and professional colleagues who have had first-hand dealings with the candidate will be helpful in evaluating legal knowledge and ability.

3. PROFESSIONAL EXPERIENCE

A candidate must have been a licensed attorney in this state for at least ten (10) years.

A candidate must have been admitted to practice law in New Jersey for at least ten (10) years (N.J. Const., Art. 6, Sec. 6, para.2). The length of time that a lawyer has practiced is a valid criterion in screening applicants for judgeships. Such professional experience should be long enough to provide a basis for the evaluation of the candidate's demonstrated performance and long enough to ensure that the candidate has had substantial exposure to legal problems and to the judicial process.

It is desirable for a candidate to have had substantial trial experience. This is particularly true for a candidate for the trial bench. Trial experience includes the preparation and presentation of matters of proof and legal argument in an adversary setting. The extent and variety of a candidate's experience as a litigator should be considered in light of the nature of the judicial vacancy that is being filled.

Although substantial trial experience is desirable, other types of legal experience should also be carefully considered. An analysis of the work performed by the modern trial bench indicates that, in addition to adjudication, many judges perform substantial duties involving administration, discovery, mediation and public relations. A private practitioner who has developed an active practice, a successful law teacher and writer or a successful corporate, government or public interest attorney all may have experience which will contribute to successful judicial performance. Outstanding persons with such experience should not be deemed unqualified solely because of lack of trial experience. The important consideration is the depth and breadth of the professional experience and the competence with which it has been performed, rather than the candidate's particular type of professional experience.

For a candidate for the New Jersey Supreme Court, additional professional experience involving scholarly research and the development and expression of legal concepts is especially desirable.

4. JUDICIAL TEMPERAMENT

A candidate should possess a judicial temperament, which includes common sense, compassion, decisiveness, firmness, humility, openmindedness, patience, tact and understanding.

Judicical temperament is universally regarded as a valid and important criterion in the evaluation of a candidate.

Among the qualities which comprise judicial temperament are patience, openmindedness, courtesy, tact, firmness, understanding, compassion and humility. Because the judicial function is essentially one of facilitating conflict resolution, judicial temperament requires an ability to deal with counsel, jurors, witnesses and parties calmly and courteously, and the willingness to hear and consider the views of all sides. It requires the ability to be even-tempered, yet firm; openminded, yet willing and able to reach a decision; confident, yet not egocentric. Because of the range of topics and issues with which a judge may be required to deal, judicial temperament requires a willingness and ability to assimilate data outside the judge's own experience. It requires, moreover, an even disposition, buttressed by a keen sense of justice which creates an intellectual serenity in the approach to complex decisions, and forebearance under provocation. Judicial temperament also implies a mature sense of proportion; reverence for the law, but appreciation that the role of law is not static and unchanging; understanding of the judge's important role in the judicial process, yet recognition that the administration of justice and the rights of the parties transcend the judge's personal desires. Judicial temperament is typified by recognition that there must be compassion as the judge deals with matters put before him or her.

Factors which indicate a lack of judicial temperament are also identifiable and understandable. Judicial temperament thus implies an absence of arrogance, impatience, pomposity, loquacity, irascibility, arbitrariness or tyranny.

Wide-ranging interviews should be undertaken to provide insight into the temperament of a judicial candidate.

5.   DILIGENCE

A candidate should be diligent, punctual and possess effective management skills.

Diligence is defined as a constant and earnest effort to accomplish that which has been undertaken. While diligence is not necessarily the same as industriousness, it does imply the elements of constancy, attentiveness, perseverance, painstakingness and assiduousness. It does imply the possession of good work habits and the ability to set priorities in relation to the importance of the tasks to be accomplished.

A lazy lawyer is likely to be a lazy judge. Lazy judges eventually have a debilitating effect on the judicial process. Therefore, while candidates do not have to be workaholics, lazy persons are necessarily poor candidates.

Punctuality should be recognized as a complement of diligence. A candidate should be known to meet procedural deadlines in trial work and to keep appointments and commitments. A candidate should be known to respect the time of other lawyers, clients and judges.

Effective productivity is a question of time management—that is how well a candidate uses his or her time. A candidate should demonstrate such skills.

6. HEALTH

A candidate should be in good physical and mental health.

Good health embraces a condition of being sound in body and mind and with relative freedom from physical disease or pain. This is one criterion which may be capable of objective consideration. Any history of a past disabling condition or suggestion of a current disabling condition should require further inquiry as to the degree of impairment. Physical handicaps and disease which do not prevent a person from fully performing judicial duties should not be a cause for rejection of a candidate. However, any serious condition must be considered carefully as to the possible effect it would have on the candidate's ability to perform the duties of a judge. Thus, it is proper to require a candidate to provide a physician's written report of a recent thorough medical examination.

Good health includes the absence of erratic or bizarre behavior which would significantly affect the candidate's functioning as a fair and impartial judge. Addiction to alcohol or drugs is of such an insidious nature that the State and County Committees should affirmatively determine that a candidate does not presently suffer from any such disability.

The ability to handle stress effectively is a component of good mental health. A candidate should have developed the ability to refresh himself or herself occasionally with non-work-related activities and recreations. A candidate should have a positive perception of his or her own self-worth in order to be able to withstand the psychological pressures inherent in the task of judging.

Consideration should be given to the age of a candidate as it bears upon health and upon the number of years of service that the candidate may be able to perform.

7.   FINANCIAL RESPONSIBILITY

A candidate should be financially responsible.

The demonstrated financial responsibility of a candidate is one of the factors to be considered in predicting the candidate's ability to serve properly. Whether there have been unsatisfied judgments or bankruptcy proceedings against a candidate and whether the candidate has promptly and properly filed all required tax returns are pertinent to financial responsibility. So is consideration of whether the candidate has paid all taxes which are due and owing, or otherwise made satisfactory arrangements for their payment. Financial responsibility demonstrates self-discipline and the ability to withstand pressures which might compromise independence and impartiality.

8.   PUBLIC SERVICE

Consideration should be given to a candidate's previous public service activities.

Participation in public service and pro bono activities adds another dimension to the qualifications of the candidate. The degree of participation in such activities may indicate social consciousness and concern for other. The degree to which bar association work provides an insight into the qualifications of the candidate varies in each individual. Significant and effective bar association work may be viewed favorably.

The rich diversity of backgrounds of American judges is one of the strengths of the American judiciary, and a candidate's non-legal experience must be considered together with the candidate's legal experience. Experience which provides an awareness of and sensitivity to people and their problems may be just as helpful in the decision-making process as a knowledge of the law. There is, then, no one career path to the judiciary. A broad, non-legal academic background, supported by varied and extensive non-academic achievements are important parts of a candidate's qualifications. Examples of such non-legal experience are involvement in community affairs and participation in political activities, including election to public office. The most desirable candidate will have had broad life experiences.

Appendix F

Florida   1996
Proposed Interview Questions for
Judicial Nominating Commissions

PROPOSED INTERVIEW QUESTIONS FOR DCA JNC'S

1. Is the role of the Court to interpret and apply law or make policy?

2. What contributions would you bring to the bench?

3. How do you feel about the tendency of a "professional jurist" on our courts at levels?

4. Is this job a salary increase for you?

5. Should we require that our appellate judges have circuit and practical experience (i.e., real paying clients)?

6. Why do you want to be a DCA judge?

7. What is the extent of your trial experience and appellate experience?

8. Why do you think you would be a good appellate judge? Highlight any special qualities that may enhance your abilities.

9. Do you believe in the jury system?

10. What has been your greatest disappointment?

11. What has been your most gratifying achievement?

12. Do you have any personal prejudices or stereotypical beliefs that may adversely impair your administration of justice?

13. How would you handle a courtroom situation where counsel's conduct is discourteous, disparaging, discriminatory, or appears to be influenced by gender or other bias toward a lawyer, witness, litigant or courtroom personnel. Would your response be different if the comment or conduct were directed to you?

14. When is judicial intervention appropriate to correct a professional conduct problem, and how should that intervention be accomplished?

15. Do you feel that judges who manifest bias or prejudice in the official performance of their duties should be subject to discipline?

16. Are there any factors that would make it difficult or impossible for you to handle the hours necessary for the job?

17. Is there any difficulty in your personal life that would impair you physically, mentally or emotionally from committing foremost to your judicial responsibilities?

18. Are you a member of any club or organization that discriminates in its membership or otherwise based upon the applicant's sex or race?

19. Do you perceive any significant differences between female and male attorneys?

20. Does your law firm have a policy dealing with sexual harassment or discriminatory conduct? If so, please explain the policy.

21. Do you have any feeling about whether a man or woman would be generally more suitable as a primary residential care parent in a custody dispute involving young male or female children?

22. Are you familiar with the Supreme Court report on gender bias? If so, have you ever observed any of the problems discussed in this report?

23. Do you think men and women are treated equally in the courts; have you ever seen a situation in which they were not? If so, how was it handled?

24. Are you willing to limit your activities and relationships to the extent they tend to interfere with your role as a judge?

25. Will your rulings be free from racial bias? Religious bias? Ethnic bias? Bias based on sex? Bias based on social status of the parties? Bias based on the economic status of the parties?

26. Have you ever been a subject of a grievance or other complaint relative to a gender or racial issue?

27. Have you ever been involved as a plaintiff or defendant in any legal proceedings involving moral turpitude, dishonesty or unethical conduct?

28. Have any complaints been filed against you with any disciplinary body? If so, what was the nature of those complaints? Have any of those complaints resulted in discipline or sanctions? If you have been disciplined, how long ago did this disciplinary proceeding take place?

29. Have you ever engaged in any pro bono legal work? If so, please describe the nature and extent of your involvement.

30. Do you belong to any bar associations or professional organizations? If so, which ones? In addition, please tell us if you are active in any committee work for any of these organizations.

31. Are you involved in any civic or charitable activities? If so, please describe each one and the extent of your involvement.

Appendix G

Governing Principles of the Standing Committee on Federal Judiciary*

The Standing Committee on Federal Judiciary shall continue to direct its activities to evaluating the professional qualifications of persons being considered for appointment to the federal bench on the basis of predetermined and objective evaluation criteria which shall be provided prior to evaluation to persons whose qualifications are to be evaluated. The Committee will continue, if asked, to provide to the Attorney General and, following nomination, the Senate Judiciary Committee, its appraisal of the professional competence, integrity and judicial temperament of such persons.

In view of the special nature of the function performed by this Committee and the confidence reposed in the Committee's evaluations, the integrity and credibility of its processes and the perception of these processes are of vital importance.

No member of the Committee while serving as a member or within one year following such service, shall seek or accept a nomination to the federal bench.

No member of the Committee shall participate in the work of the Committee if such participation would give rise to the appearance of impropriety or would otherwise be incompatible with the purposes served and functions performed by the Committee.

Because confidentiality and discretion are of critical importance to the evaluation processes of the Committee, only the President of the Association, his designee, or the Chair of the Committee shall respond to any media or general public inquiries or make any statements to the media or general public relating to the work of the Committee.

The President of the Association shall take any action necessary to ensure adherence to these principles.

*Adopted by ABA Board of Governors
February 4, 1988.

Appendix H

United States Supreme Court 1993
Testimony on Nomination of Ruth Bader Ginsburg
July 23, 1993

PANEL CONSISTING OF PAIGE COMSTOCK CUNNINGHAM, PRESIDENT, AMERICANS UNITED FOR LIFE, CHICAGO, IL, ROSA CUMARE, HAMILTON & CUMARE, PASADENA, CA; NELLIE J. GRAY, PRESIDENT, MARCH FOR LIFE EDUCATION AND DEFENSE FUND, WASHINGTON, DC; SUSAN HIRSCHMANN, EXECUTIVE DIRECTOR, EAGLE FORUM, WASHINGTON, DC; KAY COLES JAMES, VICE PRESIDENT, FAMILY RESEARCH COUNCIL, WASHINGTON, DC; AND HOWARD PHILLIPS, CHAIRMAN, THE CONSERVATIVE CAUCUS, VIENNA, VA

STATEMENT OF PAIGE COMSTOCK CUNNINGHAM

Ms. CUNNINGHAM. Thank you, Mr. Chairman.

Mr. Chairman and members of the Judiciary Committee, I thank you for this opportunity to testify on the nomination of Ruth Bader Ginsburg to the U.S. Supreme Court.

I am an attorney, a graduate of Northwestern University School of Law. I am a wife and I am a proud mother of three children. I think all those things bear on the testimony that I am giving today, because it is likely that I have reaped in my own career from the seeds that were sown by Judge Ginsburg in her efforts to abolish sex discrimination.

As you mentioned, I am also the president of Americans United for Life, which is the legal arm for the pro-life movement, and we are the oldest national pro-life organization in this country. We are nonpartisan and we are secular, and we are committed to the protection of the vulnerable and the innocent human life from conception to natural death.

Although Judge Ginsburg may possess the credentials to sit on the Supreme Court, we are concerned about the process by which she was nominated and her views on abortion, and appreciate this opportunity to fully educate the Nation, and that is what I appreciate about this process of a thorough look and an opportunity to speak.

I am troubled because, in the first time in our history, a Supreme Court nominee has been required to pass a test, an abortion litmus test. President Clinton made this very clear before he nominated Judge Ginsburg to the High

Court. This is a litmus test which prior nominees were wrongly accused of passing, and why one of them was defeated.

I think it is a tragedy that supporting an act which ends the life of one being and scars the future of another should be considered the supreme test for the Supreme Court. And just as disturbing as this unprecedented litmus test is Judge Ginsburg's attempt to justify the decision in *Roe v. Wade* on the ground that abortion is somehow necessary for women's equality, that women cannot be equal in the law or in society, without abortion, through all 9 months of pregnancy for any reason.

Outside of abortion, *Roe v. Wade* has done absolutely nothing to advance women's rights. State and Federal courts have handed down dozens of decisions striking down various forms of sex discrimination, and few, if any, of these courts, including the Supreme Court, have relied on or even mentioned *Roe*.

The real advances in women's rights have come not through the court cases, but through laws enacted by Congress and by State legislatures. These are the laws that have banned sex discrimination in public and private employment, in the sale and rental of housing, in education, laws that mandate equal pay for equal work, to name just a few. Do you know what? Not one of those laws depends on abortion.

Judge Ginsburg has repeatedly stated that abortion is protected by the equal protection clause of the Constitution or that that ought to have been the basis, rather than the due process clause. But she has gone farther than the Court and suggested in her writings that there ought to be a public policy supporting taxpayer funded abortions.

Her writings also reveal that she would oppose laws protecting women in crisis pregnancies, laws upheld by the Supreme Court just a few months ago, last year, laws such as a woman's right to know, a 24-hour reflection period to think about information about a decision that she cannot change and that she will live with for the rest of her life, laws involving parents. These laws received overwhelming public support. After all, they are reasonable laws.

Judge Ginsburg has testified before you that abortion is central to a woman's dignity. But what is this legacy of *Roe*? Has a generation of abortion on demand solved any of the problems for which it was offered? Has abortion reduced the rates of child abuse or illegitimacy or teen pregnancy or the feminization of poverty? Has it enhanced respect for women? After 20 years of abortion on demand, abortion has flunked the test as the miracle cure for the social problems it promised to solve.

The only obvious benefit of legalized abortion is the economic one. A $300 abortion is much cheaper than a $3,000 delivery of a baby. But what about the cost to women's bodies and women's lives? Thousands of women now bear the scars of perforated uteruses, lost fertility and higher breast cancer risks. Close to 70 percent of all relationships end in the first year after an abortion. Many women are abandoned by the baby's father as soon as the crisis of pregnancy is solved by abortion.

Some women say they can't even pass a playground or turn on a vacuum cleaner, because it sounds like a suction machine. All too often, they fall into a pattern of self-abuse, that abuse which mirrors their abuse by others. The destruction and tragedy caused by 28 million abortions is a gaping national wound, a wound whose ugliness is covered up by polite tolerance and rhetoric about a woman's right to choose and keeping government out of private choices.

And make no mistake about it, coercion to have abortions is real. The coercion may be possible precisely because abortion is legal. That is the unspoken price for progress in our careers. Female medical residents, in an article in the New England Journal of Medicine, reported that tragedy. We attorneys have discovered that same price. And why not? Because if a woman demands that complete autonomy in her abortion decision, it only seems fair that she bear complete responsibility for the consequences of that, and women once again are left alone to pay the price.

Our radical abortion policy, which Judge Ginsburg apparently supports wholeheartedly, would not expand or advance women's issues. I believe it has actually set the clock back on women's dignity, including the dignity of motherhood. Children should be a shared responsibility. Our educational goals and professional dreams should not depend on an elective surgery that creates second-class citizens of the voiceless.

Abortion goes against the core values of feminism, equality, care, nurturing, compassion and nonviolence. If we women, who have so recently gained electoral and political voice, do not stand up for the voiceless and the politically powerless, who will? Those who promote abortion rights do not represent the women of America. The 1.8 million members of the National Women's Coalition for Life prove that you can be pro-woman and pro-life. Our feminist pioneers, including Susan B. Anthony and Elizabeth Cady Stanton, cited with approval by Judge Ginsburg, were strongly against abortion and recognized it as child murder and a crying evil.

Judge Ginsburg wrote that the greatest judges "have been independent thinking individuals with open, but not empty minds, individuals willing to listen and to learn." Unless there is convincing evidence that Judge Ginsburg is willing to reexamine her premises about abortion, which she has so recently stated, then we cannot withdraw our objection to her confirmation.

We ask the committee to seriously consider this statement and our more extensive written testimony. The future of women, men and generation of many yet unborn depend on it.

Thank you.

Appendix I

U.S. DEPARTMENT OF JUSTICE
QUESTIONNAIRE FOR JUDICIAL CANDIDATES

A. NAME AND POSITION
1. Name: (include any former names used)
2. Government position for which you are under consideration.
3. Address: List current residence address and mailing address.
4. List all office and home telephone numbers where you may be reached.
5. Marital status: If married, identify spouse's present employer and spouse's employer for the five preceding years
6. List all jobs held in the past 10 years, including the title or description of job, name of employer, location of work, and dates of inclusive employment.

B. PERSONAL DATA
1. Have your federal or state tax returns been the subject of any audit or investigation or inquiry at any time? If so, explain.
2. Are you currently under federal, state, or local investigation for a possible violation of a criminal statute? If so, please give full details.
3. List all memberships and offices held in professional, fraternal, scholarly and civic organizations.
4. Have you ever been disciplined or cited for a breach of ethics or unprofessional conduct by, or been the subject of a complaint to, any court, administrative agency, professional association disciplinary committee, or other professional group? If so, please give full details.
5. Have you ever been involved in civil litigation, or administrative or legislative proceedings of any kind, either as plaintiff, defendant, respondent, witness or party in interest, which may be appropriate for consideration by the Committee of the Senate to which your nomination will be submitted? If so, please give full details.
6. List all offices with a political party held during the past 10 years.
7. List any public office for which you have been a candidate during the past 10 years.
8. What is the condition of your health?
9. Have you had a physical examination recently?
10. Without details, is there or has there been anything in your personal life which you feel, if known, may be of embarrassment to the Administration in the event you should be nominated? What about any near relative?

C. FINANCIAL DATA

Please note that federal law and regulations governing conflicts of interest require Presidential appointees within 30 days of their entrance on duty to provide reports of specified financial interests as to themselves, their spouses and any other member of their immediate households. The initial four matters listed below are designed to elicit financial information which all Presidential appointees are required to provide by Executive Order of the President. The remaining paragraphs in this section seek elaboration on your financial status beyond that which the existing Executive Order and regulations require. The information which you provide will not be transmitted to the Senate Committee considering your nomination, or otherwise be made public, without your consent. As to all matters, please provide the requested information for yourself, your spouse, minor children and any other member of the immediate household.

1. List the names of all corporations, companies, firms, or other business enterprises, partnerships, nonprofit organizations, and education or other institutions—

(A) with which you are now connected as an employee, officer, owner, director, trustee, partner, advisor, attorney, or consultant. (Attorneys and consultants need list only their major clients, but should include all of those whom you represent on a regular basis or which might give rise to an appearance of bias on your part in connection with your proposed appointment):

(B) in which you have any continuing financial interests, through a pension or retirement plan, stock bonus, shared income, severance pay agreement, or otherwise as a result of any current or prior employment or business or professional association. As to each financial arrangement, provide all details necessary for a thorough understanding of the way in which the arrangement operates, including information concerning any renewal right you may have if the arrangement is allowed to lapse and whether lump sum or severance benefits are available in lieu of continuation of the interest;

(C) in which you have any financial interest through the ownership of stocks, stock options, bonds, partnership interests, or other securities. Any interests held indirectly through trusts or other arrangements should be included. (Please provide a copy of any trust or other agreement.)

2. Provide a complete, current financial net worth statement that itemizes in detail:

(A) the identity and value of all assets held, directly or indirectly. This itemization should include, but not be limited to, bank accounts real estate, securities, trusts, investments and other financial holdings;

(B) the identity and amount of each liability owed, directly or indirectly, which is in excess of $1,000. This itemization should include, but not be limited to, debts, mortgages, loans and other financial obligations for which you, your spouse or your dependents have a direct liability or which may be guaranteed by you, your spouse or your dependents. In identifying each liability, indicate the nature of the liability and the entity or person to which it is owed.

A sample net worth statement is attached for your convenience. You may use any form you like.*

(C) List sources and amounts of all items of value received during calendar years 1984 and 1985 (including, but not limited to, salaries, wages, fees, dividends, capital gains or losses, interests, rents, royalties, patents, honoraria, and other gifts other than those of nominal value).

(D) Please provide for review by this office (but not for submission to Senate Committee staff or to the public) copies of your federal income tax returns for the preceding three-year period.

D. FUTURE EMPLOYMENT RELATIONSHIPS

1. Will you sever all connections with your present employers, business firms, business associations or business organizations, if you are confirmed by the Senate?
2. Do you have any plans, commitments or agreements to pursue outside employment, with or without compensation, during your service with the government? If so, explain.

E. POTENTIAL CONFLICTS OF INTEREST

1. Describe all financial arrangements, stock options, deferred compensation agreements, future benefits and other continuing relationships with business associates, clients or customers.
2. Describe any business relationship, dealing or financial transaction which you have had during the last five years, whether for yourself, on behalf of a client, or acting as an agent, that could in any way constitute or result in a possible conflict of interest in the position to which you have been nominated.
3. Describe any activity during the past five years in which you have engaged for the purpose of directly or indirectly influencing the passage, defeat or modification of any legislation or affecting the administration and execution of law or public policy.
4. Explain how you will resolve any potential conflict of interest, including any that may be disclosed by your responses to the above items.

Appendix J

United States District Court 1985
Testimony of Alan A. McDonald before a Sub-Committee of
Senate Judiciary Committee (Oct 2, 1985)

Senator McCONNELL. I would like to call now Mr Alan McDonald. Mr.
McDondald, if you would raise your right hand, do you swear that the testimony
you give in this hearing will be the truth, the whole truth, and nothing but the
truth, so help you God?

Mr. McDONALD. I do.

Senator McCONNELL. Mr. McDonald, you have been a practicing attorney for
over 30 years. Now, you have been nominated to be a Federal district judge for
the Eastern District of Washington. I wonder if you foresee any difficulty in the
transition from private practice to that of trial judge at the Federal district level.

**TESTIMONY OF ALAN A. McDONALD, OF WASHINGTON, TO BE
U.S. DISTRICT JUDGE FOR THE EASTERN DISTRICT OF
WASHINGTON.**

Mr. McDONALD. You mean other than the time involved in making the
transition?

Senator McCONNELL. Yes.

Mr. McDONALD. I do not. Protocols, of course, are different, and it comes at
a time in my life when that challenge should prove interesting. But I have been
involved in a decision-making role in my own practice, in my own law firm, and
in my own community, and I regard that as basic to the posting.

Senator McCONNELL. Would you tell the committee what procedures you
will follow in determining any potential conflicts of interest and how you intend
to resolve them?

Mr. McDONALD. I think like most private practitioners, I am more than
sensitive to the difference in the way that matter is handled between State and
Federal courts. Certainly, I feel very strongly that the appearance of justice
would be best served by recusing when that is obviously the thing to do.

Senator McCONNELL. Mr. McDonald, are there ever any circumstances under
which a judge should attempt to establish new judicial precedent, and if so what
are the criteria that you would consider in order to determine the propriety of
reversing existing precedent?

Mr. McDONALD. Well, that is an area I would approach gingerly. I think,
again, calling upon my experience as a practicing lawyer all these years that

predictability is so important to those who labor in the vineyards of the law. And I think those occasions are going to arise only when the precedent is either nonexistent of ambivalent.

And I suppose as far as the factors are concerned that those would isolate themselves in the usual fashion to somebody who has a feeling for the law. The notion as to what is right always becomes evident.

Senator McCONNELL. In response to a portion of the committee questionnaire concerning judicial activism you stated, in part,

While judicial legislation is inevitable to some degree if the common law is to provide growth and flexibility, the grand plan of our Constitution should inspire caution in providing that vitality.

Under what circumstances would you consider the matter of judicial legislation to be inevitable?

Mr. McDONALD. As I have indicated, I think it should occur in those situations, and there are enough of them. That is just a product of the evolutionary nature of the law, the common law. I think it should occur when precedent is either nonexistent or honestly ambivalent.

Senator McCONNELL. Senator Simon

Senator SIMON. Thank you, Mr. Chairman.

You heard me ask one of the previous nominees a question about membership in clubs that discriminate. Do you belong to any clubs that discriminate?

Mr. McDONALD. I belong to at least one club in my community where there are no lady members. I find nothing in its constitution or its bylaws or membership application that prohibits that.

Honestly, Senator, other than myself, the memberships is so composed that it is possible that no other-that women would not care to join. But I think that as a matter of fact that they are not encouraged to join.

Senator SIMON. And do you intend to continue your membership?

Mr. McDONALD. Oh, yes. I do not-if there is to be a change made in that situation, if that is warranted, I say very seriously that the nature of it is such that I am not so sure that it would be interesting to someone of the other sex. But if it were and I were to support that, I would do it in a much better fashion were I a member of that organization than if I were someone who withdrew from it in some sort of meaningless protest.

Senator SIMON. You heard the bar association's concerns here and the judicial code of ethics, canon of ethics, that would indicate that it probably would be wiser for you not to continue that membership?

Mr. McDONALD. Yes, sir; I am aware of that before coming here.

Senator SIMON. Yes; I notice in your information you provided, you are a member of the Yakima Country Club, the Royal Duck Club, and the 26A Dining Club, and I do not know enough about any of those three to-which one are you talking about, the one that does not-

Mr. McDONALD. The last one, Senator, the one that is designated 26A.

Senator SIMON. You might want to reflect on that membership and inform the committee of whatever decision you make in that area.

Mr. McDONALD. All right.

Senator SIMON. I have no further questions, Mr. Chairman.

Senator McCONNELL. Thank you, sir.

Name Index

Subject Index

abortion controversy, 191-195, 197, 265-267

accountability, judicial, 19, 31-32, fig 2.2, 64, 71-72, 88, 106
   see also Judges' Dilemma

ACLU v. Florida Bar (1990), 52n

affirmation of judicial candidates
   federal Courts of Appeals, 187-188, 196-197
   federal District Courts, 200-203
   federal recruitment process, table 8.1
   federal Supreme Court, 171, 179-180
   Florida Merit Plan, 142-143, fig 7.2
   gubernatorial appointees, 107, fig 6.2
   New Jersey courts, 122
   South Carolina courts, 100-101, fig 5.2
   Texas courts, 81-83, fig 4.2, 85
   Washington courts, 62-64, 208

age requirements, 3, 99

Alabama, judicial selection, 3, 34, 69

Alaska, judicial selection, 34

American Bar Association, 5, 6, 126-127, 164, 207, 208
   Standing Committee on the Federal Judiciary, 149, table 8.1, 263
      lower court nominations, 153-154, 187-189, 197, 202, 205
      Supreme Court nominations, 154-155, 164, 167, 169, 172, 177-180

American Judicature Society, 5, 6, 125, 126, 128n, 133

Americans for Life, 192

appointments, judicial
   by governors, 21, 22, 30, 47, 105-123

by legislature, 30

by presidents, 9-11, 21, 22, 30, 147-151
   to federal courts, 153-156
   to state courts, 64-66, 105-123

Arizona, judicial selection, 21n, 34-35, 45

Arkansas, judicial selection, 35, 69

Articles of Confederation, 2

articulation levels, 27-33, 108, 211, 214, 217-225
   federal Courts of Appeals, 188-190, 197-198
   federal District Courts, 203-204
   federal Supreme Court, 171-172, 180-181
   Florida Merit Plan, 145
   New Jersey courts, 122
   South Carolina courts, 102
   Texas courts, 84-85
   Washington courts, 67-68, 208-209, 217-225

Asian Bar Association, 59n, 61

at-large judicial districts, 52-53

Baker v. Carr (1962), 118n

bar associations, 5, 46, 47
   see also association names

Buckley v. Illinois Judicial Inquiry Board (1993), 52n

Buckley v. Valero (1976), 76n

California, judicial selection, 7, 21n, 35, 45, 105, 126

campaign activities, table 3.1, 131-132

campaign financing, 58, 75-76, 80-81, 85, 131-132

Canon 7, 50-51, table 3.2, 52n

Walsh Commission, 67-68, 227-235
Washington
  affirmation of candidates, 62-64, fig
  3.2
  appointments by governor, 56, 64-66
  articulation levels, 62-64, 67-68
  bar associations, 59-61, 65-66, fig
  3.2
  county commissioners, 64, 66
  court system, 53-55, 204-209
  initiation of candidates, 56, 57-58,
  fig 3.2
  judicial selection, 21n, 22n, 23, 40
  nonpartisan elections, 44n, 48, table
  3.2, 53-68
  primary elections, 217-225
  screening of candidates, 56, 59-62,
  205-207
Washington Court of Appeals, 53, fig
  3.1, 57n, 59, 60, 65
Washington District Courts, 54, fig
  3.1, 57n, 60, 66, 204-209
*Washington Legal Foundation v. U.S.
  Department of Justice* (1989), 153
Washington Municipal Courts, 54, fig
  3.1, 60
Washington State Bar Association, 59,
  65, fig 3.1, 204n
Washington State Constitution
  Commission on Judicial Conduct,
  212
Washington Superior Courts, 53, 54,
  fig 3.1, 57n, 59, 60, 65
Washington Supreme Court, 53, fig
  3.1, 55, 57n, 59, 63, 65, 67
Washington Women Lawyers, 59n, 61
Wells v. Edwards (1973), 53n
West Virginia, judicial selection, 22n,
  40, 69
White House staff, 149-151, table 8.1,
  152
  federal Courts of Appeals
  candidates, 184-186, 188, 197

  federal District Court candidates,
  200
  federal Supreme Court candidates,
  164-165, 167-168, 172-173, 180
  Office of Legal Counsel, table 8.1,
  152
Wisconsin, judicial selection, 40
Wyoming, judicial selection, 40